THE HEART GROWN BRUTAL

Peter Costello

THE HEART GROWN BRUTAL

The Irish Revolution in Literature, from Parnell to the Death of Yeats, 1891-1939

GILL and MACMILLAN
ROWMAN and LITTLEFIELD

First published in Ireland 1977 by
Gill and Macmillan Ltd
15/17 Eden Quay
Dublin 1
With associated companies in
London and Basingstoke
New York, Melbourne, Delhi, Johannesburg

7171 1234 5

First published in the United States in 1978 by
Rowman and Littlefield
81 Adams Drive, Totowa, N.J.
ISBN 0-8476-6007-9

ACKNOWLEDGMENTS

The author and publisher express their thanks for permission to use copyright material as follows: extracts from THE COLLECTED POEMS of W. B. Yeats and from the VARIORUM edition of W. B. Yeats's poems, by permission of M. B. Yeats, Miss Anne Yeats and the Macmillan Co. of London and Basingstoke. Selections from COLLECTED POEMS of W. B. Yeats: 'The Dedication to a Book of Stories Selected from the Irish Novelists', 'The Valley of the Black Pig', 'To Ireland in the Coming Times' (© 1906 by Macmillan Publishing Co., Inc., renewed 1934 by William Butler Yeats); 'Upon a House Shaken by the Land Agitation' (© 1912 by Macmillan Publishing Co., Inc., renewed 1940 by Bertha Georgie Yeats); 'September 1913' (© 1916 by Macmillan Publishing Co., Inc., renewed 1944 by Bertha Georgie Yeats); 'The Second Coming' (© 1924 by Macmillan Publishing Co., Inc., renewed 1952 by Bertha Georgie Yeats); 'Nineteen Hundred and Nineteen', 'Meditations in Time of Civil War', 'Leda and the Swan' (© 1928 by Macmillan Publishing Co., Inc., renewed 1956 by Georgie Yeats); 'Death' (© 1933 by Macmillan Publishing Co., Inc., renewed 1961 by Bertha Georgie Yeats); 'The Statue', 'Cuchulain Comforted' (© 1940 by Georgie Yeats, renewed 1968 by Bertha Georgie Yeats, Michael Butler Yeats and Anne Yeats); and from THE VARIORUM EDITION OF THE POEMS OF W. B. YEATS, edited by Peter Allt and Russell K. Alspach: 'Reprisals' (© 1957 by Macmillan Publishing Co., Inc.). Selections from THE COLLECTED POEMS of Austin Clarke, Dolmen Press © 1974. Selections from THE COLLECTED POEMS of Thomas McGreevy, New Writers' Press. Selections from Francis Stuart, *We have kept the faith*, Oakleaf Press © 1923. Selections from Sean O'Faolain, *Vive Moi!* Rupert Hart-Davis Ltd/Granada Publishing Ltd; Little, Brown and Co. in association with the Atlantic Monthly Press © 1963, 1964 by Sean O'Faolain.

Printed by Bristol Typesetting Co. Ltd
Barton Manor, St Philips, Bristol

For the memory of my grandfathers
Denis Costello
Matthew Walsh

'I have suspected that history, real history, is more modest and that its essential dates may be, for a long time, secret.'
Jorge Luis Borges:
'The Modesty of History' in *Other Inquisitions*

We had fed the heart on fantasies,
The heart's grown brutal from the fare;
More substance in our enmities
Than in our love; O honey-bees,
Come build in the empty house of the stare.
W.B. Yeats:
Meditations in Time of Civil War (1923)

Contents

Contents continued

List of Illustrations

12 *St Patrick's Purgatory* (1930), painting by John Lavery. (Hugh Lane Municipal Gallery, Dublin)

13 Sir Horace Plunkett's house *Kilteragh* burned down 29 January 1923 by Republican force.

14 Sato's sword, sheath and wrapper. (Collection Senator Michael Yeats)

15 Women scouts of the Republican Army, in action in Cork 1923.

16 *Communicating with the Prisoners, Kilmainham Jail*, painting by Jack B. Yeats. (Yeats Memorial Collection, Sligo County Museum. Photo: *Illustrated London News*)

17 *John M. Synge*, painting by John Butler Yeats. (National Gallery of Ireland)

18 *Lady Gregory*, painting by Antonio Mancini. (National Gallery of Ireland)

19 *Arthur Griffith*, painting by John Lavery. (National Gallery of Ireland)

20 *Kevin O'Higgins*, painting by John Lavery. (National Gallery of Ireland)

Preface

'Wenn ich Kultur höre . . . entsichere ich meinen Browning.'

Hanns Johst : *Schlageter* (1934)

THIS book is about Irish culture and violence, and deals with the literature of the Irish Revival of fifty years ago and its record of the contemporary political revolution.

I hope that few of my readers, on hearing the fatal words 'Irish culture', will react by reaching for their revolvers. I have written this book with the hope of disarming the past by understanding it. For as we have seen in recent years, in Ireland the past, uncritically recalled, still has a powerful influence on current affairs.

When I began this book it seemed to me that the events I was reading about were fast becoming of academic interest only. That was in 1966. That year saw the ill-considered celebrations of the 1916 Rising in the south of Ireland, and shortly afterwards in the north the first stirrings of the Civil Rights movement, which began the present turmoil there.

Inevitably the present events have altered our perspectives on the events of 1916 and afterwards. The glamour of guerrilla warfare, which was part of Irish mythology, has faded, and the Civil War, which seemed such an aberration in 1923, seems now to be the way in which most political movements in Ireland that appeal to violence will end.

But it will be for others to draw lessons for the present from the past described in this book. My interest is entirely in the culture and violence of yesterday. The thesis of this book is that the cultural revival made possible the political revolution by creating a new ideal of Ireland, and that the literature of the revival provides what might almost be called 'the secret history' of the Irish revolution.

Though the central part of the book deals with the period between 1916 and 1923, the first and third parts which survey the rise and fall of the Revival, are not so easily tied down to dates. Thus the book covers the half century between the death of Parnell and the death of Yeats, for cultural and political movements have long roots and their consequences often linger for decades. My treatment of social and political events during this period may sometimes seem too schematic, but this is only to allow more room for a detailed treatment of the literature and art of the period.

The interaction of culture and violence in any society is a complicated thing. I hope that those who are not fully convinced by my treatment of them here, will nevertheless feel that political events alone are not the determining influence on a country's people. Sometimes a people's poetry is a more critical thing than their politics.

Though there have been many useful surveys of the Irish Revival, discussions of the interactions of politics, culture and violence are few. T.R. Henn's British Academy lecture on 'W.B. Yeats and the Poetry of War' proved to be a stimulating starting point. William Irwin Thompson's *Imagination of an Insurrection* deals only with the Easter Rising. As the Rising was only a preliminary to much more important events—the author does not deal with the Civil War, the formative experience of modern Ireland—the book is only of limited use. Political themes in modern Irish poetry are discussed by Robert Loftus in his book *Nationalism and Irish Poetry*. But 'nationalism' *sensu stricto* plays only a small part in the literature discussed in this book.

In writing this book I have been far more influenced by Frank O'Connor's seminal survey *A Backward Look*, which is I think one of the best books on Irish literature published in recent years.

This book was originally begun as an academic exercise at the University of Michigan, and though the present version bears little resemblance to its original form, I would like to thank Franklin Fisher, Frank Brownlow, Leo MacNamara and Marvin Felheim for the attention they gave me then. Their patience must often have been tried. Over the years I have incurred other debts. I would particularly like to thank my parents for their memories, which have made this period a part of my own past rather than a part of history. I should also like to thank Donal

McCarteny, L.M. Cullen and Terence Brown for their helpful advice. Senator Michael B. Yeats was gracious enough to allow me to photograph his father's Samurai sword; and Mr and Mrs Donal O'Donovan allowed me to photograph a portrait in their possession. Mrs Jennifer O'Donovan showed me her materials on Gerald O'Donovan, and Professor R. Dudley Edwards allowed me to use the Archives Department of University College Dublin. Hubert Mahony has been involved with this book since its more tentative beginnings, and has been very patient about the whole thing.

And a final thank you to my wife Mary for telling me every morning that I ought to try and finish that book as soon as possible. If it were not for wives, there would be no end to the making of books.

Peter Costello
Monkstown, Co. Dublin
1977

Introduction

THE DEATH OF CUCHULAIN
History and the Imagination

IN THE central hall of the General Post Office in Dublin there stands a bronze memorial to the leaders and men of the 1916 rebellion against British rule in Ireland. Created by the Irish sculptor Oliver Sheppard, it portrays the Celtic warrior hero Cuchulain dying in the defence of his country. He is tied to a stone pillar facing his enemies, with the raven goddess of war perched on his shoulder.

The artist had been a student at the Metropolitan School of Art in Dublin with W.B. Yeats in the 1880s. It was this statue, unveiled in 1936, that prompted Yeats in one of his last poems to reconsider the connection between what had been for him a powerful literary image, and what the heroic ideal of Cuchulain had inspired in 1916 and the years that followed.

> When Pearse summoned Cuchulain to his side,
> What stalked through the Post Office? What intellect,
> What calculation, number, measurement, replied?[1]

Patrick Pearse, he knew, had been fascinated by blood and violence : but what had been the outcome of his alliance with the spirit of the ancient hero? Yeats does not answer this question directly, but he implies that the imaginative response to that summons had a major effect on the making of modern Ireland.

That is the question which this book seeks to answer by tracing the interwoven histories of the revolution which Pearse inspired and the literary movement which Yeats dominated. I hope to show just what sort of intellectual and artistic response there was to Pearse's invocation of the Celtic gods on that now far distant Easter Monday in Dublin.

Pearse was clearly one of those who had helped to bring about the Irish revolution, both by his journalism and poetry, and by actual plotting. But did some responsibility also lie with others who had encouraged the ideals of Irish nationalism? Where, for instance, did Pearse's ideas about Celtic Ireland and its heroes come from? These ideas were not original. They were part of the intellectual baggage of the Irish revolution, and they came to him through the writers of the Irish revival, from Yeats among others. Without the Revival, the revolution would not have taken on the mantle of the past, nor would the revolutionaries have acted as they did.

This connection between the two movements worried Yeats. Towards the end of his life, his memory running back over the turbulent events of the previous decades, he asked himself an even more pertinent question:

> Did that play of mine send out
> Certain men the English shot?
> Did words of mine put too great a strain
> On that woman's reeling brain?
> Could my spoken words have checked
> That whereby a house lay wrecked?[2]

He was thinking here of Maud Gonne, the great unrequited love of his life, playing the part of Cathleen ni Houlihan, the personification of Ireland herself, in the play of that name which he had devotedly written for her in 1902, as a contribution to the cause of Irish freedom; also of the Abbey actor Sean Connolly who was supposed to appear in a revival of the play on Easter Monday 1916, but instead died fighting with the Irish Citizen Army in the street outside the Dublin City Hall. And he was thinking too of the end of those great houses where he had passed so many long summers in his youth: Coole, Moore Hall, Tillyra, Lissadell and all their days of spacious leisure. By 1930 these were either burnt out, demolished, or bankrupt. Had that been what he had intended when writing his play?

Did Yeats's poetry contribute to what these people did, to those events, the fate of those houses? Could he really have spoken out to prevent or change what happened? Auden writing after Yeats's death thought not: 'Poetry makes nothing happen.' And this is a view widely held in Ireland today. It was not Yeats's opinion, however. Soon after the Rising he wrote to a friend: 'I count the links in the chain of responsibility, and wonder if any of them ends in my workshop.' He realised only too well that a poet could not write poems and plays vivid with nationalist feeling, and expect his readers to be unmoved. Had he himself not written, back in 1886 when he was twenty-one and the Revival hardly even under way, that 'Irish singers who are genuinely Irish in language, thought or style must, whether they will or no, nourish forces that make for the political liberties of Ireland.'

More convincing evidence that there is a real connection between poetry and politics is provided by that play in which Maud Gonne appeared in 1902, *Cathleen ni Houlihan.* Here poetry did make something happen. The play dealt with the Rising of 1798 and the appeal of an old woman (Ireland herself) to one of her 'sons' to free her from the bondage of British rule— at any time a powerful theme in Ireland. One member of the inner council of the Irish Republican Brotherhood, the secret society that plotted the Rising in 1916—it was far from being the great popular rebellion of legend—confessed that prior to seeing *Cathleen ni Houlihan* he had 'never had a political thought'. The writer Stephen Gwynn, then Nationalist M.P. for Galway city, recalled that he went home after seeing Miss Gonne's powerful impersonation 'asking if such plays should be produced unless one was prepared for people to go out to shoot and be shot'.

As Auden again remarked about Yeats, 'the words of a dead man are modified in the guts of the living' : in Ireland this often means an expanding bullet in the large intestine.

Though immediate violence was not part of Yeats's intention in writing the play, the appeal to force of arms was latent in every line. This production, which initiated the long history of the Abbey Theatre, also prepared many imaginations for the coming revolution. No matter what he did later, these particular words of his would indeed be strangely modified in the guts of the living. Yeats's poetry helped to nourish forces which were making for the political liberties of Ireland.

So poetry went to the making of modern Ireland as we know it, because it went to the making of the imagination that fostered the revolution. One historian of the Sinn Fein separatist movement, P.S. O'Hegarty, for whom the play had been 'a kind of sacrament', recognised this when he wrote soon after Yeats's

death that 'Ireland in the coming times will understand that the
great poet who worked for a national culture was during the
whole of his life one of the most revolutionary influences in
Ireland. He worked for a revolution of the spirit, and it is the
spirit that moves the body.'

This may be obvious enough now, and even at the time was
clear to many Irish writers. But the significance of what was
going on in Ireland around 1902 was not clear to the British
authorities in the Irish government. They were aware of the
revolution of the spirit, but when the political revolution came in
1916, it took them by surprise.

Giving evidence before the Royal Commission investigating
the rebellion in Ireland, the Irish Secretary Augustine Birrell
made some remarks about the literary situation between 1896
and 1916.

> This period was also marked by a genuine literary revival in
> prose, poetry and drama, which has produced remarkable
> books and plays and a school of acting, all characterised by
> originality and independence of thought and expression quite
> divorced from any political party, and all tending towards and
> feeding latent desires for, some kind of separate national
> existence.[3]

This was a curious situation to watch, he admits, but there was
nothing in the movement 'suggestive of rebellion, except in the
realm of thought'.

Birrell could only see political consequences in political actions.
He typified the British authorities in failing to see what effect the
literary revival might have on politics. But it was just because
the Revival was a revolution in the realm of thought—what
Yeats means by intellect, calculation, number, measurement—
that it became an influence in Ireland.

Birrell thought that if the Abbey, the epicentre of the revival,
did have any effect on life in Ireland, it would be to ameliorate
the political tensions of the country by its wit. A popular comedy
such as Lennox Robinson's *Patriots* (1912), which made fun of
harmless ageing Fenians in rural Cork, would not seem to have
encouraged revolution in any way at all.

Yet this was not so. Both Sean O'Faolain the writer, and
Michael Collins the patriot, were affected by the play, as we

shall see in chapter seven. In influencing such young minds Robinson's play was yet another (though unlikely) source of nourishment for the changing politics of Ireland. In those politics poetry found an expression of its power. That Irish school of acting which Birrell admired did not confine itself to the stage, but acted out the dramas of the national imagination on the streets of Dublin and the back roads of Cork.

Revolution, like tragedy, takes place in the imagination. A revolution in thought or feeling—that is, in what people know about themselves or imagine that they know—is the prerequisite for any revolution. The Literary Revival was part of a real revolution because Irish writers and artists were able to express, in a completely new way, a new feeling about the country and its people, quite different to what had been thought or felt previously.

The heroic image of Cuchulain which Sheppard used in his 1916 memorial was a part of that new knowledge, and is a good example of the interaction of poetry and politics which we shall be exploring in this book. As Frank O'Connor observes in *A Backward Look*, 'sometimes one gets the impression that all the vital political issues of the time were unimportant compared with the task of bringing the name Cuchulain into English literature'.

Originally resurrected by scholars and writers in the course of historical and literary research during the nineteenth century, this Celtic Iron Age warrior came to inspire not only poets like Yeats, but also some of the 1916 men such as Pearse. He became an actor in the new national drama, as well as in the plays of the Abbey Theatre : a role far removed from the original version of the legend in which he was the tribal hero of Ulster. (It is one of those odd and bitter ironies of Irish history that Cuchulain should now stand in the south as an image of patriotic sacrifice for a cause which modern Ulster hates and fears.)

There are disturbing parallels between the ancient myth and modern events. Cuchulain is one of Ireland's greatest heroes, yet in the saga he is known as the 'Contorted One'. In battle his anger rises uncontrollably while 'the champion's light' shines around his head. In his frenzy he strikes out wildly with no regard for friend or foe, and much is made of his divided loyalties. He is forced to kill a strange boy who will not give him his name—the boy is his only son sent to him by his wife from abroad. He carries the body back to the tribe: 'There, men of Ulster, is my son.'

After this, in a legend adapted by Yeats for a play, Cuchulain is bewitched into fighting the sea, for fear that he would kill the men of Ulster in his angry grief.

In his final battle Cuchulain kills his childhood friend Ferdia. Neither son nor friend can survive the warrior's battle frenzy.

A peculiarly Celtic view of life is contained in these myths (and in those about the Fianna, a wandering band of warriors, from whom the nineteenth-century terrorist group, the Fenians, took their name). When Cuchulain was a child a druid prophesied that that he would have a short life. 'Better a short life and fame forever', the boy replied, 'than a long life without glory.'

This was an ancient morality that appealed to Pearse: Cuchulain and the Fianna are the pagan heart of Christian Ireland. They represent the triumph of the will and the worth of feeling, of the romantic and the heroic, important aspects of the Irish revolution.

The character of the isolated hero, and the deeds of the outlaw band of fighting men, whether of Cuchulain or Pearse, the Fianna or the IRA, continue to fascinate the Irish imagination, as we shall see in the course of this history of the revolution and the literature it inspired.

The life and death of Cuchulain is fearsome and tragic. The ideal of his heroic death appealed to Patrick Pearse, but did he ever ponder, as Yeats did in his plays and poems, the meaning of those other deaths, of Cuchulain's only son and his closest friend? The burden of the saga seems to be that all battles end with the deaths of sons and friends, the destruction of all that one loves best.

To Pearse the revolutionary, it was the rigorous life and the heroic death that appealed; Yeats the poet was more moved by the pity of Emer's love, the son's fate, the curse of friendship, and not the death, but the afterdeath, as revealed in that strange valedictory poem 'Cuchulain Comforted'. These contrasting attitudes and sympathies already separated the rebels and the writers, even before the revolution began.

Ideas of the heroic and the romantic absorbed both the

patriots and the poets. But in both the Revival and the revolution there were realists, men who saw perhaps more clearly the real horror of trying to live according to a prehistoric code of morals in the modern age. These men, mostly novelists and democrats rather than poets and revolutionaries, also suffered a seachange in the course of the revolution. Eventually, as we shall see, romance and realism reached a compromise, as did revolution and democracy.

This dramatic struggle as seen by Irish writers and artists is the subject of this study. I hope to show that the Literary Revival in Ireland created the possibility of the political revolution; that the writings of the revival record the true reality of the war; and that the literary movement emerges from the disillusioning events of the Civil War with its integrity intact, which is more than can be said for the politics of Irish nationalism.

The book begins with a survey of the social and cultural ethos of Ireland during the nineteenth century from which grew the two branches of the Revival, the romantic and the realistic, and the complicated politics of the decade before 1916. This survey is necessarily brief; the period presents many as yet unsolved problems which cannot be discussed here. The central chapters deal with the course of the revolution itself and with various aspects of the literature surrounding it. Finally, after describing the Civil War and its impact on several writers, the book concludes with an account of the new literature of the early thirties, which dealt largely with the sterility of the new state in the eyes of its writers. A sense of exile dominated the work of many writers of that period. In contrast to this are the magnificently affirmative poems of the last years of W.B. Yeats and the later paintings of his brother Jack B. Yeats.

When going back through the history of the period between the death of Parnell and the death of Yeats we must look for the roots in Irish life which the revolution in literature shares with the revolution in politics. If after the profound events of the revolution and the great achievements of the writers and artists, there seemed to be little poetry in the new Ireland, it was because the Irish imagination and the heart that fed it had grown coarse and brutal in the heat of the long struggle.

Cuchulain, despite what he stands for in the Irish imagination today, belongs to the literature of an earlier, more primitive

Ireland. How was this potent legend revived and why did it become of vital concern to poets and patriots in modern Ireland? The answers to these questions are to be found in the society and literature of nineteenth-century Ireland, and to the formative years of the Irish Revival. To that period we will now turn.

PART ONE: REVIVAL

The event was one thing, the way the event was imagined another thing, and more powerful. And there were men and women who lived through the event, *and* through the imagining of the event. Their lives, marked by this double experience, marked mine. And both the event and its imagining, and the consequences of the way in which it was imagined, helped powerfully to shape what happened in Ireland in the early twentieth century, and what is happening there now.

Conor Cruise O'Brien: *States of Ireland*

The Memory of the Dead

SOCIETY AND LITERATURE
IN NINETEENTH-CENTURY IRELAND

CHARLES STEWART PARNELL died on 6 October 1891. His
sudden death was the climax of a political crisis which had split
the Irish Parliamentary Party at Westminster, and also divided
public opinion sharply in Ireland itself. The events of the previous months: the divorce writ by Captain O'Shea naming
Parnell, the denunciation of Parnell's leadership by the Irish
Catholic Hierarchy, the meeting in Committee Room 15, these
events passed into folklore. Dying, Parnell passed into legend.

The death of Parnell was a turning point in Irish history. Not
merely was it a critical moment in the long struggle to break the
union with Great Britain which had created the modern democratic movement in the country; but it was also an event from
which many later movements would trace their rise to influence.
So it is a good moment to look back over the nineteenth century
to trace the origins of the Revival and the revolution.

In 1801, the year of the union with Great Britain, Ireland had
been a semi-feudal country. The land was owned by a small
number of aristocratic landlords, mainly Anglo-Irish Protestants,
but also by an important sprinkling of Catholics. These great
estates were let out into smaller and smaller units, often through
sub-lettings, until in the west of Ireland many holdings were little
more than tiny plots of rock-bound earth. By 1891 the situation
was very different, the country and the people radically changed.

A major influence on the condition and outlook of the Irish
people had been the experience of the Great Famine. Since the
introduction of the potato as the common food of the people about
1750, the population had risen from two million to about eight
million in 1845. When the potato crops failed that year and for
several years running, the result was an unparalleled social disaster. A million people died of hunger and disease, another

million emigrated. And afterwards further millions continued to leave for America and the Colonies, and the population fell to below four million at the turn of the century.

The Famine was the beginning of the end for the landed gentry. The demand for land reform grew until the Land War of the 1880s brought about the first of an almost continuous series of reforms, which turned Ireland from a country of large estates into a nation of small holdings. The demand for a greater share in the actual running of the country increased as the nation grew more self-confident and politically organised. Land reform could only end in Home Rule.

Despite set-backs, the country's prosperity increased during the century, and new classes began to appear. On the land the strong farmers and graziers were becoming more important than the old landlords. In the cities there was appearing, due largely to the drift from the land after the Famine, a new urban working class. The new prosperity also produced a new middle class, largely small traders and manufacturers, in which Catholics were forming an increasing part.

The Catholic Church was a dominant influence in Irish life. During the eighteenth century Catholicism had been on the decline, and church-going had fallen off, especially in the towns. The clergy had then been members of the old landed Catholic families, mainly educated abroad in Irish colleges on the Continent. But in 1795 the British government, disturbed at the ideas these priests might be bringing back, established a national seminary at Maynooth. From this college, which had been originally staffed with Jansenist exiles from France, a different kind of priest was sent out. They were drawn largely from a different class than before, from the sons of strong farmers rather than the landed gentry. The influence of these new priests was very strong.

Their ideas were narrow and puritanical due to their Jansenist training, their social attitudes those of their class, strongly conservative, even reactionary. The increasing puritanism of Ireland during the nineteenth century was due partly to this new influence, but also to the aftermath of the Famine. A natural revulsion against breeding seems to have swept the country. Though Irish families remained large, the marriage age rose and fewer people married. A puritan outlook suited a people practis-

ing, as James Meenan observes, the only means of birth control
open to them as Catholics. But the emotional nature of the Irish
people was warped by these changes, or so it seemed to many
later writers, especially the novelists of the Irish Revival. Sexuality had become for the Irish an actual threat to their material
safety, even to their very existence, as the horrors of the Famine
had shown them. If sex was a serious sin in the eyes of the
Church, in the minds of the people it was a social menace.

Social attitudes altered in little more than a generation. Daniel
O'Connell, embedded in the last days of the old Gaelic culture,
was notorious (in Irish folklore at least, for the real facts were
different) for his priapic adventures. Parnell, a product of the new
Ireland created by Emancipation, the Land Acts and the Home
Rule movement, fell from power when his most circumspect
ménage was revealed to the public.

This newly established Church grew in power and influence
during the course of the century. The local priest was often the
only man of education from whom people could obtain advice,
and his views carried weight, especially in rural areas. Though
there was always a considerable amount of poverty in the
country, Ireland still had enough of an economic surplus after
the 1850s to support the widespread building of churches and
convents. The numbers of Catholics to one priest went from
1,978 in 1849 to 927 in 1901. These efforts in building and
training were funded by the farmers and the new middle class,
and not by the old Catholic gentry. As George Moore, a landed
Catholic from Mayo, remarked in *Parnell and His Island*
(1887), 'priesthood and patriotism are the only ways of advance-
ment open in Ireland to those who are not landlords'. The
Church and the new nationalism, neither of which Moore cared
for, would remake the country in his lifetime.

These social and emotional changes coincided with a cultural
transition from Irish to English. Here also the Famine was a
great divide. Before 1849 large areas of the country were still
Irish-speaking; afterwards English, which was encouraged in the
new National Schools managed by the local clergy, gained ground
continuously. There were clear social and political advantages in
speaking English, and the majority of Irish people were not slow
to grasp them. Gaelic came to be regarded as the badge of the
Bog Irish, the ignorant unredeemed.

Gaelic Ireland had been a traditional culture with its own largely oral literature, which was rooted in the life of a rural society. Now the people were learning a new language in an Ireland dominated by Victorian bourgeois decorum and the Jansenist outlook of the Catholic Church. That language was the English which Thackeray raged against because it restricted the nature of what he could write about, in contrast to the freedom of expression found in Fielding. This radical change in the nature of the language they spoke had a serious effect on Irish writers and their work. Indeed, because of the language question there is really nothing that can be called 'literature' in Ireland during much of the nineteenth century.

The peculiar features of Irish and English, and the nature of their literatures, are well illustrated by Brian Merriman and Maria Edgeworth.

Merriman's poem *The Midnight Court* was a witty, earthy poem dealing frankly with the sexual dilemmas of women in his native Clare. His open frankness reflects the attitudes of pre-Famine Gaelic Ireland (the poem is set in the 1780s), and his freedom of expression is quite representative of the Gaelic temperament. The influence of Swift and Goldsmith on his work shows that Merriman was open to cultural exchanges between Gaelic and English on an equal basis. But he belonged to a dying culture, which was effectively destroyed by famine and emigration.

Maria Edgeworth's *Castle Rackrent* (1800) is the first real Irish novel and in its own time was very influential, for it inspired Scott to write his series of historical novels, and Turgenev his sketches of rural life in feudal Russia. This tradition of the realistic novel, which Maria Edgeworth began, was brought back to Ireland at the time of the Irish Revival by George Moore, who had been influenced by Turgenev. Such are the complex connections of European and Irish culture.

The themes of Merriman and Edgeworth, the Gaelic theme of the social dilemmas of the individual and the Anglo-Irish theme of the decline of the gentry in the Big House, were themes to which the Irish revival returned at the end of the nineteenth century. By then the old ways of life were dying but there had been a growth of interest in Gaelic, begun by scholars on the Continent, and popularised by several Irish writers.

Many manuscripts had survived from earlier periods of Irish history, but many of them were in Old Irish which was quite unintelligible to modern speakers of Irish. In 1855, however, Johann Zeuss, after extensive studies of continental Irish manuscripts, published his *Grammatica Celtica*, which provided the key to reading the earlier forms of Irish. Thus began the intensive investigations by German and other scholars into the literature of ancient Ireland which eventually compelled the respect, even of the English, for the old culture of the country.

A poem such as Sir Samuel Ferguson's *Congal* (1872) would have been quite impossible without all this previous scholarly research, without the basic facts. These facts, as Ferguson observed as early as 1840, were allowing the people of Ireland 'to *live back* in the land they live *in*, with as ample and as interesting a field of retrospective enjoyment as any of the nations around us'.

The translations of histories, sagas, and most importantly, of poetry, followed naturally. These provided the basic materials at last for both historians and writers. Eugene O'Curry's pioneering book *The Manners and Customs of the Ancient Irish* appeared in 1877, but was based on lectures given at Newman's Catholic University in Dublin in 1852.

Popularisations such as P.W. Joyce's *Old Celtic Romances* (1879) as well as his more scholarly *Irish Names of Places* (1869) and *A Social History of Ancient Ireland* (1903), brought the work of the academics to a wider audience. But in this field the books of Standish O'Grady, beginning with his *History of Ireland: Cuchulain and His Contemporaries* (1880), were the most influential. These books with their grand compelling manner, were the basic background reading of most writers of the Irish revival, who saw O'Grady as their founding father.

However, it was an English critic who first recognised the peculiar nature of this rediscovered Celtic literature. Matthew Arnold's lectures as Professor of Poetry at Oxford on *The Study of Celtic Literature* (1867) constituted a major step towards the creation of modern Irish literature. Arnold himself actually wrote an 'Irish' poem in 1869 about St Brendan, and persuaded Tennyson to try an Irish subject, which resulted in that strange poem *The Voyage of Maeldun*. These efforts by English poets, which were part of the general revival of interest in

B

things medieval and gothic in Europe, helped prepare the way for the publication of Yeats's first major work *The Wanderings of Oisin* (1889), by adding dignity to Ireland (the phrase is Lady Gregory's) and by introducing Celtic themes to a wider audience.

Yeats recognised three poets as his peers in the nineteenth century, Thomas Davis, James Clarence Mangan, and Sir Samuel Ferguson, and they are indeed representative writers, in whom we can find the elements of much later writing.

In Davis there is the conscious use of nationalist politics in poetry; his poems and ballads are still popular today among those otherwise uninterested in poetry. Aside from his sweeping, powerful rhetoric, there is nothing in his work that we can recall as real poetry but he brought politics to Irish poetry, to remain for a long time.

With Mangan we have a different case. Translating from the Gaelic with passionate freedom, he also utilises the fervid emotions of patriotism. But Mangan was a real poet, and what persists in the memory after reading him is the sense of tortured self, a tone to become familiar in later Irish literature. His insistence on the supremacy of the artist appealed to both Yeats and Joyce, and has kept him a reputation.

Ferguson rejected nationalist politics, and was so reticent about himself and his work that Standish O'Grady, though a frequent guest at his house, was unaware that his host had written poetry at all. In contrast to Mangan, he used the sources of Irish history, not for the projection of self, or for obvious political ends as Davis had, but to recreate some sense of the living legendary past of the country. Yeats was influenced by him at an early stage of his career—the comment on the political effect of Irish verse quoted earlier in the Introduction is from an essay on Ferguson's poetry—and applied for his own ends the peculiar effect of Irish themes that he learnt from Ferguson.

The elements of Irish writing in the revival, the personal intentness, the emotions of politics, the legends of history, exist separately in these writers. When, as in Yeats, these elements merge, we get the powerful sensual political poetry of his old age. For this miracle to occur, and it is the greatest achievement of the Irish revival, the sources of the Irish tradition from which the legends came had to be discovered, cleared and tapped.

This work was done partly by archaeologists and partly by philologists and other literary scholars. A new idea of Ireland, far removed from the current one of ignorance and poverty, was built up. By the time of Parnell's death in 1891, the sources and elements of a new Irish literature were in existence. A new image of the country had been established, partly the creation of scholarship which had revealed the ancient Celtic civilisation with which the modern Irish might claim a continuity, and partly due to the self-confidence bred of the Land War and other political events. It seemed to Yeats that all a new Irish literature needed for full expression was a new language. Gaelic was dead; the English of the Ascendancy was, as it was used, a foreign language. To express anything new about the country something quite different was needed. This was how it appeared to Yeats, Moore and Synge. The actual interrelationship of Irish and English was not so schematic. Though there is a Gaelic accent to much modern writing in Ireland, some write in the usual mode of English.

In 1893, two years after Parnell's death, Douglas Hyde, a mild-mannered Protestant gentleman, did two significant things. The first and more obviously important to historians, was to found the Gaelic League. He intended this organisation to be non-political, embracing in a love of the Irish language all the classes of Irish society. At first he was successful, but as the membership of the League grew, politics soon entered into its affairs. Later many were to claim that Hyde's efforts to revive Irish as a living language partly inspired the ideology of those who planned the Easter Rising in 1916.

But secondly, and far more relevantly for us here, he published a slim volume of poems translated from the Gaelic, printed with the originals. The book was called *The Love Songs of Connacht*, and it contained some of the finest of Irish poetry. But these poems were, as the title announced, love songs: not songs of patriotism, but of more intimate emotions.

The authentic voice of the Irish people, Brian Merriman's voice, had reasserted itself in the language of Maria Edgeworth. The literary translation of the nation was complete. The English language in Ireland had reached maturity after a century of struggle. The vigour and freedom of the Gaelic language had been imported into English. Yeats was later to claim, quite rightly, that parts of Hyde's book marked 'the coming of a new power into our language'.

It was now possible, using this language, these elements and sources, as Yeats and his friends hoped at the time, to create at last a real literature for Ireland. But much of the force of their creations depended on the energies released by the concurrent rise of Irish democracy. The Irish Revival was only one part of a general alteration of feeling in Ireland affecting not only literature but also politics.

An important factor in the origins of the Revival (and the politics of Home Rule also) was the creation of the new middle class which formed a new audience for literature, as well as for painting and music. The audience for the old traditional Gaelic literature had been a rural one. The audience for the Revival was the respectable bourgeoisie of the cities and towns; certainly Yeats and Moore were more read in Dublin and Cork, than in Aran or Dingle. Before the emergence of this new middle class, the literary and social revolution at the turn of the century would have been impossible. The modern prosperity of the country had brought about an increased literacy, and this increased the appetite not only for Irish literature, but also for self-government.

A general improvement in Irish culture also resulted. In architecture and painting, the two arts most dependent on wealth, there had been a sharp decline from the elegance of the late Georgian. In the buildings of Dublin, for example, there is a long gap between the last of the large town houses built in the Georgian style and the late Victorian suburbs, with their quiet charms, which were built for the new middle class, where the families of Yeats and Joyce lived. In painting too there is a dearth of both talent and interesting pictures in the middle of the century, so much so that pictures such as Daniel Maclise's *Marriage of Strongbow and Aoife* and Frederick W. Burton's *The Aran Fisherman's Drowned Child*, stand out as almost revolutionary. The Aran painting presages the interest of the Revival in the Western peasantry; while the Maclise picture represents the consummation of the union which the politics of Irish nationalism was bent on breaking.

The ideas of the Irish Revival were acceptable to the new Ireland because they confirmed their political aspirations, especially those of the new middle class. But that same middle class was often to be distressed at the working out of those ideas in plays, poems and novels during the next generation.

By the death of Parnell Ireland was, then, a very different place, both socially and culturally, from what she had been two generations before. The old opposition of Castle and Cabin (though it would play a large part in the imagination of the Literary Revival) was less significant, except in the West of Ireland. New political ideas were emerging (the first stirrings of the revolution), which the Irish Parliamentary Party represented.

However there also existed a more radical, revolutionary tradition, especially in the poorer parts of the country, in Connaught, Donegal and the south-west. For those who could not find a place in the democratic movement, the old Republican conspiracy remained a vital form of political action. During the Land War, when Parnell was creating the basis for a new nation, a gang of terrorists murdered the Chief Secretary and a colleague in the Phoenix Park. Those Invincibles with their surgical knives may have seemed a small and unimportant faction, but they represented the 'physical force' tradition which would eventually cut the country apart in the Civil War. Though the Fenian tradition had little real support, it had a powerful hold over the Irish imagination. *The Memory of the Dead*, from which the title of this chapter comes, was only one of many songs that helped to keep the revolutionary tradition alive until 1916. Such brooding over historical injustice was an important factor in the political attitudes outside the middle class in Ireland, in the nineteenth century and even today.

Parnell had now become part of the memory of the dead, many felt in 1891 : the Famine dead, the Fenian dead, the dead Celts in Maclise's picture. Parnell haunts the memory of a generation : every book Joyce wrote, the later poetry of Yeats, the early fiction of O'Faolain. What Irish person of that generation ever forgot, as the boy James Augustine never did, that terrible scene in the Joyce house at Christmas 1891, when Mr Casey in a passion shouts 'No more God, away with God', and collapses weeping on the table for 'Poor Parnell, my dead king'.

Yet the fall and death of Parnell, though so like the final fatal act of some tragedy, was really only the prologue to a greater drama. 'The modern literature of Ireland,' Yeats recalled for the Swedish Academy in 1923 after receiving his Nobel Prize, 'and indeed all that stir of thought that prepared for the Anglo-Irish war, began when Parnell fell from power in 1891. A disillusioned and embittered Ireland turned from Parliamentary politics; an event was conceived; and the race began, as I think, to be troubled by that event's long gestation.'[1]

The Return of the Native (1)

POETRY AND THE IDEAL OF IRELAND

THAT great stir of thought which Yeats described in 1923 can
be traced through the course of his own career and his relations
with other Irish writers during the decades before the Easter
Rising.

The literary revival over which he presided had two main
streams: a romantic thesis led by Yeats himself, and a realistic
antithesis inspired by George Moore; one concentrated mainly in
poetry, the other in prose, with both experimenting in drama.
Both of these groups rejected any mere imitation of the contemporary English literary modes. Drawing on the modern continental techniques of the Symbolists, and of Ibsen and the Realists,
they applied these to Irish themes and to Irish society. In the
context of the English literary scene at the time, theirs was a
revolutionary departure.

We will begin, in this chapter, with Yeats and the Romantics.
Yeats published his first collection of poems *Crossways* in 1889.
He was then only 24, and the indecisive title was an appropriate
one for that strange *mélange* containing the thoughts of the
Indian upon God and the tale of a Sligo priest. Yeats was still
searching for some personal style, still hesitant which road he
should take, the one to India or the other to the West of Ireland.
His route was soon settled for him, as he tells us in his memoirs:

It was through the old Fenian leader John O'Leary I found
my theme. His long imprisonment, his longer banishment, his
magnificent head, his scholarship, his pride, his integrity, all
that aristocratic dream nourished amid little shops and little
farms, had drawn around him a group of young men; I was
but eighteen or nineteen. . . . He gave me the poems of Thomas
Davis, said they were not good poetry but had changed his life

when a young man, spoke of other poets associated with Davis and *The Nation* newspaper, probably lent me their books.[1]

O'Leary had been one of the original Fenians in the 1860s, but he did not hold with a careless resort to violence as did others in the movement. In his sage-like old age, he tried to exert a pacific influence over younger people such as Maud Gonne and Yeats, and to divert their energies into what he saw as constructive paths. It was O'Leary who encouraged Maud Gonne in her early politics; and who sent Yeats to read Eugene O'Curry on the ancient Celts. Some other friend suggested he read O'Grady's versions of the Celtic myths and sagas. All of this reading had its due effect. Just as Maud Gonne became almost the personification of Irish nationalism, so Yeats was identified with the older, Celtic Ireland of myth.

By 1893, when his next collection *The Rose* appeared, Yeats was establishing himself as a poet. Now, however, his symbolic rose of poetic beauty was dedicated to the themes suggested by his reading :

> I would, before my time to go,
> Sing of old Eire and the ancient ways.[2]

Ireland had acquired him as her poet. From his childhood Yeats had been conscious of his peculiar identity as only an Irish boy reared in England could be. In his imagination he fell back on the happy memories of his summer holidays in Sligo. In his poetry, however, he had to struggle hard against the influence of Spenser, Shelley and Blake, and to expand the limits imposed by Symbolism. Irish themes and imagery liberated him from too rich, highly coloured and mystic verses, and from the easy facility of the decadent.

From the first he wanted his poetry to have its own inherent unity. 'Have not all races', he thought, 'their first unity from a mythology that binds them to hill and rock?' On his annual holidays among the people of Sligo he sought out some of the stories for his book *The Celtic Twilight* (1893), the unfortunate title of which became attached to the whole literary movement. But there was nothing arch or fey about those gritty peasant stories, or about the movement itself which was full of practical people who got things done. Yeats was seeking deliberately among the rocks and hills of his own home country for a mythology to nourish his poetry, to bind him to Ireland. He became self-consciously an *Irish* poet. Anglo-American critics often underestimate just how Irish he was, a poet working deliberately in a national tradition which he was to completely transform.

The poetry of Young Ireland had attempted by using Irish history to create a national consciousness. Yeats was not led, as so many others were, to admire Davis and the others merely because they were suitably patriotic. They were of great interest to anyone concerned with the course of Irish literature, but he saw all too clearly their deficiencies as poets. To them the old legends were nothing more than stories to stir up latent patriotism. To Yeats, who saw them as the scattered fragments of a lost religion, there were 'heart-mysteries there'.

Though he read scholarly works or serious popularisations of scholarship, Yeats used them for quite unscholarly ends. Cuchulain was to him no mere barbaric curiosity. That intensity of feeling which we find in later poems like 'Cuchulain Comforted' and the play *On Baile's Strand* has its origin in such earlier work as 'Cuchulain's Fight with the Sea'. This was the first appearance of the hero in Yeats's poetry and the poem reads almost prophetically. Cuchulain, bound by an oath, slays his own son and is stricken by remorse. For fear that in his anger he would kill all of them, the druids cast a delusion over him:

> Cuchulain stirred,
> Stared on the horses of the sea, and heard
> The cars of battle and his own name cried;
> And fought with the invulnerable tide.[3]

The hero had returned with a vengeance. Soon the name of Cuchulain would be cried among the armoured cars of a modern war, other only sons would die, other heroes fight with the 'invulnerable tide' of history: when this poem was published, Patrick Pearse was at the impressionable age of thirteen.

The Dublin of the 1890s in which Yeats and his friends were trying to create a modern literature from the materials of the ancient sagas and peasant folklore, was a quiet place, Joyce's 'centre of paralysis' in a country where nothing seemed to be happening. Yet the forces of change were already at work which would raise Pearse to the stature of a Cuchulain.

The fall of Parnell had split the Irish Party. Young men of nationalist sympathies, as Yeats suggested to the Swedish Academy, finding no outlet for their natural idealism in the sordid post-Parnell party politics—evoked for us in all their sterility by Joyce in his story 'Ivy Day in the Committee Room'—turned instead to literature. Others equally idealistic turned to more revolutionary politics. Yeats dabbled in both. Through his friendship with John O'Leary and later with Maud Gonne, he joined the oath-bound Irish Republican Brotherhood, though whether he was ever sworn is uncertain. This political activity on the poet's part was by no means due to his infatuation with Maud Gonne. He was a convinced nationalist, and subtle enough in his politics to gain what he wanted for the cause of literature. He had also a politician's love of controversy. The simplicities of life may often have bewildered him, but he delighted in conspiratorial complexities. For a while he enjoyed the stir and activity of involving himself with organised politics, until the type of person they naturally attracted disenchanted him.

Granted his nationalist sympathies, what was the position of the artist in relation to the revolution? In *The Rose* Yeats included not only that poem on Cuchulain's fight with the sea, which suggests the futility of all struggle if it destroys what one loves, but also a poem he originally prefaced to a selection from nineteenth-century Irish novelists he had made for an American publisher. In it he contrasts the poet at home with the Irish political exiles in the United States:

> Ah, Exiles wandering over lands and seas,
> And planning, plotting always that some morrow,
> May set a stone upon ancestral sorrow!
> I also bear a bell-branch full of ease . . .
>
> Gay bells or sad, they bring you memories
> Of half-forgotten innocent old places:
> We and our bitterness have left no traces
> On Munster grass and Connemara skies.[4]

He is playing here on the sentimental feelings of his Irish-American readers, who would have been content to have poets and writers provide only the familiar sentiments of Carleton and Griffin. Yet Yeats himself never limited his poetry to such a narrow notion of the poet's art. In the same collection he addresses Ireland in the coming time, and makes clear where his loyalties lie :

> Know, that I would accounted be
> True brother of a company
> That sang, to sweeten Ireland's wrong,
> Ballad and story, rann and song;
> Nor be I any less of them,
> Because the red-rose-bordered hem
> Of her, whose history began
> Before God made the angelic clan,
> Trails all about the written page.[5]

And as if his patriotism was in doubt—as it was, for many nationalists distrusted on principle both poetry and Protestants —Yeats compares his own poetry with that of *The Nation* poets, finding its true value only in its arts :

> Nor may I less be counted one
> With Davis, Mangan, Ferguson,
> Because, to him who ponders well,
> My rhymes more than their rhyming tell
> Of things discovered in the deep,
> Where only body's laid asleep.[6]

True to this artistic creed, at the same time as he was involving himself in politics, Yeats was organising the Irish dramatic movement. The first production, his own play *The Countess Cathleen*, was presented in 1899 in Dublin.

Irish drama, if it meant anything at that date to foreigners, meant Boucicault. Irish nationalists hated his plays as degrading the real Irishman with the image of the feckless drunken 'stage Irishman'. Yet oddly Boucicault was a notably patriotic person. In *Arragh-na-Pogh*, produced in Dublin in 1865, at the time of the Fenian troubles, he sang with reckless defiance his own version of 'The Wearing of the Green' at one of the most melodramatic moments of the play. For a modern audience his plays are fine entertainment. Certainly his delineation of character is on the level of a strip cartoon, but there is nothing derogatory about his Irish people. What Irish nationalists really hated may well have been his laughter, when they required serious purpose. Today his plays are interesting for their influence on later playwrights like Shaw and O'Casey who also made the serious-minded uneasy with their laughter.

Yet for Yeats, Boucicault was not what was wanted. He wanted to create a dramatic poetic theatre, devoted to high thoughts and fine poetry. His *Countess Cathleen* was an example of what he wanted, but his allegory of the noblewoman who sells her soul to save her peasantry in a time of famine was roundly denounced by patriots and churchmen as being derogatory to the character of Catholic Ireland. It was not going to be easy for Yeats to give his people the theatre he thought they ought to have.

1899 also saw the publication of *The Wind Among the Reeds*, which was a considerable advance on his earlier work, and was remarkable for the complete absence of political themes. These were mostly love poems, and the lover was concerned completely with the torments of his unrequited love. This was strictly poet's poetry, for lovers rather than politicians, for Deirdre rather than Cuchulain.

Maud Gonne was the tormenting inspiration of these poems. The passion here was singularly one-sided. She admired Yeats in a rather off-hand way : after all, however silly, Willy was useful to the cause. But as she already had a French lover, who was the father of her romantically named daughter Iseult, her emotions were never involved with Yeats.

Yeats the politician was active in organising the 1798 Centenary, and in boycotting Queen Victoria's visit in 1900, an event enlivened by Maud Gonne flying a black article of ladies underwear over her house as a flag of shame to greet the 'Famine Queen'. Yet the creations of the Irish dramatic movement were perhaps more politically influential than these acts, and of deeper consequence than pious memorials or amusing ruderies. They were at least *creative*. The ideal of the Abbey was to add dignity to Ireland and to the Irish people by making them the subjects of dramas, to do away with the image of the stage Irishman.

Yeats contributed to a volume edited by Lady Gregory called *Ideals in Ireland* (1901) as did nearly everyone associated with the literary movement. AE, George Moore, Synge, Horace Plunkett : they are all in it. The book, though little mentioned now, was a kind of manifesto of the movement's intentions. They were all idealists of a kind (even George Moore), with visions of Ireland's possibilities which they would try and realise as best they could. The key word is *ideal*, for theirs was very much an idealised version of Ireland and her future.

Plays were a means of presenting that ideal and of creating political passion. To the political cause Yeats contributed his play *Cathleen ni Houlihan*, which was produced in April 1902 with Maud Gonne in the role of the old woman lamenting over her four green fields. However maudlin the play now appears to us, at that moment it was staggering in its effects. The curtain rose on the interior of a small cottage near Killala Bay in 1798, at the time of the expected French invasion. The son of the house follows the old woman out to join the invaders and the younger coming in is asked if he has seen them. 'I did not,' he replies, 'but I saw a young girl and she had the walk of a queen.' Irish nationalism had for some, it seemed, a rarefied sex appeal.

The play created a sensation. An image of Ireland worthy of worship captivated many imaginations that night. P.S. O'Hegarty confessed that to him the play 'was a sort of sacrament', and the grace transmitted through it inspired many to revolution. 'Miss Gonne's impersonation had stirred the audience as I have never seen another audience stirred.' One wonders if Maud Gonne's imagination, inflamed at the best of times, ever recovered from that impersonation; whether in later life she was not continuing the same dramatic performance on other more public stages.

The plays were to have an objective political effect, just as Yeats had thought they would. Yet what were Yeats's political ideas at this time? In a speech in New York in 1904 he outlined some of his ideas about the Ireland in the making. He was at this time still deeply influenced by the ideas of Ruskin's *Unto This Last*, which he had read when about twenty-four, and also by his friendship with Morris at whose house he came in contact with other British Socialists and Fabians. His mind was still pliable enough to be easily changed by his friends' opinions. In his speech he sees the conflict between England and Ireland as a 'war between two civilisations, two ideals of life'. Ireland, unlike England, was not an industrial country, and he claims that the Irish had no desire to build up a very rich or a very poor class, or to have whole counties blackened with the smoke and grime of factories.

> I think that the best ideal for our people, an ideal very generally accepted among us, is that Ireland is going to become a country where if there will be very few rich, there will be nobody poor. Wherever men have tried to imagine a perfect life, they have imagined a place where men plough and sow and reap, not a place where there are great wheels and great chimneys vomiting smoke.

He goes on to elaborate this pastoral vision of an Ireland in which he clearly sees no place for the industrialised Lagan Valley around Belfast.

> And this Ireland too, as we think, will be a country where not only will the wealth be distributed but where there will be an imaginative culture and power to understand imaginative and spiritual things among the people. We wish to preserve an ancient ideal of life. Wherever its customs prevail, there you will find the folk song, the folk tale, the proverb and the charming manners that come from an ancient culture. . . . In Ireland alone among the nations that I know you will find, away on the western sea board, under broken roofs, a race of gentlemen keep alive the ideals of a great time when they sang the heroic life with drawn swords in their hands.[7]

The ideal of Ireland espoused here is one which would attempt to overthrow English rule. His suggestions for revolution, if that is what a return to a heroic life with drawn swords would mean, are put off to a suitably vague date in the future, but he sees the poetry and the politics of the present as a preparation for tomorrow's fight. In 1886 he had seen that Irish poets merely by writing on Irish themes in an Irish style contributed to political ends. At the centenary celebrations in 1898 he had spoken of building the nation 'to noble ends'. There was an old story, he had related on that occasion, of a ship running onto rocks in a storm, 'and almost on the rocks a mysterious figure appears and lays its hand upon the tiller'. This was Manannan, the Celtic god of the sea. 'So it is with nations, a flaming hand is laid suddenly upon the tiller.' Can his audience have doubted the meaning of his words: Ireland would be saved by the intervention of the old gods, high culture would return to the country, when the peasant way of life was restored to respectable prominence; all this after the fiery intervention of a revolution. Putting this ideal into action was another matter.

In 1903 Yeats and Maud Gonne finally parted when she married, against all her friends' advice, Major John MacBride, a hero of the Boer War prominent in Nationalist affairs. The marriage was not a success. After the birth of her son Sean, she left her husband in 1905. These years were a critical period for Yeats. When his old love threw herself with passionate energy into the founding of Sinn Fein with Arthur Griffith, he could not follow. He turned away from politics in such a style, and absorbed himself in the Abbey Theatre, plays and poetry.

The West of Ireland, on whose lifestyle the notions of political utopia quoted above were based, was a stimulating discovery for Yeats. In August 1896 he had visited the Aran Islands with Edward Martyn and Arthur Symons. He was working on *The Speckled Bird* at the time, a novel in which the principal characters alternate between the mystical cults of Paris and the stark simplicity of Aran, rather like Madame Blavatsky in a shawl and red petticoat. Yeats made two trips to the islands that summer in fishing boats, gathering background colour for his book.

The novel came to nothing, and Yeats was to make little direct use of what he had seen on the islands. But the scenery of their life had become the central background to the work of the literary movement he was creating. In August the party called on Lady Gregory at Coole, and Yeats began the most productive friendship of his life. Lady Gregory was a diplomat's widow with literary ambitions. Her house provided the poet for many years with a refuge where he could work in peace. With Lady Gregory he went around the cottages of Kiltartan Cross, listening while she collected folktales. Her use of the local dialect impressed him greatly, especially when she used it in the early 1900s to retell the old sagas in modern form; her versions became his indispensable source.

Along with Edward Martyn and his cousin George Moore, Yeats and Lady Gregory began the Irish Literary Theatre in 1899, producing the controversial play *The Countess Cathleen.* Without Martyn and Moore, the Irish National Dramatic Society was formed which later moved into the Abbey Theatre in 1904. It was Lady Gregory who lightened the tone of the theatre with her little farces, though later these became a tiresome feature of the theatre's fare. However, among the first plays produced by the new company was one by a young writer named Synge.

In December 1896, Yeats had met Synge in a students' hostel in Paris. He had just come from the Aran Islands and his imagination was full of those grey islands 'where men must reap with knives because of the stones'. In a moment of inspired insight, he told Synge: 'Give up Paris, you will never create anything by reading Racine, and Arthur Symons will always be a better critic of French literature. Go to the Aran Islands. Live there as if you were one of the people themselves; express a life that has never found expression.'[8] If he could not get the place down on paper in his abandoned novel, Yeats was determined that someone should.

Charles Lever had set part of a novel on the islands in 1865. He saw the place with the eye of a decayed romantic 'that great mountain rising abruptly from the sea ... those wild fantastic rocks, with their drooping seaweeds; those solemn caves, wherein the rumbling sea rushes to issue forth again in some distant cleft'. This was to miss the essential life of the islands. Another visitor, who described his visit to the islands for the readers of *Harper's Magazine* in 1881, saw only the ancient ruins and the modern poverty but nothing of the real life of the people. The revival would change all this.

Synge saw the islands more soberly, the grey rocks lit up for a moment by the flash of a woman's red petticoat. The people there were certainly to find expression through him, for on the islands he got hints for three plays, *Riders to the Sea, In the Shadow of the Glen,* and *The Playboy of the Western World.* The emergence of the shy and sickly student Synge as a writer was as remarkable as his subjects. He was, in the neat phrase of Conor Cruise O'Brien, dominated by 'mother's tongue'; his family and the Irish language.

His family were gentry come down in the world. They had once owned estates in Wicklow, but Synge's father had died when he was two, and Synge was brought up in near-suburban Dublin. From the dusty gentility and religious gloom of his Rathfarnham home he would escape into the Wicklow hills, a com-

pletely different world. In his unfinished autobiography he
describes his close friendship with a girl his own age. 'I was a
sort of poet with the frank imagination by which folklore is
created,' he writes. 'We were always primitive. We both understood all the facts of life and spoke of them without much
hesitation but a certain propriety that was decidedly wholesome.
We talked of sexual matters with an indifferent and sometimes
amused frankness that was identical with the attitudes of folktales.'[9]

This passage explains the grown man's love of the peasantry.
They were not only the complete antithesis of his mother's way
of life, they were still living a real folklife and talked of their
affairs 'with an amused frankness' which he found intensely satis-
fying as a writer. They also gave him their language, their
imagination 'fiery, magnificent and tender'. The tone here is
that of Brian Merriman, returned again to Irish literature.

Because Yeats's expression 'the Celtic twilight' had come to
cover the whole of the Irish literary movement, it is often thought
that there is something fey and other-worldly about the entire
literature it produced. But this is not so. There was indeed a
certain amount of ingenuous feyness in Yeats and much more in
George Russell, but just as Russell as a man was intensely practical, so in Synge the movement had its gritty, sweaty side. Synge
expressed the differences between his style and theirs in a poem
written after looking at one of AE's pictures, *The Passing of the
Shee* :

> Adieu, sweet Angus, Maeve and Fand,
> Ye plumed yet skinny Shee,
> That poets played with hand in hand
> To learn their ecstasy.
>
> We'll search in Red Dan Sally's ditch,
> And drink in Tubber fair,
> Or poach with Red Dan Philly's bitch
> The badger and the hare.[10]

That was just what Synge put in his plays, those peasants and
the painful squeals of the dying hare.

His first play, *In the Shadow of the Glen*, was produced in
January 1904. A Dublin critic called it 'a farcical libel' and Maud

Gonne led a walkout protesting against 'a decadent intrusion where the inspiration of idealism rather than the downpull of realism was needed'. On the third night of the *Playboy* in 1907 Lady Gregory telegraphed Yeats: *Audience broke up in disorder at the word shift.* The audience were not only shocked by the public use of such an indelicate word, but also by an Irish girl passing the night unchaperoned under the same roof as a strange man, an event which renewed their disgust in the earlier play at Nora's passionate desire to escape from her loveless marriage to an old man and go off with the tramp. Dublin audiences, anxious to do the proper thing, found Synge's amused and open frankness quite indecent.

Arthur Griffith denounced the play in his paper *The United Irishman* as un-Irish, by which he meant that it was a betrayal of the national cause. Yeats replied that the purpose of his theatre was artistic not propagandist. Maud Gonne, in turn, retorted scathingly in terms that some still repeat:

> A play which pleases the men and women of Ireland who have sold their country for ease and wealth, who fraternise with their country's oppressors or have taken service with them, a play that will please the host of English functionaries and the English garrison, is a play that can never claim to be a national literature. . . . The centre of the national life is still among the poor and the workers, they alone have been true to Ireland, they alone are worthy and they alone are capable of fostering a national literature and a national dream.[11]

This opposition of ideas has since become more familiar to us. What Maud Gonne and her allies wanted was a form of 'socialist realism' which might be called 'nationalist idealism', a notion which has blighted the humanity of so much radical writing. Where Synge delighted in the incipient anarchy of the Irish, Maud Gonne wished to formalise their passions to one end only.

Synge was attempting to give the peasants of Ireland a dramatic existence which would give their whole life a perspective of humanity. He hungered for 'harsh facts, for ugly surprising things, for all that defies our hope'. He realised the real life and feeling of his people more truly than Maud Gonne did, for all her work among them in the famine-ridden areas of Donegal.

She saw them always in political terms, he only in human terms. Theirs was a life he knew well, perhaps better than Maud Gonne. *The Aran Islands*, published in 1907, was based on his diaries of his annual visits to the islands between 1898 and 1902. It was illustrated with twelve drawings by Jack Yeats, one of the artist's first important commissions, which were based on photographs by Synge himself. Jack Yeats was one of Synge's few close friends, and we shall see how the painter's work often echoes the poet's. In the summer of 1905 they were asked by the *Manchester Guardian* to travel through what were then called 'the congested districts', the crowded impoverished areas of Connemara and Mayo, and to report on the social distress there. Synge was well aware of the realities of Irish life.

> There are sides of all that western life [he wrote to his friend Stephen MacKenna on 13 July 1905], the groggy-patriot-publican-general shop-man who is married to the priest's half-sister and is second cousin once-removed of the dispensary doctor, that are horrible and awful. This is the type that is running the present United Irish League anti-grazing campaign, while they're swindling the people themselves in a dozen ways, and then buying out their holdings and packing whole families off to America.[12]

Yeats, thinking of some ideal of the playwright, which he had invented, claimed that Synge was 'unfitted to think a political thought'. The passage above shows this was not so. Nor is it unique. After the riots that greeted the *Playboy* he became even more disgusted with 'the scurrility and ignorance and treachery of some of the attacks' made upon him by middle-class Dubliners. 'As you know,' he wrote again to MacKenna, 'I have the wildest admiration for the Irish peasants, and for Irish men of known or unknown genius—do you take a bow?—but between the two there's an ungodly ruck of rat-faced sweaty-headed swine.'[13]

In keeping with this rejection of his own class, like Yeats Synge was a socialist in his political sympathies. As a student in Paris he read the basic texts of socialism and had been to hear lectures given by the anarchist Faure. Was Synge then a revolutionary? When writing to Maud Gonne resigning from her Paris-based *Irlande Libre* society, he claimed that if he became involved with a militant revolutionary movement such as hers, he could not work for Ireland's regeneration in his own way. His socialism was, like Yeats's, more of the Morris than the Marx variety, interested in the brotherhood of man rather than in the union of the workers of the world. He told his mother, who needed reassuring about the wild ideas of her strange son, that he was not a rebel because in 'years to come when socialistic ideas spread in England' Ireland would get her rights. Things could 'change of degrees in the world' without fighting; 'equality and no more grinding down of the poor' could be achieved by reform.

The poverty of the west was a grinding down of the poor that came home to him. He describes in his book an eviction in the Aran Islands, but without mentioning that his brother was an agent responsible for similar outrages. Such sympathies in the man and the writer quite cut him off from his own class, for he understood as they did not why people turned to rebellion. Jack Yeats records how the two of them were told by a local politician in Mayo how he became a nationalist.

> I was but a little child with my little book going to school, and by the house there I saw the agent. He took the unfortunate tenant and thrun him in the road, and I saw the man's wife come out crying and the agent's wife thrun her in the channel, and when I saw that, though I was but a child, I swore I'd be a Nationalist. I swore by heaven, and I swore by hell and all the rivers that run through there.[14]

That he was able to recall this incident years later shows the impression it made at the time on the painter himself. Synge can have been scarcely less moved.

Seeing and hearing such things, it is not surprising that both the writer and the painter should have come to feel as they did : for both of them the peasant, the man of the west, became the embodiment of all that was noble, heroic and fine in human nature. 'I think', Jack Yeats continues about Synge, 'the Irish peasant had all his heart. He loved them in the east as well as he loved them in the west, but the western men on the Aran Islands and in the Blaskets fitted in with his humour more than any; the wild things they did and said were a joy to him.'[15]

The key words here—heart, love, humour, wild things, joy— describe well enough the emotions of Synge's plays. He was well versed in political theories, knew all about the poverty of Mayo, the 'rightness' of the Irish cause. But he did not choose to write plays about such things. He learnt Irish, and by doing so reverted to the essential themes of Gaelic literature : love and women. All his plays have one theme in them all : love of women. To this theme the Western world and all that horrified the original audience who had expected pious uplift, were very relevant. If Yeats found 'heart-mysteries' in the ancient sagas, Synge found heart wonders in the Western peasants. From Nora going off with the tramp at the end of *In the Shadow of the Glen*, to the final line of the *Playboy*, where Pegeen realises her loss, all Synge really ever writes about is the intercourse of men and women, the fine words of the one, the hard-to-please hearts of the other. In his last play *Deirdre*, this theme is raised to a tragic level, ending as the others had not with a grand defiance of death. That was the final gesture of the dying man to his theme. Synge objected to Yeats's idea of a theatre based only on Cuchulain (so to speak), so this play was his only attempt at a story from the sagas. In it he celebrates the triumph of love over death, of Deirdre over Cuchulain. His heroes are never heroes on any battle-field, their victories are over human hearts by fine words.

Synge died in 1909. His last play was produced the following year. Because of his death, 1910 seems to mark the end of a period in Irish writing, the end of a decade or more of high literary achievement, as well as political tranquillity.

For Yeats it was another moment of crisis. Maud Gonne was long lost. Now Synge was dead. When he later published it he called the diary for that year a record of *Estrangement*. He felt at odds with the society around him. He was bitter and despondent, and told Robert Frost that he might not write more poetry. George Moore reported in *Hail and Farewell*, his comic account of the literary revival and his role in it, that Yeats's Dublin friends felt that he was written out as a poet. This was not to prove true, but it was some time before his poetry began to move in a new direction. His least important work was written between 1910 and his marriage in 1917. Yet even so, we find he was already beginning to elaborate his major themes.

One of these was the image of the aristocratic peasant, who under the influence of Synge's plays took on a more superior aspect in contrast to the now increasingly despised bourgeoisie, as indeed did the warrior heroes of the sagas. A third theme now gained his imagination, which also owes much to Synge : the theme of the Big House.

Though the Yeats family were small landowners and shippers, the artistic poverty of his own father had given the young poet a healthy respect for those who were not well off. His early work contains little about aristocracy. This now changed.

In the summer of 1895, when he visited the Aran Islands, he also stayed at several of the great houses of the West. As well as Coole, which he was to return to for many summers, there were Tillyra where Edward Martyn lived in ascetic comfort, Moore Hall where George Moore's soldier brother Maurice lived and looked after the family estate. And that winter while he was staying with his cousin Henry Middleton at Thornhill outside Sligo, he visited the Gore-Booth family at Lissadell, an evening to be commemorated evocatively in his maturity :

> The light of evening, Lissadell,
> Great windows open to the south,
> Two girls in silk kimonos, both
> Beautiful, one a gazelle.[16]

These were Constance and Eva Gore-Booth, two high-spirited women, whose lives were to twine with Yeats's for decades to come.

Yet at the time this visit was not an occasion for verse. Yeats was still the mystical admirer of the peasantry. His love of the Big House had to wait for Synge. The playwright's articles on the West were well liked by the editor of the *Guardian*, who published more of his essays. In May 1907 (three months after the *Playboy* riots) Synge published a sketch written in 1903 describing a landlord's garden in County Wicklow. He had spent a great deal of time in Wicklow, sometimes staying near the old family home at Castle Kevin, which inspired this piece.

Everyone is used in Ireland to the tragedy that is bound up with the lives of farmers and fishing people; but in this garden one seemed to feel the tragedy of the landlord class also, and of the innumerable old families that are quickly dwindling away. These owners of the land are not much pitied at the present day, or much deserving of pity; yet one cannot quite forget that they are the descendants of what was at one time, in the eighteenth century, a high-spirited and highly-cultivated aristocracy. Still, this class, with its many genuine qualities, had little patriotism, in the right sense, few ideas, and no seed for future life, so it has gone to the wall. The broken green-houses and mouse-eaten libraries, that were designed and collected by men who voted with Grattan, are perhaps as mournful in their end as the four mud walls that are so often left in Wicklow as the only remnants of a farmhouse. The desolation of this life is often of a peculiarly local kind, and if a playwright chose to go through the Irish country houses he would find material, it is likely, for many gloomy plays that would turn on the dying away of these old families, and on the lives of one or two delicate girls that are left so often to represent a dozen hearty men who were alive a generation or two ago. Many of the descendants of these people have, of course, drifted into professional life in Dublin, or have gone abroad; yet, wherever they are, they do not equal their fore-fathers, and where men used to collect fine editions of *Don Quixote* and Molière, in Spanish or French, and luxuriantly bound copies of Juvenal and Perseus or Cicero, nothing is read now but Longfellow and Hall Caine and Miss Corelli. Where good and roomy houses were built a hundred years ago, poor and tawdry houses are built now; and bad book-binding, bad pictures and bad decorations are thought well of, where rich bindings, beautiful miniatures and finely-carved chimney pieces were once prized by the old Irish landlords.[17]

This essay contains the germ of whole literatures, of Chekhov's themes in *The Cherry Orchard* or Turgenev's in *Nest of Gentle-folk*. Synge brooded on his own family history, and would no doubt have turned to such a theme if he had lived. The seam of dramatic material in Irish peasant life was narrow and he had almost exhausted it himself. To find another way of life as varied and rich, and as full of dramatic potential, he would have had to turn either to the Dublin slums (as he is thought to have intended) or to the decayed old houses of his class and family.

This was not a new theme : Maria Edgeworth had defined the fall of the Anglo-Irish in 1800 in *Castle Rackrent*. George Moore had given moving descriptions of the same life in his first novel *A Drama in Muslin* (1884) and in his collection of sketches *Parnell and his Island* (1887), where some of the originals of his characters are described. Moore himself appears, as a landlord newly returned from Paris with a volume of Verlaine in his pocket. He describes Moore Hall as it appeared to him on his visit during the Land War, when he found it falling into disrepair.

> And the great wide green path of the race-course that wound in and out through the woods and fields is now overgrown and lost; and the garden where several generations of children played and grew amid everchanging ideas and desires from childhood to manhood, is now but a wild, a sad, and savage place—a strange place where strange weeds over-top the apple closes, and where the roses have returned to the original eglantine. ... And upon the tall and morose walls, wet with rain that drips from the overhanging beeches, a peacock—the last of the many generations of peacocks that in gladder days decorated the terraces and the long lawns—now cries dolorously for the pea-hen *morte d'antan*.[18]

This as we shall see in the next chapter was not to be a theme Moore would devote much attention to; he was more concerned with the revolution which would overthrow that house. So it was left to Yeats to elaborate the themes of folly, grandeur and decline, the extinction of the Great House in Irish life and literature : we shall hear echoes of that peacock on the long neglected lawns of a rich man in his later poetry. For Yeats those two girls at Lissadell that evening, so briefly met, the last delicate lives left of a line of hearty men, were to be an image of all this.

In his depressed mood after Synge's death, when it seemed that the hope of continued genius had passed from the literary movement, Yeats turned back into his own family tradition. He began now to talk about being related to the Butlers, and of being the true Duke of Ormonde if his claim were recognised— much to Moore's amusement, who pointed out that his father might be in the way of Willie's title. He also recalled his ancestors who fought at the Boyne, though this too was confused, for at first he imagined they had fought with James and had to correct the reference when he was told they had in fact been Whigs with King William.

The lover of mankind of the New York speech was being

replaced by the gentleman of feeling. In writing of his early years in *Reveries over Childhood and Youth*, he made a hero of his uncle George Pollexfen and his other gallant, dashing, hearty forebears. He used their lives and those of his grandparents to unite the small book, their lives having had much of the colour he felt lacking in his own.

All of this had been on his mind since the death of Synge shortly after which the theme of the great house enters his poetry for the first time. His poem 'Upon a House Shaken by the Land Agitation' was written in April 1909, within a fortnight of Synge's death, a period of deep melancholy as he recorded in his diary. In the poem he is thinking of Coole House.

> How should the world be luckier if this house,
> Where passion and precision have been one
> Time out of mind, became too ruinous
> To breed the lidless eye that loves the sun?
> And the sweet laughing eagle thoughts that grow
> Where wings have memory of wings, and all
> That comes of the best knit to the best? Although
> Mean roof-trees were the sturdier for its fall,
> How should their luck run high enough to reach
> The gifts that govern men, and after these
> To gradual Time's last gift, a written speech
> Wrought of high laughter, loveliness and ease?[19]

This was to be the staunch conservative attitude he was to maintain to his last days, when he himself had some chance to exercise the gifts that govern men and declaim his own written speeches in the Irish senate.

In other poems written earlier in the year he compares his love of Maud Gonne to Homer's love of Helen: with the result

> That life and letters seem
> But an heroic dream.[20]

Here the destruction of the Great House which represented all that Maud Gonne hated in politics, is absorbed into an image of the destruction of Troy through Helen's pride:

> Why, what could she have done, being what she is?
> Was there another Troy for her to burn?[21]

It seemed to him then that there was not; but, for something magnificent to burn, there *were* the great houses.

In these poems we find an altered attitude to his art. Once he could have been tempted from his poetry by the beauty of Maud Gonne and 'the seeming needs of my fool-driven land'. He had in youth admired a poet whose poetry was such that 'one believed he had a sword upstairs'. Now at Galway races he ponders the crowd, so representative of the new Ireland, swayed with one mind by the running of the horses. He and his verses had once done that, as when a small boy at a public meeting in the 1890s had shaken his hand and shyly said how much he admired his poetry.

Now 'the merchant and the clerk', not to speak of the gentry drifted into the professional classes, had altered everything. Yet once again 'the whole earth might change its tune'

> And we find hearteners among men
> That ride upon horses.[22]

He turned in scorn upon the new middle-class Ireland, so piously Catholic and stolidly commercial, on Paudeen and his Ireland. These feelings of disgust came to a head during the great lockout of 1913 in Dublin when he wrote in support of the workers, and were summed up in 'September 1913':

> What need you, being come to sense,
> But fumble in a greasy till
> And add the halfpence to the pence
> And prayer to shivering prayer, until
> You have dried the marrow from the bone?
> For men were born to pray and save:
> Romantic Ireland's dead and gone,
> It's with O'Leary in the grave.[23]

O'Leary, who had died in 1907, had been his own personal image of what a reawakened nationalist Ireland might have become: proud, cultivated, aristocratic, honourable. O'Leary and those other patriots, 'those names that stilled your childish play', had had no time to pray, to save anything at all from the fate of failure and the hangman's rope. Yeats, remembering the ideals they had all had back in the 1890s, looked around him at what nationalist Ireland was becoming, at Redmond's party,

Griffith's Sinn Fein, William Martin Murphy's Dublin, and shuddered.

> Was it for this the wild geese spread
> The grey wing upon every tide;
> For this that all that blood was shed,
> For this Edward FitzGerald died,
> And Robert Emmet and Wolfe Tone,
> All that delirium of the brave?[24]

The poets of the revival, among whom we must count Synge, created in their work an ideal of Ireland based on the ancient sagas and the life of the peasants in the West. It was an anti-industrial, reactionary ideal, even though its ideas were heavily influenced by the pervasive socialism of the period. Theirs was a literary ideal. The natural audience for their literature, then busy making good, either by leaving the land or in commerce, was either shocked by what the poets were doing or contemptuous of it. What most people did not see was how the poets' ideal would work its way into political action, how the peasant and the heroes of the sagas would be as influential in remaking Ireland as Redmond, Griffith or Martin Murphy ever were. But that was only one side, the poetic side, of the Irish literary revival. There was another, equally important, to which we will now turn.

3

The Return of the Native (11)

REALISM AND THE IRISH NOVEL

'The sceptre of intelligence has passed
from London to Dublin.'[1]

THIS was the brief text of the momentous telegram sent by
Edward Martyn which brought his cousin George Moore back
in 1901 to live and write in Ireland.[1] Yeats thought the message
was invented by Moore himself for *Hail and Farewell*, as it was
more in his style than Martyn's. This may well be so: Moore
was often accused of rearranging reality to suit his fancy. What
is true is that the words set the tone for what Moore and Martyn
wanted to do for literature in Ireland: against the ideal which
the poets and dramatists around Yeats were so busy creating,
they opposed an image of reality in their own plays and novels.
Here the native returns in quite a different guise: in the land of
heart's desire, they were aware of the pain and heart-ache of life.

We have followed till now, in tracing the rise of the literary
revival, the course of Yeats's own career, for to a great extent
he *is* the movement. Almost, but not quite, as we shall now see.
There is a tendency, especially among admirers of Yeats and
Synge, to see their romantic thesis, with its warriors and peasants,
and latterly its aristocrats, as representative of the feeling of the
entire movement. But there was also, in opposition to their
Protestant thesis, a Catholic antithesis. This stream includes
George Moore, James Joyce and other novelists. Though Catholicism has a large part in their world view, the contrast is also
between imagination and intelligence; between poetry and the
novel; between romanticism and realism; between the brief glory
of the heroic and the devouring entanglements of social life.
These realists were also trying 'to express a life that has never
found expression'.

Yeats, in starting the Irish Literary Theatre, wanted to create a poetic drama; so he wrote *The Shadowy Waters* and *The Countess Cathleen*. Douglas Hyde, in wishing to revive the Gaelic language, wanted an Irish theatre; so he wrote his first play *Cashad an tSugan*. Edward Martyn in joining with Yeats and Hyde in this venture, wanted something quite different again : an intellectual theatre, influenced by Ibsen. Because he was wealthy, he was welcomed by the other two for a while. But unfortunately he was a failure as a dramatist, so his kind of theatre came to nothing. The Abbey became a theatre of poetic drama, in which Ibsen would never be played.

Edward Martyn—the familiar 'dear Martyn' of *Hail and Farewell*—was an extraordinary character with very varied interests. He was an inveterate celibate, and lived a life of almost monastic discipline in a tower of his Galway mansion Tillyra Castle, which was only a few miles from Coole. He was a Catholic, but of a type more common on the Continent than among the landed gentry of Ireland. He hated women, but passionately loved Ibsen, Wagner and the polyphonic music of Palestrina. He asked Aubrey Beardsley to design a window for his castle, admired the Japanese artist Utamaro, and collected paintings by Degas, Monet and Corot. Yet despite all this aesthetic cultivation, Yeats thought his Catholicism remained 'a peasant religion'. But Yeats is not always a good witness. Martyn was obstinate in his insistence on the trivialities of his religious practice; mere aesthetic religion was no use to him. Martyn's religion was more serious than Yeats cared for.

As an artist Martyn was an amateur. 'A beginner', Moore thought, 'in danger of remaining a beginner.' His first plays *The Heather Field* and *Maeve*, were pulled into better dramatic shape with the help of Yeats and Arthur Symons. But though he could not handle plot very well, Martyn did have some talent for writing. That first play *The Heather Field* was far more popular with Dublin audiences than the scandal-provoking *Countess Cathleen* (hence Yeats's dislike of Martyn).

Influenced by Ibsen, Martyn had tried to write an Ibsenian play. The plot was simple enough. An idealistic dreamy Irish landlord, falling on hard times, attempts a practical solution to his problem by ploughing up the wild heather field and sowing it. All this improvement is done at great expense. His hard and materialistic wife, realising that the scheme is a folly, tries to have two doctors commit her husband. But they delay giving a final opinion. Spring comes : his small son returning from a ride in great excitement, cries : 'Ah, Papa, it is beautiful in the Heather Field. The heather is coming up everywhere.' And he drops at his father's feet a bunch of sprigs. His dream destroyed, the father goes mad at last.

Curiously the play was a failure in London, the critics seeing the husband as 'a dangerous impractical person', the wife as a sensible realist. In Dublin the Irish audience had grasped the author's essential hatred for her, and admired the attractive figure of the husband and his wild hopes.

Such fatal dreaming was the theme of Bernard Shaw's *John Bull's Other Island*, originally written for the Abbey in 1904. This was another Ibsenesque attempt to expose with laughter the hopeless, unchanging situation in Ireland. Though Larry Doyle is obviously intended as a practical-minded scourge of the feckless Irish, it is Keegan the spoilt priest with his poetic idealism who carries the play. Broadbent as the Englishman who becomes almost more Irish than the Irish themselves was also a not untypical figure. Shaw knew what was the matter with Ireland, and that little would change it. His play was not produced by the Abbey until 1916, an appropriate year in view of what other poetic idealists were planning.

The play was not liked by Yeats. Shaw, he felt, lacked a passionate 'vision of life', his mind was logical and mechanical, his plays the didactic dramas of a social reformer. All of which (Shaw would gladly have admitted) was true. Yeats hated the whole influence of Ibsen on modern writing. This hatred was a basic division between the romantics and the realists of the revival.

Martyn's later plays live only in the peculiar vividness of his personal views and not as dramas. He is now remembered (if at all) more as patron than as a writer. He paid for the productions of the national theatre until he felt in conscience bound to withdraw when he found the theme of *The Countess Cathleen* heretical. Interested in art, he encouraged painters like Dermod O'Brien. He discovered John McCormack as a schoolboy and set him on his singing career. He endowed the Dublin Pro-Cathedral to employ a conductor to train the choir in plain chant so that the capital might enjoy the ineffable pleasure of his beloved Palestrina. He also took a personal interest in the building of the new cathedral at Loughrea in Galway, where the work of so many fine Irish artists was used.

Martyn was much like his own creation, an idealist looking for a practical solution to his country's problems. He continued his efforts to found a theatre along his own lines, ending with the Irish Theatre founded in 1914 with the help of the poet Thomas MacDonagh. His search for a practical solution took him eventually into politics. In 1905 he joined Arthur Griffith and Maud Gonne in founding Sinn Fein, the party which was to spread Griffith's ideas of a separate national existence for Ireland (a dual monarchy was at that time the end in view). 'Ourselves Alone' was Martyn's motto for life as well.

Bringing back his cousin George Moore, whom he regarded with good nature as a pagan damned for his sins and his greatest friend, may well have been as important as anything else that Martyn did. Though he himself was unable to imitate the austere model of Ibsen, his theory was sound. Provincial Ireland ought to have provided a dramatist with as much material as Norway (then in much the same relationship to Sweden as Ireland was to England). Martyn's play *The Tale of a Town*, about people and politics in a western town not unlike Galway, was derived from *An Enemy of the People*. But even when reworked by George Moore as *The Bending of the Bough*, the play did not work well. Yeats did not care for Ibsenesque dramas. He preferred his own plays or Synge's, or others such as Lady Gregory's *The Rising of the Moon* or Padraic Colum's *Broken Earth*, with their romantically conceived characters and peasant language. Martyn, an outsider to this group, fell away from the Yeatsian literary movement. He was a good man with the right ideas who had chosen to work for his social realism in drama, but drama was the wrong medium in Ireland's circumstances. If he had been a novelist he might have succeeded, which brings us back to his cousin.

When George Moore returned to Dublin in 1901, led he later confessed by the alluring vision of a reawakened Ireland, it was to conduct the literary revival in his own way—anything so important could not be left to people like Yeats. If anyone at that time thought about 'the Irish novel' perhaps only the names of Somerville and Ross would have come to mind. Though they were outside the literary revival, in an odd sort of way their literary career answers back to Yeats's own.

Their first book appeared in 1889, the same year as *Crossways*; their most important book, *The Real Charlotte*, in 1894, the year after *The Rose*; and *Some Experiences of an Irish R.M.* in 1899, the year of *The Wind Among the Reeds*. The novels and poems may only be related by having Ireland as their subject, but in describing the literature one cannot neglect such a remarkable contrast.

They have been dismissed casually in the past as presenting merely a comic and feckless picture of Irish life, showing the Irish as the ineffectual idiots that the English would have liked them to be. Yet they belong, if anyone does, to the real world of the revival. Their story 'Lisheen Races, Secondhand', where the jockey Driscoll rises 'from the dead' seeking vengeance on Slipper, who has been relating his demise with extravagant gusto, has a striking parallel with the resurrection of the Da swathed in bloody bandages in *The Playboy of the Western World*. Conor Cruise O'Brien, who noticed this, wondered if they had been read by Synge. Even if such a notion seems to stretch the effect of influence too far, the backgrounds and the attitudes displayed by their characters show how close the authors were, not to each other, but to the realities of Irish life. Far from being 'unIrish' (whatever that may mean), Somerville and Ross have caught the whole flavour of Ireland in their tales, a light laugh at death's door.

But they had their more sombre side as well. This was fully explored in *The Real Charlotte*, a study of obsessive jealousy which was compared with Balzac's *Cousin Bette*. It was also a brilliant portrait of rural Irish society in Parnell's island. For they were aware, in their own way, of those divisions of feeling which lay beneath the easy heartiness of the hunting stories. Hunting was the one occupation in Ireland which united the various classes; the meet a place where many differences were dropped for a day's sport. Somerville and Ross preferred the heartiness, but could not completely avoid the occasional note of real bitterness.

In *The Silver Fox* (1897), a sort of fox-hunting ghost story, the peasants hold in fear the phantom animal which the gentry pursue with wasteful recklessness. Maria Quinn, whose family's ruin and brother's death she blames on the hunt, discovers Lady Susan, an Englishwoman, fallen from her horse near the cottage.

The Englishwoman is distraught about her horse's death. This Mary regards as a childish, almost sinful parody of the feelings properly reserved for people. Lady Susan attempts to thank her for her help with a gift of money.

> Their eyes met, and it seemed as if till then Lady Susan had not recognised Maria Quinn. She visibly flinched, and her flushed face became a deeper red, while the hand that had begun to feel for her purse came out of her pocket empty.
>
> 'Little ye cried yesterday whin ye seen my brother thrown out on the ground by the pool,' said Maria, with irrepressible savageness, 'you that's breakin' your heart afther yer horse.'[2]

The English had always found it easier to cry for animals than for their fellow men. Maria's is the real voice of Ireland, in dialogue with the English. 'Little ye cried yesterday' might have been the bitter words of many angry nationalists, words which brought on that flush of fearful recognition which came occasionally to the English.

Yeats was not an admirer of Somerville and Ross. He did not read novels, and they were not the kind of people he could use for his own purposes, as he used so many others. When inviting Edith Somerville to join the Irish Academy of Letters in 1932, he even managed to spell her name incorrectly, an error which offended her greatly. Not that she warmed to his literary circle herself. She thought the Dublin poets were remote from the reality of Ireland, the very charge now often levelled at her. Political changes, the product of the irrepressible savageness she had observed in Maria Quinn, were to change completely the society she wrote about in west Cork. Literary critics of a nationalist bent, such as Daniel Corkery, would not consider Somerville and Ross serious writers at all. Yet, as we shall see, they have their part in chronicling the downfall of Anglo-Ireland and the emergence of the new nation.

Certainly from George Moore's point of view in 1901 they would have been of no consequence. The comic Irish story was not what he wanted to work with. Their novels he would have considered clumsy, old-fashioned and even inartistic. However keen their social observation, their novels were still bound by the conventions of fiction which he had rejected. He wanted to create something new and fresh.

C

George Moore, though sprung from the landed gentry of Mayo, was reared as a Catholic. His creative imagination was dominated by that one big fact of Irish life, which Yeats, Synge, and Somerville and Ross tend to neglect or ignore, the stern religion of the people. Moore's father had been a horse-racing MP (almost a character out of the Irish R.M. stories indeed). But he had also been one of the leaders of the Irish Independent Party in the 1850s. And his grandfather had been President of the short-lived Republic of Connaught during the rebellion of 1798. The boy grew up in the company of gamekeepers and jockeys at Moore Hall in Mayo. He was educated in England at Oscott College, but on coming into his inheritance went off to Paris to study art—or, rather, Art, for Moore would have always given it capital emphasis. He became friends with the leading Impressionists of the day, and with writers such as Zola, Turgenev and Dujardin.

When his Irish rents failed during the Land League agitation in the early 1880s, he moved to London to try and write, having failed as a painter. *A Drama in Muslin* (1884) was set in County Galway in the countryside near Gort, but for the most part his early books were set in England. He introduced into the comparative gentility of the English novel the then startling techniques of the French and Russian realists. Moore, together with Thomas Hardy, fought against the censorship imposed on writers by the powerful circulating libraries; *Literature at Nurse* attacked the pretensions of those who would set bounds to what a novelist might deal with. *Esther Waters* (1894), the story of a servant girl with a love child set against a background of racing stables, is his finest *English* novel, though it is strikingly more humane and gentle than the pervasively deterministic novels of his master Zola. Moore had discovered England as a subject of fiction for himself. When the idea of Irish life as a suitable subject was suggested to him by Yeats and Edward Martyn, Moore was uncertain about it. He had dismissed Ireland in *Parnell and his Island* (1887), a collection of sketches of Irish life, mostly dismal, which brooded on the pervasive influence of the Catholic Church; Ireland was not associated in his mind with anything artistic. As a leading English novelist of the day Moore lived only for his art.

But Moore had been too hasty (influenced by the loss of his

rents from the estate in Mayo), and Yeats and Martyn seemed to be right about a revival in the country. What finally brought Moore back to Ireland was the appealing possibility of renewing the English language from Gaelic sources. In his technique Moore was the most advanced English novelist of his day, aiming at a complete and penetrating realism. The writers of the revival, in contrast, were heavily imbued with idealism, and from the background of an older culture were creating a new form of language. Moore's contribution to *Ideals in Ireland*, the manifesto of the movement published in 1900, was an essay on 'Literature and the Irish Language', which outlined his ideas on the significance of the language revival begun by the Gaelic League. He rightly saw this as one of the most important developments for Irish literature, because it would free writers in a way no longer possible in England.

> The healthy school is played out in England; all that could be said has been said; the successors of Dickens, Thackeray and George Eliot have no ideal, and consequently no language. . . . The reason of this heaviness of thought is that the avenues are closed, no new subject matter is introduced, the language of English fiction has therefore run stagnant. But if the Realists should catch favour in England, the English tongue may be saved from dissolution, with the new subjects they would introduce, new forms of language would arise.[3]

The Irish revival seemed, then, to present an opportunity for literature which should not be neglected.

For Moore, literature was the short story and the novel. His slight contribution to the dramatic movement was in imitation of Ibsen, in reworking *The Bending of the Bough*, and in writing *Diarmuid and Grania* with Yeats. But this is of no consequence compared with what he did for Irish fiction, especially the short story.

His first Irish novel, *A Drama in Muslin* (1884), is the story of the efforts of Mrs Barton, the wife of a Galway landlord, to launch her daughters, who are of course Catholics, into polite Castle society. The novel contains what we get nowhere else, a trenchant and witty portrait of the landed gentry only slightly perturbed as yet by the Land League, unaware of their impending doom. The intelligent, free-thinking daughter, Alice Barton, marries the local doctor and escapes to a new and better life in London.

Now in 1900, influenced by the ideas of his friends in the revival, Moore grasped the possibilities for fiction which existed in that rural society that Alice Barton (and Moore himself) had escaped from, especially when seen through the eyes of an admirer of Turgenev. Moore set out firstly to apply his realistic technique to that society; and secondly, to throw open the resources of the new continental manner to other Irish writers who might be inspired to write fiction again.

Moore made the highest claims for literature. In a passage from *A Drama in Muslin*, he describes the task of the novelist quite clearly.

> The history of a nation often lies in social wrongs and domestic griefs as in the story of revolution, and if it is for the historian to narrate the one, it is for the novelist to dissect and explain the other; and who could say which is of the most vital importance, the thunder of the public against the oppression of the Castle, or the unnatural sterility, the cruel idleness of mind and body of the muslin martyrs who cover with their white skirts the lawns of Cork Hill.[4]

This conception of the novelist as a kind of historian is one which we shall follow up in the course of this book. In overthrowing the political oppression of the Castle, the social and emotional martyrdoms of other men and women would be described by George Moore's successors with the harsh reality of cold prose.

Moore's first contribution was the short stories in *The Untilled Field*. As these were intended to provide 'the young Irish of the future with models', Moore had them translated into Gaelic and first published in book form in Dublin in 1902 under the title *An t-Úr Gorta*. His own models were the type of sketch which Turgenev had created in *A Sportsman's Notebook*, which had been a seminal work in its time. But Moore's Irish version was not a success, and the book had to be brought out again in English in 1903 before it made its mark.

The Untilled Field seems to have had little effect on writing in Gaelic; Peadar O'Leary's *Séadna* (1904) was far more influential; only Padraic O Conaire seems to have learnt from Moore. In English, Moore himself claimed later that his book directly inspired Synge's use of dialect in his plays—a possibility which no critic seems to have taken up. It does seem certain, however, that Moore's modern example set James Joyce writing those mordant studies of Dublin life which he began publishing in 1904, in the unlikely pages of George Russell's farming journal, *The Irish Homestead*. Moore's influence on Joyce was considerable, though critics eager to emphasise his originality have tended to play this down. The name of his friend Dujardin was always on Moore's lips in Dublin; it was from a neglected novel of his, *Les Lauriers sont coupés*, as well as from early attempts by Moore himself, that Joyce derived the device of interior monologue which he elaborated in *Ulysses*. Indeed Joyce so admired the ending of *Vain Fortune*—'fine original work' he thought in 1901 —that he rewrote it for the celebrated conclusion of his own story 'The Dead'. Moore was the only contemporary Irish writer who could rival Joyce, hence his later denigration of *The Lake* and *Celibates*.

The intention of *The Untilled Field* may have been exemplary, but the result was quite different. The book is one of those few collections of stories which are complete in themselves, a unique work on a par with *Dubliners* or *Winesburg Ohio*. The untilled field of the title suggests not only the unploughed acres of Irish fiction, but also the uncultivated Irish heart. The stories turn over and expose various aspects of Irish rural life and the peculiar conscience of the people. A pervasive image is the abandoned fields of the West from which the people have been driven out, not by the landlords but by the priests, the guardians of that conscience.

Again and again Moore returns to what he sees as the stifling influence of the Church on people's lives. In *Hail and Farewell* he comments on the great change in the country since he knew it as a boy in the 1860s. Instead of providing the people with spiritual comfort, the priests were dictating to them, either driving them into exile in America or reducing them at home to sullen conformity. Exile and conformity are the basic themes of the stories. In 'The Exile', the eldest son has the choice of becoming a policeman or a priest; he avoids both, marries the girl his brother loves, and so sends the younger man into exile. The demands of family and society had become twisted, and were thwarting the emotional life of the country.

In an Ireland coerced by police and priests—the agents of Stephen Dedalus's two mistresses—not everyone had such a choice as the two brothers. In other stories a sense of isolation becomes exile at home. Again and again, and in more and more sombre terms, Moore shows how the possibilities of life were narrowed. He contrasts two priests: Father Tom Maguire, on the one hand, with his harsh domineering ways to the people in the little village near Dublin, and Father McTuran, on the other hand, living in saint-like simplicity in his Mayo wilderness. But goodness gets nowhere, and for most people exile was the only choice.

In the final stories in the collection 'In the Clay' and 'The Way Back' (later combined as one tale called 'Fugitives') a sculptor is asked by a Father McCabe to make a statue of the Virgin Mary for the church he is building in Galway. The artist requires a model, and he persuades a niece of the priest's to pose for him in the nude. But her family discover what is happening, and her brothers destroy the statue in the clay. (The artist was modelled on Moore's friend John Hughes, who was responsible for both an altar-piece, *The Man of Sorrows*, showing the Resurrection and a Virgin and Child in the new cathedral of Loughrea; Father McCabe is drawn from Father O'Donovan, the Administrator in Loughrea, of whom more is said below.) The opposition of art and life to the power of conformity is underlined. The priests might be able to coerce the people, but Moore as an Irish artist would not allow them to treat an artist in such a way. But in the end both the girl and the artist leave Ireland, one for marriage in Chicago, the other for the Continent. (Hughes did in fact die in France.)

Moore had originally intended to include another story in the collection, but he expanded it into a short novel which he published in 1905 as *The Lake*. The novel describes the spiritual crisis of a young priest named Oliver Gogarty. (Much to his mother's distress, Moore borrowed the name of the young poet who was to be the original of Buck Mulligan in *Ulysses*.) This is resolved in the closing pages when the priest strips off his clerical clothes and swims to freedom across the lake to a new life with the woman he loves in a new country.

In his stories and novel, Moore explores that great theme neglected by Yeats and Synge, the effect of their religion on the lives of the Irish people. Moore, in true realist fashion, acts as a naturalist as well as an artist, by investigating as well as describing the society around him. This concern with man as a social being, and the effect of religion and community on him, distinguishes the novelist from the more romantically inclined poets of the literary revival.

This approach was part of his view of the novelist's purpose, that of dissecting and explaining the country's social wrongs and domestic griefs. For a novelist these wrongs and griefs are of necessity the wrongs and griefs suffered by the characters he creates. In one story, 'Home Sickness', a barman in New York returns home to his native parish, where he meets a girl and intends to settle down. But he finally realises that having escaped into exile he cannot now live at home under the control of the local priest, and so he returns to New York. Yet Moore concludes:

> There is an unchanging, silent life within every man that none knows but himself, and his unchanging silent life was his memory of Margaret Dirkin. The bar-room was forgotten and all that concerned it, and the things he saw most clearly were the green hillside, and the bog lake and the rushes about it, and the greater lake in the distance, and behind it the blue line of the wandering hills.[5]

This invocation of the typical landscape of the poets' imagination should not blind us to Moore's very different purpose. That the emotional life was a secret life seems to have been felt by all the novelists of the time. Just as there was a political underground plotting the political liberty of the country from the British, so the novelists were part of an emotional underground plotting the liberation of feeling: or so the writers felt. This subversion is most fully elaborated in the work of James Joyce, the most important writer of the period following that of Moore himself, and by Gerald O'Donovan, one of the more minor writers.

In contrast to Moore, the Mayo landlord, James Joyce was the archetypal urban writer. Though city people were to a great extent free from the direct surveillance of the police and clergy, the themes of Moore fiction are reworked by Joyce's peculiar genius in his stories of the Dubliners he knew. This was also a life which had 'never found expression'.

Joyce had no time for the rural ideal which dominated the literary revival. He hated and feared the country, as that tart passage at the end of *A Portrait of the Artist* on the return of John Alphonsus Mulrennan indicates. Yet earlier in the novel there is the story Davin tells Stephen, where Joyce casually shows himself equal to Synge or Moore in evoking the peculiar western landscape of the romantic imagination, in which the young country wife, alone in the house, invites the passing stranger in to comfort her bed. For a moment Joyce surrenders to the rural ideal (his truest friends were both countrymen), yet infuses it with a curious melancholy quite different from what we find in Synge or Moore. Yet beyond the Pale there was no salvation for Joyce. When George Russell, the arch apostle of an ideal rural-ism, requested some stories for *The Irish Homestead*, he asked Joyce to write something characterised by 'simple, rural, live-making, pathos' which would not shock his readers. Joyce wrote at once 'The Sisters', 'Eveline' and 'After the Race'. These bitter little stories were printed before the complaints grew too numer-ous for Russell to ignore. The stories were neither rural, nor simple, nor conventionally pathetic, and Joyce cared too much about the reality of what he was writing to care whether it was thought shocking or not.

Joyce cared to write only about city people : their life, society, art and women. This was the explicit reversal of all that the Yeatsian stream of the revival stood for. By his admiration for Aristotle, for Ibsen, and for the realistic novel, Joyce allied him-self with the literary tradition which was anathema to Yeats. As a student Joyce wrote what Moore called 'a preposterously clever' article on Ibsen's play *When We Dead Awaken*. This was an early indication of the cast of his imagination. His first effort at drama was a play in Ibsen's manner called *A Brilliant Career*, which seems to have been inspired by *An Enemy of the People*. But it was fiction which gave him the freedom of expression he needed. George Moore was the only novelist of the revival that Joyce admired, indeed more than admired, actually imitated. The sense of the stifling effect of the Church on Ireland in Moore, becomes quite explicit in Joyce, providing *A Portrait* with its main theme of the artist escaping from faith and fatherland.

Such themes were the quintessence of Ibsen. Moore pointed out that the theme of *Muslin* was similar to that of *A Doll's House;* and Joyce in attacking the new Irish theatre, specifically cast himself in the role of a successor to 'the old man dying in Christiania'. The seminal influence of the Norwegian permeated the modern movement in European literature, but had little effect in Ireland. Joyce's remarkable play *Exiles* (again a theme derived from Moore) was a calculated imitation of Ibsen : it was rejected by the Abbey. Joyce felt even in 1901 that Yeats and his friends were out of touch with what was most distinctively modern in European literature : Joyce was not.

Joyce's Dublin was not so up to date. His city is as much a static world as the countryside of Somerville and Ross. For Joyce Dublin was 'the centre of paralysis'. And though this harsh judgment was softened in the broad humanity of *Ulysses*, life in that book was stopped forever on 16 June 1904. This stasis and the conventionally squalid topics of the book and its language were too strong meat, at least for the vegetarian who had fled with squeamish horror from the poverty of the city in 1876. In Shaw's opinion

> James Joyce in his *Ulysses* has described, with a fidelity so ruthless that the book is hardly bearable, the life that Dublin offers her young men, or if you prefer it the other way, the life its young men offer to Dublin . . . a certain futile derision and belittlement that confuses the noble and serious with the base and ludicrous seems peculiar to Dublin.[6]

This was a peculiarly wrongheaded judgment, but Shaw felt he had to defend his own exile from his native city. It had offered him nothing when he was twenty, it could have offered Joyce less, and he could not allow that despite the eternal stasis of the characters, *Ulysses* was indeed noble and serious in its own way.

Joyce was born in 1882, and grew up in the post-Parnell period. His first published work (of which now no copy survives, except perhaps in the Vatican library, for his father sent a copy to the Pope) was a pamphlet poem in which the precocious genius excoriated Tim Healy for betraying Parnell. The politics of his short stories are the impotent politics of the split in the Dublin wards described in 'Ivy Day in the Committee Room'. The scene, described so vividly in *A Portrait*, of the Joyce household in Bray at Christmas 1891, shows that for his father's generation there was no way on from that fatal fall. Later in the novel we meet in fictional form two of Joyce's college friends, who present the views of a younger generation which Stephen also rejects. The two friends were Tom Kettle, the Catholic Conservative, and Frank Skeffington, the ardent Socialist, feminist and pacifist. The haughty Stephen turns aside from their political blandishments to foster his art in exile. (Later Joyce himself seems to have been a mild supporter of Sinn Fein before the Rising, though he did not admire Griffith much.) The artist as Joyce saw him has his own priestly function : the transubstantiation of reality. 'I go to forge in the smithy of my soul the uncreated conscience of my race,' Stephen says while packing for Paris. Joyce, ever the pedantic theologian, uses conscience (the inbit of inwit) in its exact sense, of that most intimate knowledge of our own selves, our faults, virtues and abiding natures. His knowledge of politics is this kind of moral knowledge, the only kind an artist possesses.

Though the theme of the artist runs through *Ulysses* too, Joyce deals also with politics and history as sub-themes on which both Stephen and Bloom ponder in their own ways. To the pompous Englishman Mr Deasy who employs him to teach school, and who says he is his own master, Stephen replies that he is, in contrast, the servant of two mistresses, 'the imperial British state ... and the holy Roman and Catholic church'. Stephen sees the old crone who brings the morning milk to the tower where he is staying with Malachi Mulligan, as the figure of Ireland herself, in her desire to please mistaking Gaelic for French, and having to serve her conqueror and her 'gay betrayer'. (Joyce's dislike of Gogarty here found full expression, for he thought that Gogarty would betray Ireland, as indeed the Republicans later felt he had.) Irish art is described by Stephen as the cracked looking-glass of a servant : with the implication that Stephen's book would be the clear mirror of a master. History, which Stephen finds himself having to teach at Mr Deasy's school, is a nightmare from which he is trying to awaken, a nightmare of squalid horrors :

Glorious, pious and immortal memory. The lodge of Diamond in Armagh the splendid behung with corpses of papishes.

Hoarse, masked and armed, the planters' covenant. The black
north and the true blue bible, Croppies lie down.[7]

Like all his countrymen, Joyce carried in his imagination the
short hand of the Irish revolutionary tradition.

With that image of the rebellion of 1798 running in his mind,
Stephen hears the unctuous Mr Deasy outline his conservative
beliefs.

—But one day you must feel it. We are a generous people but
we must also be just.

—I fear those big words, Stephen said, which make us so
unhappy.[8]

Such big words as Peace, Freedom, Revolution, Republic.

In the Cyclops episode, where the wandering Bloom ventures
into the cave of Barney Kiernan's pub, Joyce for once deals
directly with politics. The Citizen (a figure modelled on Michael
Cusack, the eccentric founder of the GAA) and his dog Garry-
owen are described in mock heroic epithets derived from the old
Irish sagas. The Citizen sets upon the mild-mannered Bloom with
malicious gusto, when Bloom remarks that persecution per-
petuates national hatred among nations.

—What is your nation if I may ask, says the citizen.

—Ireland, says Bloom. I was born here. Ireland.[9]

But the Citizen, a reader of Arthur Griffith's paper *The United
Irishman* and a staunch Irish Irelander, will not accept the notion
of a Jewish Irishman. So that when Bloom responds to a set
piece of patriotic nonsense, speaks about the persecution of the
Jews, he is jeered at again. Here, for once, he gets angry.

—But it's no use, says he. Force, hatred, history, all that.
That's not life for men and women, insult and hatred. And
everybody knows that it's the very opposite of that that is
really life.

—What? says Alf.

—Love, says Bloom. I mean the opposite of hatred.[10]

From that point we move on through the book towards the
affirmative encounter of Stephen and Bloom, and finally to
Molly's rambling night thoughts.

Big Words are what the Citizen and Mr Deasy, the Nationalists and Arthur Griffith, the Church and the British, all specialise in. Those men in the pub express their fear of the Jewish peril, while the figure of Bloom passes through the city concerned only with small words for the smaller but essential emotions of the ordinary man. Joyce sees through those big words. His characters all belong to the shabbier end of the middle class, interested in music, sex and children. This was an easy convivial life, with minor triumphs and tragedies, which lasted until the 1920s.

Joyce rejected the heroic of Yeats and the peasantry of Synge. His hero is not Hector the Tamer of Horses, but Ulysses the man who survives, recreated in the staunch figure of Mr Bloom. The search for sexual freedom in Joyce's work reflects not merely his personal situation, but something at the very core of Irish life as seen by the novelists. Joyce's interest in life's circulating course seems far removed from the ethos of the revolution. We must remember however that it was not the return of the uxorious Ulysses that Dublin waited for, but the coming of Hector. The concern of *Ulysses* with common humanity was to be spurned in favour of the high heroic of another burning Troy.

The concerns of Moore and Joyce in their fiction were shared with quite minor writers, however, and so must be representative of a wide current of feeling. Dublin in June 1904, while not perhaps the centre of paralysis it seemed to Joyce, was a city where serious-minded men were at work to set the body politic moving again. The Literary Revival, Sinn Fein, the Co-operative Movement, were all active, practical and even realistic affairs. These movements, close to the heart of the country, also have their historian in fiction.

Given his concern in *The Untilled Field* with the effect of the Church on Irish life and the frustrated feelings of both priests and laity, it is fitting that one of Moore's followers in fiction should have been a priest who left his orders to marry and write in England. In Moore's story 'Fugitives' the artist was modelled on his friend John Hughes, as we have seen. Father McCabe, the priest who commissions the sculptures, was drawn from Father Jeremiah O'Donovan, then the Administrator at Loughrea. In writing of this enthusiast, Moore reveals a neglected side of the Irish Revival, which is summed up by the work of the novelist that Father Jerry became, Gerald O'Donovan.

This will not be a familiar name. As a consequence of the Yeatsian version of Irish literary history gaining dominance in academic circles, whole aspects of Irish life and culture in this period have been either neglected or forgotten. Gerald O'Donovan's is one of the bodies buried at dark of night in the shadow of Ben Bulben. He has been effectively 'unpersoned' by both the Church and the critics, because he chose to go into exile rather than lapse into silent conformity, because as a writer he chose to use his intelligence rather than his imagination, because he was a realist when heroic poetry was the order of the day.

Not much is now known about him, so some of what follows may well be mistaken in the details. (A biography of O'Donovan is in preparation by Mrs Jennifer O'Donovan, in which more light will be cast on his life.) He was born in County Down in 1871; his father was an ex-army man, then a building contractor, who settled in the West of Ireland. His mother seems to have been a devotedly pious woman, who hoped her son would be a priest. He was intended for one of the religious orders, perhaps the Carmelites, but chose instead to be a secular priest and entered Maynooth in September 1889. He was ordained on 23 June 1895 for the Diocese of Clonfert. For two years he was parish priest at Portumna, before becoming Administrator at Loughrea under Bishop Healy.

O'Donovan was an exceptional man, intelligent, artistic, impassioned. He was a genial and attractive personality, who threw himself into many schemes for the improvement of the country. It was he who persuaded Bishop Healy to employ Irish artists on the new cathedral then being built at Loughrea, and from his correspondence he seems to have been given a free hand in commissioning their work. The design was by the only architect associated with the revival, Professor William Scott; the decorations and carvings were by Sarah Purser who did the stained glass, Jack Yeats and John Hughes. Hughes's Virgin and Child was a controversial work, which some people thought vaguely pagan. (This is hinted at in Moore's story 'Fugitives'.)

The cathedral was only one enthusiasm. It was O'Donovan who brought John McCormack as a schoolboy to sing in the new cathedral choir. He also brought down to Loughrea in 1901 the Irish National Theatre Company, which played to packed houses, for their solitary performance in the provinces. He threw himself into the social life of the town, helping the poorer workers, organising a non-denominational club for them which he made them run themselves, much to the horror of his colleagues. He wrote in favour of Catholic social action, radical reform, industries for rural Ireland, reform of the workhouses, better convents and practical schools for girls. He was a contributor to the Jesuit-run *New Ireland Review,* and with Father Tom Finlay S.J. was deeply involved in the Co-operative movement. He was a close friend of Sir Horace Plunkett, who singles him out by name from among the young priests that he knew in his important book *Ireland in the New Century* (1904), as one of bright hopes for a socially minded Church.

The slightly anti-clerical tone of Plunkett's book drew down the wrath of the Catholic hierarchy—he was another who felt that the Church was largely to blame for the inertia of rural Ireland. Soon O'Donovan himself was in trouble. He was one of a number of young priests who were greatly influenced by the radical thoughts of the Modernist movement on the Continent. These new ideas were in contrast to the stale conservatism of what they had been taught at Maynooth. In his first novel, the highly autobiographical *Father Ralph* (1913), he goes so far as to claim that Modernism represented twenty-five years of the best thought in the Church. This was not the opinion of the Vatican. In 1907 the Papal encyclical *Pascendi Dominici Gregis* condemned Modernism, outlining a budget of errors which were not in fact held as a system by any one person. The leaders of the movement on the Continent were excommunicated. In Ireland the hierarchy decided that young priests thought to be tinged with any modernist ideas should be required to submit themselves to the terms of the encyclical. The climax of the novel is Father Ralph's refusal to do so, and his consequently abrupt, departure from the priesthood into exile in England. The cool anger of these chapters marks them as very personally experienced.

As the novel more or less re-creates O'Donovan's own childhood, education at Maynooth and years as a priest, I once thought that *Pascendi Dominici Gregis* was also the reason for his own exile, but it seems that personalities played a larger part than dogma. O'Donovan's relations with Bishop Healy and other priests in the diocese seem to have been very good. Healy was moved to Tuam in 1902, and Dr O'Dea became Bishop of Clonfert. Many of his progressive friends had hopes that O'Donovan, young as he was at 31, would be the next Bishop, and he was actually the selected candidate of the priests of the diocese. Now he found himself Administrator to a man put in over his head. Their relations were not good, it seems. Soon after O'Dea's consecration in 1904, O'Donovan left Loughrea for good. His last baptism was in August 1904; by December the new Administrator was in office. Leaving Loughrea, Jeremiah O'Donovan left his orders. He changed his name to Gerald O'Donovan and went into exile.

George Moore provided O'Donovan with a letter of introduction to his London publisher T. Fisher Unwin, in which he commended the young priest's extensive knowledge of literature and his just critical appreciations. Moore, who was kinder to his friends than is often said, hoped that Unwin might find some reading, or other work, for O'Donovan to do. 'I believe him to be a man of great ability,' Moore concluded, but in going to London O'Donovan was another talent lost to Ireland.

After leaving Ireland O'Donovan may have joined the British Army; at least I have lost track of him until 1910.* He does not seem to have returned to Ireland again. Yet in a series of novels published between 1913 and 1922, his imagination was preoccupied with the problems of Ireland, with what Moore had called the history of 'social wrongs and domestic griefs', which O'Donovan tried to the best of ability to portray and explain.

His second novel *Waiting* (1914) deals with the personal difficulties caused for a young politician of liberal views by that other important encyclical of the period, *Ne Temere* (1904), which put severe restrictions on the marriages of Catholics and Protestants. In Ireland this upset the delicate *modus vivendi* established by custom that in matters of religion the sons followed the father, daughters the mother. In future, the Vatican ordered, all children of the marriage must be brought up as Catholics. This encyclical is well remembered in Ireland because of the great

---

*In that year he married and became sub-warden at Toynbee Hall. Later he worked in the Italian section of the British Department of Propaganda, and was later still a reader for Collins. For many years he was a beloved friend of Rose Macaulay, who was much influenced by him. He died in 1942. Rose Macaulay wrote his obituary for the London *Times*: she concluded that 'to know him was to love him'.

bitterness it caused in many families by interfering in the intimate affairs of the laity. The novel closes on an optimistic note.

On the other hand, *Pascendi Dominici Gregis*, affecting as it did only the priestly intelligentsia—always a small, if influential, number in Ireland at any time—is now quite forgotten. Recent accounts of the role of the Catholic Church in Ireland ignore it, and never even mention Modernism. Yet the triumph in 1907 of the reactionary elements over the more liberal-minded minority set the tone of the Irish Catholic Church for the coming decades of revolution. Those tendencies which Moore had detected in the country and which Joyce had rejected, became entrenched and no other views were allowed. This, to say the least, was to have unfortunate social consequences.

Father O'Donovan has been neglected as a religious person because his views, which have now become the commonplace opinions of many Catholics, had until recently no apparent relevance for the Catholic Church in Ireland. A generation living after Vatican II and concerned with revitalising Catholicism in modern society, may wish to recall his name to memory as a brave pioneer for social justice.

Why Gerald O'Donovan as a writer is forgotten is a different matter. He is the victim of a false view of Irish literary history, in which the novelists receive scant attention. Yet O'Donovan's novels were well received at the time : *Waiting* was reviewed in the *Times Literary Supplement* on the same page as a curious collection of short stories entitled *Dubliners*, the author of which got only half as much space as O'Donovan, and little praise.

He is no Joyce, needless to say, but he writes well of bourgeois Dublin and small-town Ireland at a level unknown to Joyce. He is not interested, as Joyce so happily is, in the psychological perversities of Irish Catholicism. The childhood chapters of *Father Ralph* are like nothing else in Irish literature in describing the pressures brought on a boy towards a vocation. Like Moore, O'Donovan is concerned with the social effects of religion. As a writer he has not that compelling mastery of technique which is so important to Moore and Joyce, but he does apply a civilised intelligence to the re-creation of rural Ireland. Using the example of Moore's technique—there seems to be no other model in his mind—he shows the achievements of what is essentially the good will of the outsider against such obstacles as the local canon's prejudices. Only an internal change, he implies, will bring about the desired social revolution. His insight into the politics of a small town is keen—this is where he follows up on Edward Martyn—and ranges from the parish priest to the paupers in the workhouse.

His first two novels deal with the frustrating effects of the Church; the last two, *Vocations* (1921) and *The Holy Tree* (1922) deal with love gained and then lost, the first in the context of a priest's loss of faith, the second in a woman escaping from an unhappy marriage into a doomed love. O'Donovan was, as the moving final pages of *Waiting* suggest, optimistic enough to expect that internal change to come about, to hope for a new dawn in Ireland, an escape from unhappiness into love. In this he was too hopeful.

His six novels were written between 1910 and 1919 when it was still possible to be optimistic in Ireland. After all, there had been nearly a generation of peaceful progress. But this was soon disrupted. *Conquest*—the Irish *Uncle Tom's Cabin* according to Norryes O'Conor the American critic—dealing with the divisions between Green and Orange, Catholic and Protestant, came out in 1920. Its liberal tolerance reads ironically beside the events of that year which were rapidly heading towards the creation of a Catholic nationalist state and a Protestant dominion in Ulster. In one passage, Arabella watches a small stream flowing into the broad smooth-flowing river, and thinks of hate losing itself like that in love, the minority disappearing into the majority.

> There was her father-in-law with his little bundles of hate, and her own father at Lissyfad with his : mere bundles of Green and Orange misunderstandings and pitiful spites. They were blind and couldn't see. How alike they were, too, in all essentials, generous, lovable, different though they thought themselves. Would love, the solvent, ever do for them what it had done for her and her husband?[11]

This tone, with its honest liberalism and concerned intelligence, at once forward looking and confident of people's good faith, soon goes out of Irish writing. The short story and the novel would, like the country, take another direction. How painful it must have been for men like O'Donovan. There would be no place for the intelligent liberal in the new country, no solving love in the Ireland in the making.

However, in the novels and short stories of the coming decade, which deal with the events of the revolution, we shall see how the romantic thesis of Yeats and Synge, which was so much a part of the revolutionary ethos, becomes tempered by events with the realism of George Moore, the humanity of Joyce, the generous compassion of Gerald O'Donovan.

Joyce and O'Donovan went into exile in 1904. They were followed in 1910 by George Moore. In London Moore began to publish the trilogy *Hail and Farewell*, his comically conceived but convincingly perceptive account of the Revival and the varied personalities of its writers. It was George Moore who made Yeats and Synge, AE and Edward Martyn into the characters we all remember. To Moore it was quite clear that Synge's early death had marked the end of a period. Nor was he alone in thinking this.

Yeats, writing to Joyce in August 1917, refusing to produce *Exiles* at the Abbey, as it was 'too far from folk drama', admitted that the theatre did not even play its own dramas very well. There was a slackening of intellectual tension in Ireland. And though James Stephens suddenly emerged from the Dublin slums like some gifted elf, there was nothing really new on the literary scene.

Yet a theatre had been brought into existence, where Irish playwrights could dramatise the experiences of Irish life. An audience for drama had been created. Yeats and AE had also inspired a host of imitators and followers. The Irish novel and short story had been created almost single-handedly by George Moore, and were now open to further explorations by younger writers. Then means of art were ready to hand. Now only a subject fitting for the creation of great art was needed.

The Literary Revival had shaped an ideal of Ireland, and also in novels and stories described some of the realities of Irish life. Now it was for others, inspired by that ideal of Ireland to attempt to change that reality. So the intellectual initiative passed from the poets, novelists and painters into the activities of the prospering bourgeoisie, to the militant workers, and to small groups of politically motivated men in back rooms dedicated to hastening change by force of arms.

4

The Thing that is Coming

POLITICS TOWARDS THE EASTER RISING

So far we have followed the slow gestation of the literary ideas of an Ireland moving towards revolution. The long slow stir of thought which produced Yeats and the Abbey Theatre, and Moore and modern fiction, both with their new images of Irish life, had its political counterpart in the trends away from the parliamentary politics of the Irish Party towards the resort to armed rebellion. Here also there were new images of Irish life and what it might become, in the ideas of Sinn Fein, the Socialists and the Republicans.

Ourselves Alone: by 1900 the now reunited Irish Party, under the leadership of John Redmond, held the great majority of the Irish seats at Westminster. The country as a whole was overwhelmingly nationalist in sentiment, except for the north-east which was staunchly Unionist. It was clear that sooner or later Home Rule would be wrung from a Liberal government in need of Irish support. Then a re-established Irish parliament in Dublin would take charge of Irish affairs.

Expecting Home Rule to come, most people were content to wait for it. For the most part the country seemed well off enough as it was. The old power of the landlords had been broken by a succession of land Acts. The land now belonged, if not to the nation as Fintan Lalor had wanted, at least to a new breed of small proprietor. In Belfast and in Dublin new industries were growing up. Horace Plunkett was bringing the benefits of the Co-operative movement to the countryside. The nearly new Department of Agriculture and Technical Instruction was helping in the modernisation of Irish farming. Prosperity was increasing at last, and though much poverty remained, the middle classes thrived.

Not everyone, however, was content with this situation. Rejecting the satisfaction of the Irish Party, which often seemed more concerned with Westminster than with Ireland, other individuals and groups began to work for what they saw as the regeneration of Ireland.

The earliest of these, and the most popular and widespread, was the Gaelic Athletic Association. Hurling, in a disorganised way, had been an Irish game since Celtic times. In Thurles in 1884 Michael Cusack founded an association under the patronage of Archbishop Croke to organise and promote Irish games and athletics along purely national lines. The GAA was organised on a parish-by-parish basis across the country. The place of its founding is significant, as the GAA was always to be largely a rural interest. It was also, as David Greene notes, 'the first modern example of a great democratic movement, with the apparatus of committees and boards, under completely Irish auspices'. Naturally enough, this was politically significant. The hurley (or camán) became a weapon of which the police were wisely cautious, and members of the GAA were to be seen guarding Parnell's last meetings and escorting his coffin to the grave. Athletics were for all, and the GAA was notable in fostering a sense of local pride which was new to the country. In its early days, the exact history of which is none too clear, the association had in some places a mildly anti-clerical Fenian tone, but after Michael Cusack was forced to resign, the GAA became an accepted part of the Irish scene, approved of by the parish priests. The erstwhile founder of the movement remained a keen follower of the sports, and was a familiar Dublin figure, caricatured by Joyce in *Ulysses* as the Citizen. With his stout blackthorn and fierce dog, Cusack expressed the vigorous contempt that some felt for all things English. This contempt, leading to the famous and long-lived ban on foreign games and dances by the GAA, shut out from the association the Protestants, the Catholic middle classes and the city workers. The GAA was strongest in the country, and it is no coincidence that the Irish Republican Army was to organise itself in its time along the same parish-by-parish lines when forming the Flying Columns in the 1920s.

Gaelic passed into common usage as meaning football played under GAA rules: the old language of the countryside was still called Erse. But after the games came the language; after the GAA, the Gaelic League. This language movement was the direct result of the work of many scholars on the old Celtic tongue, outlined earlier. Douglas Hyde and his friends felt that only with the revival of Irish as a spoken language would the nation prosper, or find its identity. Hyde, whose father had been an Anglican rector at Frenchpark in Roscommon, called for the complete de-anglicisation of Ireland. Here was a cause which anyone could join. The League was a deliberately non-political organisation, in the sense that it did not go in for party politics, yet nevertheless its effect was political. Unlike the GAA, however, the League was an urban affair, mainly bourgeois and intellectual, with a large Protestant membership. Here at least the Protestant could find a common cultural pursuit to share with Catholics. The League was particularly active in Cork, where the great scholar Osborn Bergin was an early and inspired member, as was the writer Daniel Corkery; membership elsewhere sometimes rose to the same distinguished heights. The Gaelic League attempted to revive dances and Irish dress, but its greatest success was to have Irish accepted as a school subject and the creation of an Irish chair at the National University, where Hyde himself became professor. (The government enquiry into this matter was the occasion for Mahaffy's remarks about Irish literature 'being at base coarse and obscene'.) The League was a serious rival to the popularity of the Irish Party, for it was new and stimulating compared with the settled political party. Increasingly people tried to use it to further purely political aims, and Hyde was glad to resign from the council to devote himself to literature. In himself, as a poet, playwright, scholar, teacher and publicist, Hyde represents a great deal of what was best in the revival, and best in Ireland. It was a grand gesture on the part of the De Valera government to promote him in his last years to the distinction of the Presidency—yet when he died no member of that government would enter St Patrick's cathedral for his funeral, for fear of clerical disfavour. He had helped immeasurably in the creating of modern Ireland, yet its sectarianism could not have pleased him.

Both the GAA and the Gaelic League aimed at the creation of what had been dubbed Irish Ireland, in contrast to West Britain, by Moran of the *Leader*. And it was as the party of Irish Ireland that Arthur Griffith, with the aid of Edward Martyn and Maud Gonne, founded Sinn Fein in 1905. 'Sinn

Fein! Sinn Fein amhain,' the Citizen shouts at Mr Bloom in Barney Kiernan's pub. 'The friends we love are by our side, the foes we hate before us.' And he then goes on to read out to the public house an article from Griffith's paper *The United Irishman*. This was the belligerent tone all too common to extreme nationalism in Ireland. In the real context of Irish politics Sinn Fein was a minority party. A lone attempt to gain a parliamentary seat failed in 1908, and Sinn Fein had to be content with municipal seats and the vituperative columns of Griffith's paper. There he preached a Dual Monarchy (along the lines of the Austro-Hungarian model), protective capitalist economics, and the pressing need to plant trees in Ireland. In between, he also attacked, as we have seen, the plays of Synge and the Abbey Theatre people in general. Patrick Pearse wrote of Griffith in 1912 : 'You were too hard, too obstinate, too narrow-minded and too headstrong. You never trusted your friends sufficiently. You had too much esteem for your own opinion. You doubted people as staunch as yourself. You would praise no counsel but your own. You would agree with nothing but the thing you recommended yourself.' This harsh, but eminently just, verdict is not really softened by Pearse admitting in conclusion that Griffith had virtues no other Irishman possessed. It was not Pearse, however, who set the general tone of Irish nationalism, but the ranting Griffith. And rant, rather than hard thought, became the feature of much nationalist opinion.

None of these groups favoured revolution. They did not talk of bloodshed, except in the fantastic manner of the Citizen over his pint of Guinness. They found their support among very different groups of people, yet they shared an appeal to the new self-consciousness and self-confidence of the Irish people. Yet because, in the political sphere, both the Irish Party and Sinn Fein had their eyes set only on the independence of Ireland, they overlooked some of the more depressing aspects of Irish life and society.

The Starry Plough: 1913 was the year of the great Dublin Lock-Out, when the united employers determined by William Martin Murphy, tried to smash the newly organised Transport and General Workers Union. A new problem—urban poverty— thrust itself with ugly vitality before the public. The workers were led by James Larkin, a fiery-mouthed militant. August through October were months of battles and bloodshed, and there were vicious scenes in the streets of Dublin, which scarred themselves into working-class memories.

That a vigorous social policy should have been the first concern of any political party could have been seen by looking round the streets of Dublin. Georgian Dublin, the same city where the events of the coming decades were to be played out, was by then abysmally squalid in places. Its horrors are now scarcely believable : in 1911 the death rate in Calcutta was 27 per thousand, in Dublin it was 27.6. Arnold Wright, a hostile witness to the labour struggles of 1913, had to admit that parts of Dublin were in desperate straits :

> Sackville Street, one of the noblest of the Empire's thoroughfares, swarms with the miserable flotsam and jetsam of the darkest and dreariest depths of the social current. The Gothic pinnacles of St Patrick's Cathedral . . . look directly down on the quarter of the Coombe where the degradation of humankind is carried to a point of abjectness beyond that reached in any city of the Western World, save perhaps Naples. Hard by O'Connell Bridge, with its magnificent vista of soaring monuments and noble buildings, is a maze of streets physically and morally foul. . . . The Dublin slum is a thing apart in the inferno of social degradation. Nowhere can there be found concentrated so many of the evils which are associated with the underworld of our modern civilisation.[1]

In literature this city appears briefly for a moment on George Moore's *Muslin*, when the debutantes driving through the streets to the castle ball are struck by fear at the sight of the crowded white faces of the poor. That Dublin we glimpse in *The Real Charlotte*, hot, dusty and shabby, had by the time of *Ulysses* become sleazy, poor and wretched. Joyce describes some of the worst parts of it, especially the brothels around Montgomery Street (hard by Sackville Street) which were the familiar territory of his medical friends such as Oliver St John Gogarty. This is James Plunkett's *Strumpet City*, the streets those of Brendan Behan's childhood, the people those O'Casey knew so well, though he was not one of the most abjectly poor. And it was the city of Jim Larkin, where a third of the average wage of 17 shillings

was spent on the rent of one or two rooms; where 5,322 tenements housed 28,822 families or 87,205 people. If the conditions
for revolution existed in Ireland, they existed here where in the
classic manner of revolution, efforts to alleviate conditions merely
increased the desire for change. This desire was expressed force-
fully by Larkin, and by James Connolly who brought the revolution to the city in 1916.

Dublin had become Connolly's city, though he had been born
in Edinburgh, for which he stood as a town councillor in 1894.
He helped to found the Irish Socialist Republican Party in
1896, through which he made his own contributions to that
great stir of thought, for if Larkin was the messiah of the workers,
Connolly was their prophet. He firmly related the emancipation
of the working class to the emancipation of Ireland. For him the
cause of labour was the cause of Ireland, the cause of Ireland the
cause of labour.

> The struggle for Irish freedom [he wrote] has two aspects: it
> is national and social. Its national ideal can never be realised
> until Ireland stands forth before the world a nation free and
> independent. It is social and economic, because no matter what
> the form of government may be, as long as one class owns
> as private property the land and instruments of labour from
> which all mankind derive their substance, that class will always
> have power to plunder and enslave the remainder of their
> fellow creatures. . . . The party which would lead the Irish
> people from bondage to freedom must then recognise both
> aspects of the long continued struggle of the Irish nation.[2]

Nothing could be clearer: that was where the Irish labour movement stood on the eve of the Rising.

Connolly was associated in a small way with the national
groups which arranged the 1798 Centenary celebrations, at which
time he met Yeats, Griffith and Pearse. But in 1903 he was
forced for economic reasons to emigrate with his family to
America. There he joined the Industrial Workers of the World—
the red-scarved Wobblies—and tried with little success to spread
his socialist ideas among his fellow Irishmen in America. His
reputation grew, and in 1910 he was invited back by the Socialist
Party of Ireland. He wrote at this time his book *Labour in Irish
History*, a radical review of Irish history. In 1911 he became

secretary of Larkin's Irish Transport and General Workers Union in Belfast. Here he had to fight against the sectarianism of the Nationalists and Orangemen in the shipyards. In Clonmel in May 1912 his was the speech which closed the debate establishing the Irish Labour Party.

It was the Lock-Out that brought into the open the whole relationship of the labour movement to the progressive elements in the country. The Lock-Out was unique in rallying to the side of the workers the liberal and intellectual factions in the city, who contributed in their own ways. Orpen the painter, for instance, drew Larkin in conference at Liberty Hall, the union's headquarters, surrounded by his ragged supporters. That politically-minded hostess, the Countess Markievicz, ran a soup kitchen in the Hall's basement. Francis Skeffington helped send workers' children to England for a holiday, and was beaten up in the railway station for his trouble by Sodality men fearful of the pagan influences of England on those famished young souls. George Russell brought in the Co-operative movement and addressed an open letter to the employers on their duty to the workers. Larkin had spoken in support of the case for the return of the Lane pictures, and Yeats, still smarting about that controversy, wrote an article for *The Irish Worker* denouncing Murphy and his clerical supporters. Though less socialist than he had been ten years before under the influence of Morris, Yeats saw that the literary revival and the labour movement shared a common enemy : the crass commercialism of modern capitalism.

The Lock-Out ended and the workers were finally forced back to work, though not before achieving some improvement in their conditions of work. When Larkin departed for America himself in 1914, Connolly took over from him as leader of the trades union movement. His involvement with nationalism now increased : the Irish Citizen Army, founded to defend the Dublin workers, was to be one of the main groups involved in the Easter Rising two years later.

Almost alone among the 1916 leaders, Connolly deserves to be called an intellectual. It is this fact, and the more basic fact of his socialism, that scares the apologists of nationalism in dealing with him. They would rather concentrate on how the socialist became a nationalist, when it is his social ideas which are his great contribution to the nationalist movement. Much of his thought influenced Patrick Pearse in those last crucial months before the Rising, and is basic to the spirit of the Proclamation. Connolly called openly in his papers for a revolution by a united national front. It is often said that in contrast to Pearse, who spoke always in terms of blood sacrifice, Connolly regretted the necessity of fighting. This is not really so. He was quite ready to fight, and some of his editorials in *The Irish Worker, Honesty* and *The Spark* are just as bloodthirsty as Pearse's writings could be. Like other Irish patriots he appeals to the graves of the martyred dead :

> A Resurrection! Aye, out of the grave of the first Irishman or woman murdered for protesting against Ireland's participation in this thrice accursed war will arise anew the Spirit of the Irish Revolution. . . . If you strike at, imprison or kill us, out of our graves we will evoke a spirit that will thwart you and, mayhap, raise a force that will destroy you.[3]

Prophetic words indeed : but would the spirit of that Irish revolution be one which Connolly would desire?

Though he united himself with the more familiar line of Irish nationalism, Connolly himself represents a long line of Irish radical thought. In *Labour in Irish History* he sketches out this left-wing tradition and some of its significant figures such as William Thompson, the precursor of Marx; Arthur Vandeleur and his commune at Ralahine in Clare; Fintan Lalor and the land question. These few men were not, in the wider context of Irish history, a very central tradition. Still they were there, significant and perhaps of importance. With the establishment of the trades unions, something might be made of them. For though Ireland might have a radical tradition, it did not have a social democratic one in the European sense. Connolly hoped to create such a social democracy.

What sort of society did Connolly envisage after the revolution? It was of necessity a socialist state, but one with peculiar roots. Mixed in with his continental syndicalism and his Marxist analysis, was a very strong strain of Celtic revivalism. Connolly, as much as any other writer, was a product of the Irish literary revival. From a remarkable book by Alice Stopford-Green, *The Making of Ireland and Its Undoing* (1908), he had derived a vision of the ideal Celtic society in which all men were free, where kings were elected by the tribe, where the nation state did not exist and yet the whole island was united culturally, a place where skill, craft and learning were respected. What William Morris found in the Middle Ages, Connolly took from Iron Age Celtic Ireland. It is now beside the point to object that *Labour in Irish History* depends on an historically inaccurate notion of what Celtic Ireland was really like. Connolly was presenting an ideal model against which the inadequacies of modern Ireland could be measured. As much as Pearse did, he wished for a return to that ideal state, which rejected every English institution of law, parliament and private property which the tragic course of history had foisted on the Irish people, which had created the material and mental poverty of Dublin.

Thus it was quite in character that on Easter Monday 1916, James Connolly should have led out his Irish Citizen Army, the workers' blue flag emblazoned with the starry plough fluttering above them to join the dreamers who had begun the hard business of the revolution.

The Sacred Heart of Cuchulain: In comparison with Griffith or Connolly, Patrick Pearse, the leader of those poetic dreamers, is a very strange case. His cast of mind is so different to theirs, and so alien to our way of thinking, that often he seems quite unreal. Yet this unreality is still, unfortunately perhaps, influential today among some Republicans. As a single instance I can cite Bernadette Devlin, a disciple of James Connolly if ever there was one, who mentions in her autobiography that the initial impulse towards Irish nationalism in her life was the poetry of Patrick Pearse : a recitation of his verse won her ten pounds in a talent competition at the age of twelve.

On his mother's side, in the words of one school history, Pearse 'came of Fenian and Gaelic speaking stock'. His father however was a Cornish stonemason who had settled in Dublin where he found work on the new Catholic churches then being built throughout the country. Willie Pearse followed his father into the trade and worked in the family firm in Dublin. But it was an Irish Catholic family none the less, where the mother exerted over her growing sons an excessive emotional influence. In much of Pearse's writings, the image of his mother Ireland suffering in chains is the predominant one; so much so that one wonders whether an unhappy marriage with the English mason produced it. Pearse's identification with the suffering female figure of Ireland was so complete, a recent biographer, Hedley McCay, assures us, that as a boy Pearse took to long night walks alone through the streets of Dublin dressed in girl's clothing.

Pearse grew into one of those etiolated personalities, who fearing the emotional intimacy of individual relationships, find satisfaction in sublimating their sexuality into an excessive love of man in general. Pearse's aloof nervous energy reminds one of the late Dag Hammarskjold, a very similar type of personality, as a comparison of *Markings* with Pearse's poetry shows. The intensity of their desire for personal sacrifice and suffering drove both men to find their ends in the fire of political action. Though Hammarskjold's Lutheran background is far more self-consciously intellectual than Pearse's more emotional Irish Catholic one, the images of pain, suffering and death are strikingly similar.*

Pearse learnt Gaelic and visited the Aran Islands to improve his knowledge of it; later he bought a cottage in Connemara. Most of his imaginative writing is in Irish. Yet he never honed his language as a literary tool, and it remains simply that of a parvenu learnt from a primer. In *Isogan*, his best known story, the identification of the child Christ with a boy named Patrick jars the modern reader, though it is very relevant to Pearse's view of himself as a messiah. For Pearse writing was an extension of his politics, a means towards the regeneration of Ireland. Trained as a lawyer, he was the editor of the supposedly non-political journal of the Gaelic League *An Claidheamh Soluis*, which means the Sword of Light. (Not the light of learning as might be thought : the Sword of Light was the gift of the god Manannan to the boy hero Lugh to enable him to drive out of Ireland the evil Formorians.) Around 1907 the vigour went out of the language movement, and Pearse was not satisfied to wield a merely mythical sword in trying to revive his country. Something more was needed.

*It is worth observing also that for Casement, as for André Gide in Algeria and the French Congo, Africa liberated his emotions from the unnatural constraits of his Ulster childhood. Having come to love the Negro so intimately, it was impossible for him to maintain the attitude of imperial superiority proper to a British consul. From this sexual liberation it was but a small step to their political freedom and, in his own mind, the freedom of the Irish.

To further his own aims he founded a school, St Enda's, in 1908. This school was remarkable in the context of Irish education, then as now dominated on the one hand by the primary National Schools under the management of parish priests and on the other by the secondary schools of the Christian Brothers, where children were crammed for the British Civil Service and beaten out of any unhealthy initiatives.

Pearse had no corporal punishment in his school, which was also entirely under lay management. Pearse, however, was a natural teacher and his staff included Thomas MacDonagh the poet and Desmond Ryan, later a historian. With only a few pupils, the school could not fail. Irish was spoken in class and playground, a policy which worked well in a happy atmosphere free from coercion. The school attracted to it the children of such progressive parents as James Larkin and W.P. Ryan.

Yet there was still something in the school of the self-conscious bourgeois intellectual returning to the folk. Yeats in a diary records a conversation with Thomas MacDonagh in 1909, whom he found was very sad about the state of the country: 'Says that he finds a barrier between himself and the Irish-speaking peasantry, who are "cold, dark and reticent" and "too polite". He watches the Irish-speaking boys at his school, and when nobody is looking, or when they are alone with the Irish-speaking gardener, they are merry, clever and talkative. When they meet an English speaker or one who has learnt Gaelic, they are stupid. They are in a different world.'[4] Yeats's observations illustrate the contrast between the Irish-speaking and the English-speaking cultures in Ireland. Even with the best of intentions some barriers were still difficult to cross. The sometimes hopeless idealisation of the Irish-speaking peasants by writers was verging on cloud cuckoodom; the sharp touch of realism was lacking. Realism was not, however, the spirit of Pearse's particular experiment.

In the hall of the school was an immense portrait of Cuchulain, who was, according to Desmond Ryan, 'an invisible but important member of the staff'. For Pearse, as for Yeats, there were in the ancient myths profound 'heart secrets'. Cuchulain who had been in the poetry of the Revival a symbol of all that was distinctively Irish, became for Pearse symbolic of the struggle for freedom. He preached to his pupils the nobility of the heroes of the ancient sagas.

We must recreate and perpetuate in Ireland the knightly tradition of Cuchulain, the noble tradition of the Fianna,—'We, the Fianna, never told a lie, falsehood was never imputed to us'; 'Strength in our hands, truth on our lips, cleanness in our hearts'; the Christ-like tradition of Columcille, 'if I should die it shall be from the excess of love I bear the Gael'.[5]

That is a fairly typical passage, which shows up the curious double-think in Pearse's mind, that resolved this mixture of pagan and Christian into one coherent thought. Though it was as much a fantasy of Celtic Ireland as Connolly's tribal communism was, it was this image of heroic endeavour and sacrifice for Ireland that inspired Pearse to answer England 'with the sword's edge', to go out gladly to the ultimate sacrifice of his own life.

Writing about 'The Coming Revolution' in November 1913, Pearse claimed that 'bloodshed is a cleansing and a sanctifying thing, and that the nation which regards it as the final horror has lost its manhood. There are many more things more horrible than bloodshed; and slavery is one of them'. This high-flown and terrifying sentiment was followed by the even more extraordinary statement that he 'would like to see any and every body of Irish citizens armed. We must accustom ourselves to the thought of arms, to the sight of arms, to the use of arms. We may make mistakes at first and *shoot the wrong people*' (added emphasis).[6] Indeed there was to come a time when the Irish people were to be more than accustomed to the sight of arms, and many of 'the wrong people' would be shot before the end of the events that Pearse's imagination loosed upon the country. Whether this bloodshed was a cleansing and sanctifying experience for the Irish people we shall have to see.

In his own imagination this cleansing sacrifice was modelled on the same curious amalgam of Cuchulain and Christ that we saw above. At the end of his play *The Singer* this identification becomes explicit, when MacDara goes out to fight the foreigner and die against great odds : 'One man can free a people as one Man redeemed the world. I will take no pike, I will go into battle with bare hands, I will stand up before the Gall as Christ hung naked before men on a tree.'[7] That this was blasphemy in the orthodox Catholic view does not seem to have disturbed many admirers of Pearse. The Rising began on Easter Monday so that

in future Ireland would be unable to celebrate the Resurrection
of Christ without remembering the Insurrection of Ireland. The
Risen God became the Risen People.

That significant date was chosen by Pearse. Through his
mother he had acquired an emotional devotion to Irish nationalism; the Fenian tradition was a strong one in his family. By
1913 the Fenians had become, as Connolly remarked to a friend,
'the sort of old codgers you'd meet in a pub'. But that year
Pearse joined the Irish Republican Brotherhood and was 'rebap-
tised in the Fenian faith'. He believed in blood sacrifice, and saw
himself as a Christ figure destined to die for the salvation of his
people. That school painting of Cuchulain is now transformed
into the memorial bronze which stands in the GPO.

Poetry and Republicanism were the twin inspirations of the
1916 leaders, so before dealing with the rise of Irish republicanism, we will look into the poetry of the Rising. The messianism
of Pearse was shared by Joseph Mary Plunkett, and in a much
smaller way by Thomas MacDonagh : the three Bad Poets of the
Rising as they were once called. They are not really so much
bad poets as minor poets for whom poetry was not enough. Like
other minor artists they attempted to achieve in life the impact
they failed to have in art.

They had no illusions about their stature as poets. Thomas
MacDonagh wrote his own epitaph in a poem called 'The Patriot
Poet' :

> His songs were a little phrase
>   Of eternal song,
> Drowned by the harpings of lays
>   More loud and long.[8]

The poetry of the 1916 poets has been effectively drowned, not
only by the more distinguished 'harpings' of other poets of the
Revival, but also by the noise of the explosion they ignited.

Not for Pearse was Yeats's red-rose-bordered hem of beauty.
He had another, more awful muse : his mother Eire.

> I am Ireland
> I am older than the old woman of Beare,
> Great my sorrow, my own children
> Have sold their mother.[9]

The poetry written under her inspiration is of two kinds : a loud rhetorical verse intended to sway the heart and smother the mind, and a quieter, more personal kind. The first sort is really an extension of his public speeches, such as the famous oration over the grave of the old Fenian O'Donovan Rossa in 1915 (a piece admired by Bernadette Devlin, which still features among the samples of English prose studied by school children in the Republic for the Leaving Certificate) :

> Life springs from death; and from the graves of patriot men and women spring living nations. The Defenders of the Realm have worked well in secret and in the open. They think they have pacified Ireland. They think they have purchased half of us and intimidated the other half. They think they have foreseen everything, they think they have provided against everything, but the fools, the fools, they have left us our Fenian dead, and while Ireland holds these graves, Ireland unfree will never be at peace.[10]

Such sentiments translated easily into a public kind of poetry, such as this passage from 'The Fool' :

> O wise men, riddle me this : what if the dream come true?
> What if the dream come true? and millions unborn shall dwell
> In the house that I shaped in my heart, the noble house of
> my thought?
> Lord, I have staked my soul, I have staked the lives of my kin
> On the truth of Thy dreadful word. Do not remember my
> failures,
> But remember my faith.[11]

In this kind of poetry Pearse remains that remote figure by that open grave, shrouded from us by a cloak of nationalist piety, as if there were no human being inside it.

There was, but only in the smaller pieces of verse do we catch for a moment the anguish of an individual voice :

> Naked I saw thee,
> O beauty of beauties,
> And I blinded my eyes
> For fear of my failing . . .

I blinded my eyes,
And I closed my ears.
I hardened my heart
And I smothered my desires ...

I have turned my face
To this road before me,
To this deed that I see
And this death I shall die.[12]

This poem is entitled 'Renunciation', and its severe ideal of purity and dedication is derived from the puritan streak of Irish Catholicism and was to set the tone of the social attitudes of the revolutionary underground. Where the poets of medieval Ireland were dedicated in their purity only to Christ, Pearse was dedicated to Cuchulain 'and he crucified'. If such a sentiment verges on the blasphemous, the blasphemy is Pearse's.

His poems speak continually of his mother Ireland with an emotion proper to his own. We should not, in political characters such as Pearse's, underestimate the effect of personal experience. Perhaps the emotional confusion due to an unnaturally strong affection for his mother was only to be sublimated in a bloody gesture of revolt; the Rising was a political expression of his desire to murder his English father for the love of his mother. There is in fact a poem of his called 'The Mother', written in Kilmainham Gaol shortly before his execution :

I do not grudge them : Lord, I do not grudge
My two strong sons that I have seen go out
To break their strength and die, they and a few
In bloody protest for a glorious thing. ...
Lord, thou art hard on mothers :
We suffer in their coming and their going;
And tho' I grudge them not, I weary, weary
Of the long sorrow—and yet I have my joy :
My sons were faithful and they fought.[13]

My sons were faithful and they fought : we shall have occasion later on to contrast these feelings with those of other bereaved mothers both in life and in literature before the revolution is over.

Pearse sent his mother another poem in his last letter from Kilmainham. These last lines, free from all the posturing and

D

rhetoric of so much of his verse, are the most moving he ever wrote :

> The beauty of the world hath made me sad,
> This beauty that will pass;
> Sometimes my heart hath shaken with great joy
> To see a leaping squirrel in a tree,
> Or a red lady-bird upon a stalk,
> Or little rabbits in a field at evening,
> Lit by the slanting sun,
> Or some green field where mountainy man hath sown
> And soon would reap, near to the gate of Heaven;
> Or children with bare feet upon the sands
> Of some ebbed sea, or playing on streets
> Of little towns in Connacht,
> Things young and happy.
> And then my heart hath told me :
> These will pass and be no more,
> Things bright and green, things young and happy,
> And I have gone upon my way
> Sorrowful.[14]

These lines suggest very well the quality of Pearse's hopes for his people. He wished, as so many in the literary and political revival did, for a renewed contact with the soil. All good, they believed, as Yeats later put it,

> Must come from contact with the soil, from that
> Contact everything Antaeus-like grew strong.[15]

This reactionary agrarian ideal was shared also in the strictly political area by Michael Collins, if we can judge his hopes for Ireland from that often quoted passage where he describes cheering the donkey cart in the Shepherd's Bush Road; and of course, by Eamon de Valera. One doubts however that if by some extraordinary chance Pearse had lived he would have been able to put into political action what was essentially a poet's vision of the hopeless beauty and shadowed innocence of the world.

In the Gaelic tradition of which he saw himself as part, there had never been any bar between the love of God and the delight in nature, as the anonymous lyrics scribbled in the margins of manuscripts by early Christian monks show :

> A hedge of trees surrounds me,
> A blackbird sings above me,
> Over the lines of my book,
> The merry chatter of birds.[16]

In Pearse this innocent delight, so fresh and vital, turns into an almost decadent world-weariness. From his momentary delight in the squirrels, insects and rabbits, he turns away in sorrow for all

> Things bright and green, things young and happy,
> And I have gone upon my way—
> Sorrowful.[17]

The same passing beauty of the world which was such a delight to Yeats was a snare to Pearse. The austerity of such 'catholic' imagination is a little frightening, as when Joseph Plunkett sees in the rose tree only a remembrance of Christ's passion :

> His crown of thorns is twined with every thorn,
> His cross in every tree.[18]

To such beauty as the world held they blinded their eyes, hardened their hearts, turning to face their expected deaths. It is a chilling and inhuman spectacle.

Plunkett was as curious a man as Pearse. Having studied literature and philosophy at UCD, he helped Thomas Mac-Donagh found the Irish Theatre with Edward Martyn and edit *The Irish Review*. He, it seems, was largely responsible for the actual planning of the Rising, which he came to join from his hospital bed after an operation. His imagination is suffused with an almost Spanish sense of suffering, due perhaps to a heightened awareness of death due to his continued ill health. 'I see his blood upon the rose', he writes of Christ in one poem,

> All pathways by his feet are worn
> His strong heart stirs the ever-beating sea,
> His crown of thorns is twined with every thorn,
> His cross is every tree.[19]

These pantheistic sentiments are quite unlike the Irish nature poetry of the Middle Ages, in the tradition of which they were written. Even more strikingly morbid is 'My Lady Has the Grace of Death' :

> She found me fainting by the way
> And fed me from her babeless breast
> She played with me as children play,
> Rocked me to rest.

which has this strange final stanza :

> And when the morn rose bright and ruddy
> And sweet birds on the branch above
> She took my sword from her side all bloody
> And died for love.[20]

The night before his execution Plunkett married the artist Grace Gifford in prison : an event the poem seems almost to presage.

Thomas MacDonagh is perhaps the only real poet of the group, next to Connolly its most interesting mind, because his intelligence was not overwhelmed by either rhetoric or morbidity. A sense of humorous irony runs through much of his writing. MacDonagh, who lectured in English at University College Dublin, was a keen student of Irish : on his summer visits to Cloughjordan he and my grandfather, who taught in the National School as once MacDonagh's parents had done, used to read their way through the volumes of the Irish Texts Society, then being issued annually. As a scholar he was concerned to discover whether there was a continuity between Gaelic and English literature in Ireland. As a critic he wanted to see if there was in Irish poetry written in English such a thing as an 'Irish mode'. His criticism, which tried to continue what Matthew Arnold had begun, was not based on any narrow nationalistic ideal (as was later the case with Daniel Corkery), but on a just appreciation of literary merit.

In *Literature in Ireland*, published after his death in 1916, he tries to be definite about these points : '[Anglo-Irish literature] is distinctly a new literature, the first expression of the life and ways of thought of a new people, hitherto without literary expression, differing from English literature of all periods, not with the difference of age, but with the difference of race and nationality. That race is the Irish race, now mainly English-speaking.'[21] He sees this new literature as 'moving to the rhythm of Irish music', and is exact about its production. 'The term Anglo-Irish literature is applied very rarely to the meagre writings of the planters :

it is worth having as a term only to apply to the literature produced by the English-speaking Irish, and by these people when writing in Ireland and for the Irish people.'[22] Later we will see how these ideas were taken up by Daniel Corkery, except that in MacDonagh there is no moral disapproval of Anglo-Irish writing as there is in Corkery. These definitions are important for being made by a man who signed the 1916 Proclamation. They might have become the accepted definitions of Irish culture, but as we shall see, narrower and more bigoted canons were to be adopted in the new Ireland he helped towards its freedom.

If James Connolly was an immeasurable loss to the future of the Left in Ireland, Thomas MacDonagh was a loss to the future of literary criticism as serious study. Such intellectual losses are a serious matter in a small country, and part of the failure of the Rising must be that it led to the death of such men as these.

Pearse and his friends had no illusions about success : they knew they would fail. But they felt that someone should strike the first blow, and hoped their insurrection even if unpopular would have a catalytic effect. They hoped the precipitate would be a Gaelic Socialist Republic—the 'house of my dreams' as Pearse called their vision. Their imaginations, which were those of poets, were fed on Cuchulain and Christ and the notion of the redeeming death—even Connolly would have agreed with them about the nobility of sacrificing one's life for the cause of Ireland. Even the gentle Connolly, once opposed to war and the notion of blood sacrifice, thought in the end that theirs was the only way.

Thomas MacDonagh wrote from his cell the night before he was shot that 'it is a great and glorious thing to die for Ireland and I can well forget all petty annoyances in the splendour of this. When my son Don was born I thought that to him and not to me would this be given. God has been kinder to me than I hoped'.

MacDonagh, in completing *Literature in Ireland* shortly before the Rising, quoted Francis Thompson : 'The more a man gives himself to poetry, the less poetry he writes.' The 1916 poets exemplify this effect in themselves : that men become expressions of their own imaginations. They gave themselves to the great theme of their poetry, the cause of Ireland, and made the Rising not merely a political event but also a poetic creation. So Pearse, in a poem called *The Rebel*, put into verse some of the current feelings of immanent revolt :

And I say to my people's masters : Beware,
Beware of the thing that is coming, beware of the Risen
People,
Who shall take what ye would not give—Did ye think to
conquer the people,
Or that law is stronger than life or man's desire to be free.
We will try it out with ye.[23]

The coming event cast a long shadow before it. Austin Clarke
the poet, then a student studying under Hyde and MacDonagh
at UCD, recalls one last vivid impression of MacDonagh :

> Students watch their lecturers with close attention, so it was
> that late in the Spring of 1916, I began to realise, with a
> feeling of foreboding, that something was about to happen
> for I noticed at times, though only for a few seconds, how
> abstracted and worried Thomas MacDonagh looked. Sud-
> denly one day, during a lecture on the Young Ireland poets,
> he took a large revolver from his pocket and laid it on the
> desk, 'Ireland can win her freedom only by force,' he remarked
> as if to himself.[24]

He was not just talking to himself, but for his friends.

Drums under the Window: That force was needed to secure the
freedom of Ireland, was a feeling widely shared by different
groups. Some of these we have already looked at : the men were
to hand, now only the arms were required.

The crisis which brought on the Rising grew out of the controversy over Home Rule. In 1910 the Liberals were returned
with a reduced majority and were dependent on Labour and
Irish support to put through such measures as the reform of the
House of Lords. It was clear that a third Home Rule Bill would
be introduced and in 1912 this was done, by Asquith.

Strongly opposed to such legislation, and supported by the
Conservative Party, the Ulster Loyalists led by Edward Carson
(a Dublin man) collected half a million names on Ulster's Solemn
League and Covenant, which proclaimed their readiness to resist
by 'any means' the conspiracy—as they saw it—to set up a Home

Rule government in Ireland and pass over the control of the country to Catholics. Encouraged by the Conservative Party, the Ulster Volunteers were formed late in 1912 to back the Covenant with force.

Ulster in arms encouraged others in the South to arm also. In 1913 Larkin and Connolly formed the Irish Citizen Army partly to protect the workers during the Lock-out, and partly to provide a 'Red Army' for future revolutionary action. In November Eoin MacNeil, in an article for *An Claidheamh Soluis,* suggested the formation of the Irish Volunteers. At the inaugural meeting in December 1913 thousands joined up, and the organisation quickly spread throughout the South.

The crisis worsened. In March 1914 officers at the Curragh, the central military establishment in Ireland, refused to move against the Ulster Volunteers. The next month the Ulster Volunteers landed at Larne and Bangor a shipment of guns from Germany—putting 35,000 rifles in the hands of 85,000 men. Redmond was forced by this escalation to put his support behind the National Irish Volunteers. Ireland was now becoming an armed camp and Great Britain was teetering towards civil war.

At a meeting in London early in April, a few days after the Larne landing, a group of prominent Irish Liberals, more or less associated with the Irish Volunteers, met to discuss what was to be done. The meeting was held at the house of Alice Stopford-Green, the historian, and among those present were Roger Casement and Darrell Figgis, a writer. The argument veered backwards and forwards. At last Figgis said decisively, 'Let us buy arms and so at least get into the problem.' Casement agreed with him. It was arranged that Figgis should go to Hamburg to buy guns there.

This he did. At Hamburg he hired a tug, and having avoided the customs men, rendezvoused with Conor O'Brien's yacht off the German coast. (O'Brien was the godfather of Conor Cruise O'Brien, and well known as a nautical writer.) At Fishguard the guns were transferred to Erskine Childers's yacht, the *Asgard,* which carried them into Howth Harbour. There a large band of Volunteers under the command of Bulmer Hobson unloaded the cases, and set off with the guns over their shoulders towards the city centre. The authorities were taken by surprise. A detachment of the Scottish Borderers were called out. The soldiers met the

Volunteers on the Malahide Road, but while Hobson and Figgis argued with the officer in charge, the men and guns slipped away across the open fields into the city. Returning to barracks, the soldiers were followed by a large excited crowd, which began to throw stones at them. At Bachelor's Walk, on the Liffey quays, the rear guard turned to face the crowd. Shots were fired : three people were killed—a man, a woman and a boy of eighteen— and twenty-six were wounded. The British Army which had refused to move against the Ulster Volunteers, had proved its manhood with civilian blood on the streets of Dublin.

Two days later Austria declared war on Serbia. By August all Europe was at war. And with the war came an agreement to shelve the Home Rule Act, which had been passed by the Lords and had received the Royal Assent on 18 September, for the duration of the hostilities. John Redmond, speaking for the Irish middle classes, offered the Irish Volunteers to the British government, and most of them followed his brother to the ranks.

A rump of the Volunteers, about 10,000 out of 132,000, refused to do so, and an Anti-War Committee was set up in Dublin under James Connolly. Connolly was convinced that the war provided the opportunity for an armed rising which might not come again : now was the time for the Citizen Army to seize the initiative for revolution. This was the doctrine he preached throughout 1915 in *The Irish Worker*.

Unknown to Connolly, however, the Irish Republican Brotherhood was already at work plotting a rising, the decision for which had been taken in the first weeks of the war. For fear he would go it alone, the Army Council were forced to co-opt the not unwilling Connolly. It was their intention to use the Irish Volunteers for their own revolutionary ends, bypassing Eoin MacNeill and others like the O'Rahilly who were still opposed to hasty action.

The role of the IRB in the Rising and the intentions of their Army Council which worked in secret, are crucial to an understanding of that and subsequent events.

The Irish Republican Brotherhood saw itself as the heir to the long tradition of Irish Republicanism going back to the eighteenth century. As we saw in the first chapter this militant tradition had always existed as a minority view in the wider spectrum of Irish nationalism. At the time of the Rising there was an extra dimension of intrigue, in that Pearse and others were plotting the

Rising without the knowledge of Eoin MacNeill and those in the IRB who were opposed to immediate military action. This was what led to the confusion surrounding the orders to mobilise on Easter Sunday, and later the secrecy of the IRB was to be resented by democrats in the Dail and Sinn Fein. So for all intents and purposes the Rising was masterminded by an inner clique of the IRB, but the results of the Rising were to go far beyond their control.

Meanwhile, in August 1915 the funeral of the old Fenian leader O'Donovan Rossa—yet another of those faded figureheads, yet another of those political funerals that Republicans love—provided the occasion for a show of strength by the Volunteers and the Irish Citizen Army. They took over control of the city centre for the day, and with great panoply the old patriot was buried in Glasnevin. Some must have thought that day of Parnell's funeral a generation before. In 1891 Yeats had thought the poet might replace the patriot; now it seemed the poet was going to be replaced once more by the patriot.

Over the open grave Pearse spoke of a generation which had 'renewed its baptismal vows in the Fenian faith'. His oration was an ill omen to those who desired peace more than freedom. The poet, dressed in his Volunteer uniform, gestured across the open pit to the large crowd before him, calling on them to join him. The British, he said, had made the mistake of leaving Ireland her Fenian dead, and 'while Ireland holds these graves,' he exclaimed, 'Ireland unfree shall never be at peace'.

On Easter Monday 1916, units of the Irish Volunteers and the Irish Citizen Army occupied the General Post Office and other strategic buildings throughout the city. These included factories and mills which three years earlier had locked-out their workers, and also that symbol of Irish poverty, the South Dublin Union.

To a small indifferent crowd, gathered to watch the goings-on outside the GPO, Pearse, dressed in his olive drab uniform, read out the Proclamation of the Irish Republic. A green flag with the words 'Irish Republic' stitched in gold thread on it, flew from the roof above his head. There were a few perfunctory cheers. The crowd thought the Volunteers were either mad or playacting.

Even then it was clear that the insurrection would fail. The great drama of revolution was rapidly degenerating into a tragic farce. Eoin MacNeill, by cancelling the general mobilisation order at almost the last moment when he learned that an insurrection was planned, had brought confusion to the plans of the IRB military council. In confusion the Rising began and ended in Dublin, outbreaks in the provinces being few and small. In all only 600 men turned out to defend the Republic. The O'Rahilly who had been sent off around the country by MacNeill to ensure that no one came out, returned to Dublin and joined the rebels in the GPO. He died later in the week during the fighting in Moore Street. 'Because I helped to wind the clock,' Yeats has him say, 'I've come to hear it strike.' This mad, gallant gesture was typical of the whole enterprise.

In a few days the British authorities crushed the revolt by drafting into Dublin troops bound for France. The city centre was badly damaged by shelling and fires. (Connolly had believed that no capitalist government would destroy private property, but —just in case—he had the Starry Plough raised over the Imperial Hotel owned by William Martin Murphy.) In North King Street several civilians were killed by British troops, while in Portobello Barracks an insane officer shot three civilians, among them the well-known pacifist Francis Sheehy-Skeffington, who had been trying to prevent looting. Later the casualties during the Rising were estimated at over three thousand, though only some 627 people were actually killed.

Pearse finally surrendered on 29 April. The wretched rebels were marched off to prison to the jeers and catcalls of angry Dubliners. There was very little immediate sympathy for the Rising during those first few days. After swift courts-martial, Pearse and fifteen others were sentenced to death. The *Irish Independent*, voicing what was then the general public opinion, called for their deaths, especially that of the dangerous radical Connolly. The British military commander satisfied this wish. But the executions were drawn out over two weeks, and Connolly himself was so badly wounded that he had to be tied to a chair to be shot. Among the leaders only Constance Markievicz, the Red Countess of the popular press, and Eamon de Valera, who was an American citizen, were reprieved to serve life sentences. They were to survive to benefit from the great reversal in public opinion about the Rising which followed the executions. Dismay at the rebellion turned overnight to disgust at the vengeance exacted by the army.

The murders and executions had been intended as draconian measures to stamp out the revolutionary spark, but instead they merely inflamed the dormant emotions of many who had until then been uninterested in Sinn Fein (which, ironically enough in view of Griffith's constitutionalism, found itself blamed for the Rising), or in the ideas of Pearse and Connolly.

Their ideas had been enshrined in the Proclamation of the Republic, which is the first public document of the new revolution. Though cast in the vague general terms of all such stirring appeals to the people in time of crisis, the Proclamation nevertheless set out an ideal of the Irish Republic. The fundamental right of the Irish people to the ownership of Ireland, and to the unfettered control of the country's future, was the main declaration. The document then went on :

> The Irish Republic is entitled to, and hereby claims, the allegiance of every Irishman and Irishwoman. The Republic guarantees religious and civil liberty, equal rights and equal opportunities to all its citizens, and declares its resolve to pursue the happiness and prosperity of the whole nation and all its parts, cherishing all the children of the nation equally, and oblivious of the differences carefully fostered by an alien government, which have divided a minority from the majority in the past.[25]

In these passages nearly all the traditions of European liberal nationalism are summarised. But the thought that it might be the attitudes of the majority that had frightened the minority (rather than the machinations of the British) never seems to have passed through the minds of the authors. Though Ulster had brought on the Rising, it got scarcely a thought from Pearse or Connolly. If one considers Pearse's final thought in *The Sovereign People*, that the 'right of private property was not good against the common welfare of the people', the influence of European social democracy is also evident. Whatever their failure in arms, Pearse and Connolly had written clearly their proposed charter for the new Ireland. But their ideas were to be honoured only, and to have little influence either then or later. Liberalism and social democracy were to have small part in the new Ireland.

It has been argued that the Rising was an unnecessary act of violence. Home Rule had been achieved. A government in Dublin at the end of the Great War would have been in a position to have realised whatever further freedoms the elected representatives of the people wanted : either the Commonwealth status of Canada and Australia, or complete independence. Yet this excursion into comic opera revolution (as it seemed to the British) by a very small and unrepresentative minority would completely alter the political nature of Sinn Fein, alter indeed the whole life of the country for the next decade. In the end it was the course of events unleashed by the Rising which ensured the partition of Ireland. Despite Pearse's declared concern for the Northern people, it was this resort to revolution as a means of change that copperfastened the divisions in Ireland. The question of allegiance to the Republic was later to be the source of further divisions and further bloodshed.

This change in Irish life would affect Irish literature as well. As we have seen, the roots of the revival and the revolution are tangled together. Yeats the poet was a Republican, Pearse the Republican was a poet. The poetical and political ideas of both shared a common basis in Irish history, a belief in the special destiny of the Irish people. As Yeats would later put it in that poem inspired by the statue of Cuchulain commemorating Pearse in the GPO:

> When Pearse summoned Cuchulain to his side,
> What stalked through the Post Office? What intellect,
> What calculation, number, measurement, replied?
> We Irish, born into that ancient sect
> But thrown upon this filthy modern tide
> And by its formless spawning fury wrecked,
> Climb to our proper dark, that we may trace
> The lineaments of a plummet-measured face.[26]

The ideal of Ireland which motivated the very small group of men who plotted the Easter Rising had its origins in the materials which had been recovered by Irish scholars and recreated by Irish poets. That ideal, rather than any realistic political considerations, brought out those men the English shot. The Revival had done its work. The Revolution had now begun.

PART TWO: REVOLUTION

On the other side of the ditch which the whole party crossed, Fabrizio found himself beside a sergeant who looked a good-natured sort of fellow. 'I must speak to this one,' he said to himself, 'then perhaps they'll stop staring at me.' He remained sunk in thought for some time.

'Sir,' he said at last to the sergeant, 'this is the first time I have been present at a battle. But is this one a real battle?'

Stendhal: *The Charterhouse of Parma*

5

The Spring of 'Sixteen

IRELAND ON THE EVE OF REVOLUTION

ON 10 April 1916, just two weeks before Easter, the Director of
Military Intelligence in Ireland reported to the British authorities
that

> The general state of Ireland, apart from recruiting, and apart
> from the activities of the pro-German Sinn Fein minority, is
> thoroughly satisfactory. The mass of the people are sound and
> loyal as regards the war, and the country is in a very prosper-
> ous state and very free from ordinary crime.[1]

This prosperous Ireland—doing well out of the war by selling
food to hard-pressed Britain—seemed so calm and quiet on that
Easter Monday itself, that most of Dublin was more concerned
with the Fairy House races than with revolution. If the country
appeared so ordered to the authorities and so quiet to the man
in the street, did it appear differently to its artists? We can see
something of their island on the eve of revolution in the work of
three men : Michael Farrell, the novelist; Jack Yeats, the painter;
and Darrell Figgis, the poet turned gunrunner. These three, in
their different ways, provide images of Ireland as Arcadia.

In *Thy Tears Might Cease* Michael Farrell wrote one of the
finest of modern Irish novels. Though it was a very long time in
the making, appearing only after the author's death in 1963,
this is one of the high points of that Irish realistic fiction tinged
with romanticism, which is the peculiar literary product of the
revolution. It is, however, also a product of the disillusioned
thirties, when the vision of an independent Ireland had gone
sour, and is informed by the harsh bitterness many then felt for
post-revolutionary Ireland. The new Ireland was quite a contrast
to the provincial world of Farrell's childhood, that settled, quiet

place, like some lost domain, looked back on with the nostalgia which is so often the driving force behind the creation of the greatest fiction.

He began to write the novel when he returned from working in the Congo in 1932. He abandoned a medical career for writing, working for the radio and later on *The Bell*. The ex-colonial agent with his brown face, bright eyes and streams and streams of talk impressed his contemporaries in the Dublin literary world. He was an assertive and haughty man on first encounter, but with close friends he was amusing, cultivated and magnanimous. An American woman, a complete stranger to him, has recounted her meeting with him when he was already very ill in the 1950s, when she casually called on the weaving business he and his wife ran in the Dublin mountains. Wrapped in a dressing-gown, he re-created with his stick over the rough pile of the carpet, Sarsfield's exploits at the siege of Limerick. She thought it was almost as good as being there. This desire to *re-create* impelled him. In his house outside Dublin, the maids always appeared at table capped and aproned as before the war, as if time and change had stopped when servants were commonplace. When he began to write his novel, he tried to recapture that lost but better world with the active conviction of the man recounting Sarsfield's campaigns.

The novel opens in the Glenkilly household of the Reilly family at Christmas 1910: Martin Matthew Reilly is waiting for permission to stay up to hear the waits singing their carols through the snow-covered streets. These opening chapters describing Martin's childhood, so finely written, so masterfully evocative of a completely vanished world of country balls and sodality meetings, are the best parts of the book. With a sure hand the author guides us from the Catholic bourgeois home at Glenkilly, through the houses of their landed relatives to the easy cultivation of the Ascendancy at Keelard. There is a mystery about Matthew; he is a love child, as he later realises, the white blackbird of the family. As the orphan is passed from relative to relative we catch glimpses of the society of John Redmond's Ireland through the distancing eyes of an outsider.

One of the minor characters—who are used in counterpoint to suggest a little of the awful destiny of human life—is Tim Corbin, a nationalist town councillor in Bannow. He is described for us by a jarvey as 'Jerusalem's primest cut of a dodiddler'; he is one of those people thriving on the increasing prosperity of the country. Later we find Corbin inquiring with indecent concern into the death of Martin's father, wondering if the Reillys 'God's first-prize Catholics, had a skeleton in the cupboard'. Still later, at Keelard, Corbin arrives to take part in a meeting about a new dance hall. Here we learn the objections of the parish priest—there must be no drinking, or sitting out, and the stage must not be used for dancing or he will denounce the hall. The gentry present have some difficulty in understanding this last point, until the question of 'immorality' is explained patiently to them. During dances such as the Lancers those on the floor below might catch a glimpse of the ladies' petticoats on the stage. What begins as an argument on this point ends with bitter words when one of the Protestants calls the passionate nationalist 'an ignorant enemy of Ireland'. Yet Corbin was one of the very men who were to inherit Ireland after the revolution.

Farrell, with all the anti-clerical feeling born of a good Catholic education, despised especially this sort of mean-mouthed puritanism. The schools to which Martin is sent provide the novelist with scenes of Irish education which remind one in places of James Joyce. Here also the future of Ireland is in the making. Having been beaten by the ignorant though well-meaning Christian brothers, Martin is sent to Dunslane, where in the figure of Long Dick we are introduced to the finer type of Irish priest, to the disillusioned teacher Curran with his motto that 'the liberal tradition cannot now be diverted', and to Conroy, a boy who wears a kilt and plays hurling by himself in a dignified protest against 'foreign games'. It is here that one of the guardians of Irish purity makes unmistakable advances to Martin, kissing him on the lips. The escape from this place to Knockester outside Dublin proves little better : for there Martin's diary is discovered, and he is closely questioned on several passages in it, particularly one about sleeping one night with his cousin Sally. This piece of childhood innocence causes the diary to be burnt, and with it any hope of Martin's loyalty to the Church or what it would make of Ireland.

His love and loyalty lay rather with the great house at Keelard, with the simplicity of the country people, with Curran's liberal tradition. Farrell is honest enough to draw for us the complexity of feelings in Ireland then, where all that was good and dignified was Protestant, and all that was grubby and conniving seemed to be nationalist. In the end Martin retains his own sort of nationalism, but tempers it with his love of the life at Keelard. From that narrow home, that straitened town, from the damp dark corridors of schools haunted by unnameable sins, his imagination escapes into the wide spring fields of ascendancy Ireland.

So Ireland appeared in retrospect to the more realistic eye in 1932, but at the time a more romantic view was common as we can see in Yeats and Figgis. Though W.B. endorsed Farrell's attack on the new commercial-minded Ireland in *The Fisherman*, that figure of completeness could in fact have stepped from one of the more literary paintings of his brother Jack. The painter, though well aware of the status of his family, nevertheless celebrated in his paintings the poorer people of Ireland.

In 1910, the year after his great friend Synge had died, Jack Yeats and his wife returned at last to live in Ireland. We have met him in a previous chapter as Synge's travelling companion in the west of Ireland, but here some details of his own earlier life are needed. In his drawings and paintings Yeats was the great visual interpreter of the life that John Synge wrote about. A painting such as *The Man from Aranmore*, with that strong stalwart figure poised on the edge of the Galway quay proudly defying the outside world and its civilisation, complements the early drawings, giving the Irish peasant a new image, proud, remote, heroic.

The title of an illustrated book which Yeats published in 1912, *Life in the West of Ireland*, was the running title of several exhibitions from one of which Patrick Pearse bought a few paintings. One imagines, however, that Pearse had little sympathy with the other side of western life that Synge and Yeats relished so much, the wild fecklessness and cunning of the *Playboy* or the painting that illustrated it, *The End of the Race*.

In retrospect Jack Yeats dominates his generation of painters in Ireland. But at that time he was only one among many, and in the work of Walter Osborne, William Orpen, Paul Henry and Sean Keating, there are similar visions of Ireland as an Arcadia.

The work of William Orpen is particularly interesting. Orpen taught in the Dublin School of Art and was often in Dublin during the bright early years of the Revival. As he relates in his memoirs, he knew everyone from George Moore to John Hughes.

At this time he painted a series of pictures of life in the west of Ireland on a lavish scale. These are *The Fairy Ring, Western Wedding, The Holy Well,* and *Sowing the New Seed in the Department of Agriculture and Technical Instruction in Ireland.* Some critics then and since have reacted almost violently against these pictures. Orpen's delight in naked bodies is a little upsetting to some Irish sensibilities (Yeats for instance never painted a nude). His real attitude to his subject in *The Holy Well,* whether one of delight or secret satire, is hard to discover. *Sowing the New Seed,* with its contrast between the sharp-eyed puritans and the graceful young girl, is an amusing and accomplished jeu d'esprit. The pleasant nude casting seed on broken earth is said by Orpen to represent 'the spirit of Sinn Fein' bringing new life into Ireland. A lengthy digression could be written around this picture involving Horace Plunkett, the Co-operative Movement, the Department of Agriculture and the whole ambiance of progressive Ireland between 1900 and 1914. The sense of fun and gusto in Orpen's pictures suggests very well the atmosphere of the period when expectations of a happy future were high in Ireland. Later Orpen was to be profoundly moved by the horrors of the Great War, but unfortunately he was not to paint or draw the war in Ireland with the same vividness.

The work of Sean Keating, who studied, under Orpen, was more appealing to the 'nationally minded'. His early work, mainly portraits and scenes of life in the West, was technically very accomplished in the same manner as his mentor's, though the content was more idealised, as in *The Aran Fisherman and his Wife.* Later he was to paint the scenes and personalities of the revolution, but his work showed little technical development once he had established his individual style.

Yeats, however, was in constant evolution. In these years he was changing his style and beginning to work seriously in oils. In the events of the period Yeats formed a new ambition for his art. His sympathies were awakened by the 1913 Lock-Out, and by the shootings at Bachelor's Walk in 1915. He painted *Bachelor's Walk: In Memory,* from the actual scene later in the year. His notebooks for the period are filled with evidence of his new feelings: boys drilling, a mask of Emmet in an antique shop window, a protest chalked on the side of a goods van—'Yes we will have Home Rule in spite of Carson'. Pearse, whom he heard addressing a Volunteer meeting in Dundrum in 1914, was the inspiration of his painting *The Public Orator*. In contrast to that rhetorical painting, all action and mass, is the warm glow of the Batchelor's Walk painting, with its melancholy air and dim shadows, in which a girl throws down a rose at the scene of the incident in memory of the young man who died that day.

Yeats also went to the funeral of O'Donovan Rossa on 1 August 1915, and sketched the long procession with its flags and silent spectators on street and balcony, the Volunteers and the Citizen Army with rifles reversed, the National Foresters, Countess Markievicz and her Fianna boy scouts, and the memorial tributes again, the flowers woven into Celtic crosses.

This was a very different Ireland to Michael Farrell's, an Ireland of latent threats and violence. Yet in April 1916, as Easter approached, Jack Yeats was sketching at Greystones, a small seaside resort south of Dublin : children playing with an old bicycle wheel; a schooner under sail; Michael, his gardener clipping the hedge; local characters. All these went into his notebook, for re-creating in the paintings of later years : an Ireland of small villages and quiet lives, remote from all drama and mythology, with every appearance of continued peace.

Farrell and Yeats were artists who survived and developed 'something to perfection brought' as the painter's brother put it. Darrell Figgis was an artist who failed. But his failure, after his one brief moment of making history, is as relevant as their success. His name now seems almost forgotten, yet he is in his own way representative, as we shall see, of the writer in the revolution and its aftermath. In him the romantic tendency is carried to its extreme, with all its faults and few of its virtues.

Darrell Figgis was born of Protestant parents in Rathmines in 1882, the same year and district as James Joyce. Figgis, however, was taken to India at an early age. After leaving school there, he joined a firm of tea merchants and worked in their Calcutta and London offices from 1898 to 1910. He began writing not, like Kipling, about India, but about what were to become the familiar Georgian themes in familiar modes. His first book of verse called *A Vision of Life* was published in 1909, and brought

him a position as a reader for Dent's where he worked from
1911 for a couple of years.

At this time, as well as his own poetry and a couple of novels,
he was writing a great deal of literary journalism. Some of this,
especially an essay on Synge, was quite interesting. Thus far
then we have a familiar career, that of the Georgian literary
hack. This was the sort of trivial career that nearly killed the
talent of many writers, Edward Thomas for instance.

Figgis himself realised this, for in 1913 he suddenly came back
to Ireland to join the literary movement. He bought a cottage
on Achill Island in Mayo, to soak up the western world of Synge;
he edited a volume of Carleton's stories, as Yeats had once done;
and he got involved in politics as nearly everyone did at that
time. If we are to believe his own account, it was he who forced
the hand of those Irish liberals in 1915 who were involved in
importing the guns from Germany for the Irish Volunteers, by
offering to go to Germany and buy them himself. The guns he
bought were later carried into Ireland on the yacht of that other
writer turned Irish patriot, Erskine Childers.

After this dramatic adventure, Figgis retreated once more to
the cottage on Achill, where he was living with his wife. He was
deliberately immersing himself in that landscape (which Paul
Henry was then painting in his finest pictures). The best of his
poetry deals with the west of Ireland :

> The voices of the curlew crying on the air
> Floated about the silence of the hills.
> The brooding visage of the mountain bare
> Seemed the mute passion of a thousand wills.
>
> From the black waters of the dizzy pool,
> Cupped in the rocky sharpness of their sides,
> Enchantments curled up to their foreheads cool,
> Like a large gesture that reveals and hides.[2]

Like most second-rate writing this reduces to mere formula what
was so passionately unique in, say, W.B. Yeats. It shows more
clearly perhaps what were the commoner feelings for that
romantically seen landscape, the landscape of Yeats's poems.
Reading the comments Figgis made on his life on Achill, it is
easy to see its attractions : 'Never was the earth so savagely

turbulent as on that treeless island bare to all Atlantic storms'—
though one wonders what is owed here to English poetry? He
goes on

> And often at night I stood by the hour gazing motionless on
> the vast stretch of land and sea flooded by moonlight, the
> mountains standing up against the sky like tall ghosts, and the
> ocean glinting as far as the eye could reach like the spears of
> a countless host. Deep, inward peace pervaded such scenes,
> and if one spoke at all, one spoke reluctantly and very softly.[3]

One notes though that before the image of peace is the image
of the armed and 'countless host' : the gesture a large one that
reveals and hides.

(This admirer of the landscape was later to comfort himself
when imprisoned in 1917 and 1919 by recollecting the melodies
of symphonies by Beethoven and others and following them
through their intricacies. A theme of Brahms defeated him for
nearly a week but then 'when it was recovered, how blessed it
was, how God-like a voice it breathed, power and repose and
peacefulness'.)

These western scenes (worked up by the imagination capable
of such refined prison comforts) appeared in his novel of Achill
life *Children of Earth* written during 1915, and were to comfort
him (as much as music) in the hard years to come, assuring him
of the Earth's persistent beauty above Man's petty strife. Thus
Figgis was cut off from the real planning of the Rising he had
helped to arm, perhaps as he thought himself because he was
'judged strange and extraordinary, and therefore sinister' because
he never seemed to leave Achill. The local police had orders from
Dublin Castle to keep an eye on him; in their files he appeared
as 'an associate of W.B. Yeats'.

This beautiful, almost transcendental idyll was shattered for
him in April 1916. In his recollections Figgis recalls those last
hours of peace in Ireland, how Arcadia was invaded, how the
awful news of the Rising in Dublin was brought to them on
remote Achill by a small girl.

> Hardly could I hear her. I looked on that day of breathless
> beauty, of peace poised in perfect balance. Voices rose up from
> the land, where the spring work, long delayed after a bad

winter, was in full swing. Voices of men, voices of women, and the barking of dogs flowed over the land pleasantly. It was not strange that the mind found some difficulty in recognising the meaning of this tale of war that came like a gush of blood violently across the peace and beauty of the day.[4]

6

A Terrible Beauty

LITERATURE AND THE EASTER RISING

THE Rising came as a complete surprise to everyone, 'a gush of blood across the peace and beauty of the day'. The reaction was immediate. As at the death of Parnell, many realised that nothing could be the same again after such a bloody gesture and its consequences. The response of writers of the time was also immediate and, indeed, many later writers have found themselves obliged to give some account of the event.

We had as well begin with the idealists, who had contributed so much to the imagination of the Rising. By 1916 Yeats had little contact with the men who led the Rising. He was staying in England when he heard the astonishing news, and it took him by surprise. All that had been talked of since his youth had come about: Ireland had risen once again. To his friend Charles Ricketts who felt that the trouble would soon pass over, Yeats was insistent on the serious nature of the event: 'I was an idiot,' Ricketts was later to add beside the passage in his diary. Yeats turned out to be only too right. On 11 May he wrote to Lady Gregory:

> I had no idea that any public event could so deeply move me—and I am very despondent about the future. At the moment I feel all the work of years has been overturned, all the bringing together of classes, all the freeing of Irish literature and criticism from politics.[1]

As an artist Yeats was himself at a critical point in his life. Both the Abbey and his own poetry were at a low ebb when the Rising occurred. His last book *Responsibilities* (1914) had been full of his rage at the mental squalor of the country around him. Against the image of the money-grabbing Paudeen he had tried to set as an image of freedom his Connemara fisherman. He had thought then that romantic Ireland was dead and gone, yet here was a new gesture to equal the sacrifices of Edward FitzGerald, Emmet and Wolfe Tone, 'all that delirium of the brave'.

The new resurgence, which was to provide the Abbey with its second great dramatist in Sean O'Casey, coincided with Yeats's marriage to George Hyde-Lees in 1917. After Major MacBride had been executed he had asked Maud Gonne once more to marry him, and when she refused had asked Iseult in her turn who also refused. These pleas had been for him a last gesture to the affections of his youth. Now new relationships of art and life were beginning for him. In the same letter to Lady Gregory, he wrote that he was trying 'to write a poem on the men executed— terrible beauty has been born again'. The poem became *Easter 1916*, the first of a series on the event, which was finished, after long contemplation, on 25 September 1916.

This poem is worth looking at in some detail. Yeats had known, talked to and read the books of the men the British shot. Looking back years later he was to wonder about his own respon- sibility for the Rising, but in 1916, being then at odds with 'the seeming needs of my fool-driven land', he thought these men and he himself 'but lived where motley is worn'. He recalled how he had made fun of them and the things they thought in the usual Dublin fashion.

The Countess Markievicz was an old friend, though he had not been on close terms with her for some years; he preferred to recall how beautiful she had been as a girl when she had ridden to hounds. Pearse he had met at a meeting commemorating Thomas Davis only eighteen months before. Thomas MacDonagh he had known as a friend whose poetry he had admired :

> He might have won fame in the end,
> So sensitive his nature seemed,
> So daring and sweet his thought.[2]

And Major MacBride, who had long since deserted Maud Gonne, he had thought of only with bitterness in the past, as 'a drunken vain-glorious lout', but in the transforming alchemical fires of the Rising

> He, too, has resigned his part
> In the casual comedy;

> He, too, has been changed in his turn,
> Transformed utterly:
> A terrible beauty is born.[3]

These men of common clay were altered by the alchemy of heroic action into almost mythical figures. Pearse and they had joined Cuchulain on whom he had called. Yeats found their resort to violence disturbing, for he had his doubts about the value of the ideas behind it. Pearse he knew had written:

> I kissed thy lips
> O sweetness of sweetness,
> And I hardened my heart
> For fear of my ruin.[4]

In those months following the Rising, while it yet seemed to be merely another lost heroic gesture like those in every other generation, by which Irishmen had asserted their nationality, another gesture that had failed as the others had, Yeats felt that

> Hearts with one purpose alone
> Through summer and winter seem
> Enchanted to a stone
> To trouble the living stream . . .
> Too long a sacrifice
> Can make a stone of the heart.
> O when may it suffice?[5]

Pearse with single purpose had sacrificed his life; among his friends Yeats saw others being enchanted to stone. The danger of too long a sacrifice was all too apparent to him.

Pearse had gone upon his way sorrowful at the beauty of the world; Yeats saw that life has its own continuity outside of fanaticism and heroic sacrifice. In a passage which seems to echo Pearse's last poem in its evocation of natural life, his tone is very different:

> The horse that comes from the road,
> The rider, the birds that range
> From cloud to tumbling cloud,
> Minute by minute they change;

A shadow of cloud on the stream
Changes minute by minute;
A horse-hoof slides on the brim,
And a horse plashes within it;
The long-legged moor-hens dive,
And hens to moor-cocks call;
Minute by minute they live:
The stone's in the midst of all.[6]

The doubtful, troubled confusion that we find in 'Easter 1916' changes to something nearer to support and admiration for the Rising in 'Sixteen Dead Men' and 'The Rose Tree' (both written in 1917), moving as they do from the interior meditation on the meaning of the event in the earlier poem to a kind of political exhortation:

O but we talked at large before
The sixteen men were shot,
But who can talk of give and take,
What should be and what not
While those dead men are loitering there
To stir the boiling pot.[7]

To Yeats and MacDonagh the rose had once been symbolic of the beauty which the poet strives to bring out in his poetry. Yeats had by now grown out of that early florid style, which had been so easily imitated: now there was 'more enterprise in going naked'. So when he came to write 'The Rose Tree' he had in mind not only that symbolic rose, but also perhaps Joseph Plunkett's blood-spattered rose, and James Clarence Mangan's 'Dark Rosaleen', the little dark rose that the Gaelic poets of the eighteenth century used as a figure for Ireland.

Yeats sees Ireland as politically divided and withered by the deadening influence of England, 'a bitter wind that blows across the sea'. In the poem Pearse and Connolly discuss the remedy:

'It needs to be but watered,'
James Connolly replied,
'To make the green come out again
And spread on every side,
And shake the blossom from the bud

> To be the garden's pride.'
> 'But where can we draw water,'
> Said Pearse to Connolly,
> 'When all the wells are parched away?
> O plain as plain can be,
> There's nothing but our own red blood
> Can make a right Rose Tree.'[8]

Such words, indeed, are lightly spoken. But these rebels carried their beliefs into imaginative action. They saw the Rising as a poetic action. They shed their blood to nourish the Rose Tree, in both senses of tradition. Yeats's poems express something of the contemporary feeling in Ireland, confused but elated, proud yet anxious, that lasted until 1919. Till then it was possible to feel that the Easter Rising would be violence enough, 'that England may keep faith/For all that is said and done'. Till 1919 it was just possible for patriots and artists to believe in the same Rose Tree.

Yeats was surprised by the Rising: Sean O'Casey was not. He had been involved in the original organisation of the Citizen Army, of which he was the first and most partial historian. (The royalties from *The Story of the Irish Citizen Army* paid for his mother's funeral.) He had wanted it made into more of a Labour army, having no connections with the Irish Volunteers. He resigned as Secretary because the Countess Markievicz maintained her membership of both groups. For O'Casey there could be no equivocation; he would not have his notions of socialism corrupted by nationalism. He contributed his own small measure of confusion to the schemes of the Citizen Army before he left and became a pacifist. His vacillation is one of the most remarkable things about the early O'Casey; another is his remarkable lack of talent, shown by his truly dreadful contributions to Labour papers.

O'Casey took no part in the fighting of Easter Week however; those events he saw merely as a man in the street. His view of the Rising was as removed from the centre as Yeats's was, but he did not see it as detachedly as the poet did. For O'Casey the heroic sacrifice which had impressed Yeats was the real tragedy. He was concerned not with the hearts of enchanted stone, but with the living stream which they disturbed. Where Yeats, however, uses in his poem the images of nature to express the living nexus of life, O'Casey uses real people.

O'Casey was a working-class Protestant, and so was not moved by the same religious passions as his fellow Dubliners. Though his childhood seems to have been mildly comfortable, he himself became wretchedly poor, and though nearly blind was forced to labouring on the roads and railways to support himself. His own experiences of poverty and the dreadful squalor of the Dublin slums made him a supporter of the trades unions and a socialist. Later he liked to call himself a communist, but Irish communism of the literary variety is often merely a vigorous cover for an essentially good nature. His hero was not the martyred Pearse, but the labour leader James Larkin : 'Here', Sean thought, 'is a man who can put a vase of flowers on every table as well as a loaf of bread; here is the beginning of the broad and active day, the calm and easy evening.' If he had any really coherent political views in 1916, which seems unlikely, they would have been for a socialist Ireland. After the Rising he wrote, in praise not of Connolly, who, he felt, had betrayed the international cause of socialism by espousing nationalism, but of the brutally murdered pacifist Sheehy-Skeffington. He wanted no new state raised on the sufferings of a people who had suffered enough. He warned the Labour movement that in the end it might have to fight the nationalists if it wanted to have a say in the making of the new Ireland. (Connolly had thought this as well : his last advice to his own men was that if the Rising succeeded, they were to keep their guns for another day and another battle. They were for a socialist democracy, and those they fought with might stop before that goal had been reached.) Such was O'Casey's position in 1916 : what of his play about the event?

Published in 1926, *The Plough and the Stars* was the last of O'Casey's early plays to be produced, though it is the earliest in dramatic time, being set in late 1915 and a few days of Easter Week 1916. He wrote it deliberately to a thesis, having realised that the Rising was the one event of recent history he had not written about. (His other plays cover the war of independence and the civil war.) Coming as it did after the events of the civil war, this drama à thèse was the end of the literary period which had begun with Yeats's poem *Easter 1916*. What had begun with the poet as a sympathetic response to heroic sacrifice, ends with the dramatist's vigorous denunciation of it.

Like all O'Casey's plays of this period, *The Plough and the Stars* is a tragic comedy—what Yeats referred to in a letter as 'this tragic farce we have invented'. The reputation of the Abbey had been made by the peasant plays of Synge, but by the time of his death that pastoral theme was already exhausted and Synge had in mind an idea for a completely new departure, a play about the slums of Dublin. Such a play, the first the Abbey ever produced on the subject, was in fact presented in 1917. *Blight: the Tragedy of Dublin* was the work of two doctors, Joseph O'Connor and Joyce's sometime friend Oliver St John Gogarty. Though the play had some effect in drawing attention to the slums, the time was not ripe for this new experience, nor was the portrayal of poverty wholly acceptable even when O'Casey appeared. But whereas the doctors' play was merely bourgeois propaganda, O'Casey's tragi-comedy throbbed with the warm vitality of human life.

O'Casey's slum dwellers are at once comic figures reminiscent of the popular music hall, and tragic actors caught up in historical events they do not understand. Usually it is the men, with their bravura grandiloquence and their shuffling cowardice that are the comic characters. Fun is poked at the National Foresters and their operatic uniforms, and at the blatherings of autodidactic socialists. (Indeed the Covey who is continually quoting from Jeneresky's *Rise and Progress of the Proletariat* must sound a bit like the young O'Casey himself, but without the deplorable Gaelic that the author used to inflict on his few friends.) The women are the tragic figures, bearing the horrors of the war and the stupidities of the men on their narrow shoulders. De Valera himself told one of his officers on Holy Saturday, 'We will be alright, it's the women who will suffer. The most they can do to us is kill us. But the women will have to remain behind to rear the children.' O'Casey realises this awful fact as well. In his magnificent creations there is not a little of the courage of his own mother, to whose 'gay laugh at the gate of the grave' the play is dedicated.

When *The Plough and the Stars* was presented at the Abbey in February 1926, there were protests from some of the audience. It was said that O'Casey was out to make a mockery of the ideals for which the men of 1916 had fought. Mrs Hanna Sheehy-Skeffington and other widows were there during the opening week with their supporters and almost managed to stop the play. Just as indignation over the *Playboy* had centred on the word *shift*, these new protesters were outraged that the Republican tricolour should be carried into a *public house* in which there was, in O'Casey's gentle phrase, 'a daughter of the digs', Rosie Redmond. It was well known, was it not, that her type did not exist in Dublin, at least not since the British left—nevertheless playgoers used to be openly solicited on Abbey Street.

The demonstrators were right. O'Casey certainly intended to scorn men he thought to be wrong-headed idealists. Their ideals brought a toll of suffering and destruction, yet no amelioration of social conditions. For what little might be won, the price was too high. In the scene most objected to, the one in the public house, a meeting is going on in the street outside, at which a Pearse-like patriot is orating. Rosie's comments on his speech—adapted from Pearse's own words—put the rhetoric of nationalism into a context of human life as really lived. Like all O'Casey's women she is concerned to live rather than die. But the heart cry of romantic Ireland in revolution stirs the men:

LIEUT. LANGON : The time is rotten ripe for revolution.
CLITHEROE : You have a mother, Langon.
LIEUT. LANGON : Ireland is greater than a mother.
CAPT. BRENNAN : You have a wife, Clitheroe.
CLITHEROE : Ireland is greater than a wife.[9]

Jack Clitheroe, a bricklayer, is a Commandant in the Irish Citizen Army. He and his wife Nora live as best they can in a tottering Georgian tenement in Mountjoy Square. Nora wants him to leave the Army, and in the first scene has begged him once more so to do. But Ireland being greater than a wife, Jack Clitheroe goes out in the Rising. Nora searches the barricades for him but returns alone.

I could find him nowhere, Mrs Grogan. None o' them would tell me where he was. They told me I shamed my husband an' the women of Ireland by carrying on as I was. . . . They said th' women of Ireland must learn to be brave and cease to be cowardly. . . . Me who risked more for love than they would risk for hate. . . . My Jack will be killed ! . . . He is to be butchered as a sacrifice for the dead.¹⁰

Harsh words which must have stung the hysterical passions of the patriotic. Clitheroe then appears in retreat with Langon and Brennan. He throws his wife aside and goes on with them, leaving Nora hysterical with grief. In the last act, Captain Brennan returns from the fighting. Jack Clitheroe has been mortally wounded. Brennan has left him to die, but reports that General Connolly when he heard of it praised his death.

Nora, naturally enough, is slowly going out of her mind. Trying to get her to rest, Bessie Burgess, a Protestant neighbour with no sympathies for the Rising, is shot dead by British soldiers firing from the street outside at the figures in the window. When the two soldiers enter they are unmoved by their murder—such things happen in war—but settle themselves down at the table for a cup of tea. The curtain falls slowly on the pair of them singing *Keep the Home Fires Burning* while the streets of Dublin go up in flames behind them.

There is more to *The Plough and the Stars* than the tragedy of the Clitheroes. There is the pointless death of Bessie Burgess; Mollser's decline from tuberculosis in the wretched damp of the slums; the ineffectiveness of the Covey : these are as much to the point O'Casey is making as Jack's death for the cause. 'He took it like a man,' reports Captain Brennan. 'And when General Connolly heard of it, he said that for his wife "Commandant Clitheroe's end will be a joy when she realises she has had a hero for a husband".' But O'Casey implies that such heroism changes nothing, such deaths are pointless, as pointless as meaningless blatherings, death from disease, or stray fatal bullets.

For O'Casey the tragedy arises naturally out of the state of his characters trapped in the tide of circumstance and history. Clitheroe puts Ireland before his wife. That is the real tragedy : death before life. Faced with a choice, the Irishman accepts Thanatos before Eros, and so the purpose of life is defeated. The play is an evocation in dramatic terms of the Rising as it was seen from the Dublin slums. Though his heart might beat a little faster as he wrote down the words he puts into the patriot's mouth, there was no real meaning for O'Casey in Pearse's vision. Unlike Yeats he could not respond to the event as to some work of art and see in it only the dimensions of mythology. This city was not Troy; it was common Dublin where ordinary people lived and died. He was nationalist enough to be moved by the rhetoric of the revolution and the wild poetry, but the Dublin slums were his world and heroic martyrs were useless there. Jack Clitheroe is 'butchered as a sacrifice to the dead' on the altar of Irish nationalism, and in the end nothing is gained from the gods by the act. O'Casey's shabby idealists with their patriotic songs, his back street socialists swearing by *The Rise and Progress of the Proletariat*, his women of courage and life, these are the reality against which the myths are measured, and found wanting.

Yeats and O'Casey present in poetic and dramatic form the reactions of those who lived through the Rising: Yeats the romantic image of sacrifice while there was yet doubt as to the outcome of the revolution; O'Casey the destructive menace of the ideal, when after the Civil War the end was all too apparent.

In the half century since they wrote, the Rising has provided the material for many best forgotten novels. As a political event the Rising is of importance for what it began; it was not an end in itself. Yet for some novelists the event provides an easy, slightly exotic background for scenes of violence, torn loyalties and divided loves. We shall try in the rest of this chapter to survey what some better writers have tried to make of the event in the cooler perspective of the novel.

Yeats in 1916 is still clearly the same idealist as in 1910. O'Casey writing in 1926 is clearly related to Synge in his use of an effective mixture of what appears to be realism with the heightened style of poetic language. But we will leave for the moment the question of how drama and poetry were affected by the failure of the revolution, and turn to see what novelists in George Moore's realistic prose tradition made of this intrusion of the heroic into ordinary life.

The only fiction in Gaelic on the event which the language revival had done so much to prepare for, was a small volume of short stories by Padraic O Conaire, published in 1918 called *Seacht mBuaidh an Eirghe Amach* (Seven Victories of the Rising); it has never been put into English. His plots are rather trite—the bastard son, the heir to the Big House, coming into

E

his own; two women who hide from each other their knowledge of their men's deaths in the fighting; a bishop dealing with a young priest who has supported the rebels; a romantic poet betraying a woman. They reminded the Irish critic Francis MacManus of 'a poor Maupassant story rewritten by Ethel M. Dell'. Clearly these sketches worked up for the occasion lack the gentle charm of O Conaire's better known tales of field and road.

In English also the response was rapid. In October 1919, Eimar O'Duffy completed in Dublin a large, ambitious but dull novel called *The Wasted Island*. MacManus calls it 'the most comprehensive essay in fiction about the Rising ever attempted'. O'Duffy was critical of the whole revolutionary movement and satirises the mysticism of the poetic patriots. Against such romantic idealists he set the conservative middle classes. The novel may well be autobiographical; MacManus suggests that the central character Bernard Lascelles, son of a snobbish class-conscious pro-British Protestant surgeon and a Catholic Alice Reilly, is based on the author himself. Through his mother's brother Bernard becomes aware of the new movement reviving Ireland's past and its legends. The other main character is Stephen Ward, who is raised by a disillusioned Fenian father in a mountain cottage, for he is determined that his son shall not make a fool of himself over Ireland as he once did. Through these two young men and their touching lives we are shown the various strata of Dublin society, from the lowest slums to the genteel drawing-rooms. As a novel *The Wasted Island* fails, it is too full of long earnest debates, too schematic to re-create life as lived, is in fact more of an essay than a novel. Yet in those debates we can see O'Duffy attempting a synthesis of the elements of the revolution, of Pearse's vision and Connolly's politics. This was a very necessary debate, but debate failed and failed precisely in that 'wasted island' during the guerrilla war which followed in the years after the book's appearance.

Gerald O'Donovan's novel *Conquest* which ends with the suppression of the Dail in 1919, covers some of the same ground. It is also a poor novel, though an honest one, informed by the author's wide-ranging charity. We find in it the feelings of a man of good will, rather than a perceptive account of the actual events as they affected individuals. It too is full of long debates, needed to explain perhaps but foreign to the real purposes of fiction.

This failure of fictional perception is not confined to those who wrote, so to speak, in the heat of battle. Even writers with the leisure and perspective of long settled peace often fail as well. As mentioned above, the Rising has been the subject of several novels over the following fifty years. Most Irish people are rightly cynical about such efforts : history was never as simple as these writers suggest. Yet faced with the complexities of feeling which the event arouses, as we saw so plainly in Yeats and O'Casey, even a writer of such real merit as Liam O'Flaherty can fail to make the best of the subject, as can be seen in his last published novel *Insurrection* (1950).

O'Flaherty was born on the Aran Islands five years before John Synge's first visit : did that wild child ever set eyes on the dying man? His family intended him for the priesthood, then as now the usual fate of an intelligent younger son in poorer families in Ireland. He was sent to Rockwell College in Dublin (where de Valera had taught a few years earlier) with a view to training for his vocation. But O'Flaherty was found 'temperamentally un-suited' for the priesthood—he had organised a branch of the Irish Volunteers among the boys—and he passed on to University College Dublin. When the war broke out he joined the Irish Guards; the British Army, like the priesthood, being then for one of his class a means of escaping from the social rut. However in 1917 after the fighting at Langemarck he was invalided out with shell-shock. Though as we shall see his later adventures were to be of material use to him, his life and experience till 1919 were somewhat removed from the groundswell of revolution in Ireland. He had no direct experience of 1916, though the trenches of the Western Front gave him enough violence to surfeit most imaginations. Violence is his metier : introduced recently to another Irish writer he casually recalled a man of the same name he once knew who had been stabbed to death in a woman's bed by an irate husband in Istanbul.

The harsh, brutal, lyrical world of his childhood has been the inspiration of his finest work, his short stories and the novels *Skerrit* and *Famine*. The latter novel is one of the most moving of modern Irish books. It is part of a trilogy on the pivotal events of recent Irish history. *Land,* the second novel in the series, is

centred on the land war of the 1880s and is a minor work. The
trilogy was completed by *Insurrection* which describes the few
days of the Rising in 1916.

The central figure of the novel is Bartley Madden, a Connemara peasant who has just returned from working in England
with enough money to marry and buy a small piece of land in
his native village. He loses his money in a pub and the opening
of the book finds him wandering down Sackville Street on Easter
Monday, where he witnesses the beginning of the Rising. He is
rescued from his drunken stupor by a widow who has the odd
notion that he should join the rebels to protect her only son of
sixteen who is with them already.

So Madden joins a unit led by Captain Michael Kinsella with
whom the son is serving. Madden does this, not because of the
widow's pleas but because he is influenced by what the author
calls 'the Idea'. As Madden listens to Pearse reading the Proclamation he is deeply moved:

> At that moment, Madden threw his head forward and stared
> in rapture at the poet's face. He trembled and his face shone
> like that of the smiling woman close to him. For the first time in
> his life, his mind conceived an abstract idea that lit the fire of
> passion in his soul. Although the words he heard were beyond
> his comprehension, their sound evoked the memory of all that
> had exalted him since childhood. Like music, they carried him
> away into enchantment.[11]

His memories of his mother singing, the moonlight on the sea, the
flap of a hooker's canvas sail, larks singing over fields 'where the
shining spades were opening the black earth', the flight of wild
geese: all of these were filled with an inexpressible beauty, a
longing for which was awoken by Pearse's voice.

That is a remarkable passage, central to an understanding of
the minds and imaginations of those who went out with the
rebels. Discussing medieval Irish literature, Frank O'Connor
notes that 'the Irish had a choice between imagination and
intellect, and they chose imagination'. The same choice was made
in 1916: in the passage above we can see it actually being
made. Rather than face pragmatically the real facts of life as
the British in their wisdom saw them, the leaders of the Rising
chose the abstraction of imagination. On that Easter Monday

'the Idea' of the Republic of Ireland came into existence in many imaginations and it was to that idea that many pledged themselves with an almost religious fervour. But it was a Republic seen for many through just such images of life as ran through Madden's mind while listening to Pearse.

When Madden encounters Captain Kinsella 'the idea had found a leader for him to worship'.

> The vague mystical longings inspired in him by the poet's words had taken flesh, in this lean man with the ascetic face and the mysterious eyes of a monk. He felt taut from head to foot like a drawn bow, as he waited to establish contact with his chosen one.[12]

These passages—savouring of the fascism so clearly latent in Irish nationalism—accurately reflect the minds of many who got involved in the Rising, from Pearse himself down to the men who walked in off the street and asked for a gun.

O'Flaherty goes on to describe the fighting in Dublin. The widow's son proves to be a coward. Madden himself is shot dead at the end by British troops. For Bartley Madden, as for so many others, those sweet visions of life were shattered by a bullet through the brain.

Insurrection is an interesting novel, to damn it with faint praise, marred by its narrow scope and by the faults of the author's style. The edge of hysteria in his prose is obvious in the passages just quoted. The action is restricted to the fighting around Mount Street Bridge over the Grand Canal and the defence of Clanwilliam House. We are left wondering about the other events of the week. This of course would not matter at all if the characterisation were better. But the characters are merely lay figures : the thick, easily excited peasant; the ascetic mystical leader. We catch the right tones now and again, but for the most part O'Flaherty is not subtle enough to carry them far.

His range is narrow : 'All I know about', he once confessed to Edward Garnett, 'are cows and sea-gulls'. His stories about animals are among the finest ever written, and he is often happiest with simple people as instinctive in their feelings as animals. Madden is such a character, but his fits and moods, and especially his feelings about the Idea are not completely convincing. Certainly O'Flaherty persuades us that there were men like

Madden moved by such feelings, but he merely affirms this and does not probe into such a state of mind. This is disappointing because to have done so would have cast some curious light on the tortured motives of Pearse himself.

What then is the meaning of the Rising for Irish literature and politics?

Yeats expressed exactly its meaning for literature: 'Terrible beauty has been born again'. This was the intimation which he tried to express in his series of poems on the event. Till 1916, Irish writers had been developing their resources and techniques. Yet for all the triumphs of the Abbey, of Yeats, Synge, Joyce and Moore, theirs was a literature conjured out of the air, worked up from the meagrest of materials. Now, however, merely to live in Ireland, a writer had to come to terms with experiences that brought him into contact with the grimmest of realities, with the moral dilemmas of those lost in a world of social upheaval. Yeats's insight, 'terrible beauty is born again', is a refrain for all souls resisting the triumph of the material. It insists that from the worst of horrors we may bring substance to renew our humanity.

For Irish politics the Rising was the most important event since the death of Parnell. The event clarified the issues for many people. After the executions one was either for Sinn Fein or one was against. It was a clear choice, yet one the country only arrived at slowly. The prisoners who had been deported to Britain were released in 1917. A reorganised Sinn Fein, now with overt Republican principles and de Valera as its President emerged during the same year. The party was now broad enough to shelter most nationalist opinions, even those on the left. Such a wide spectrum of opinion was bound to fragment eventually, but in those days of eager enthusiasm no one thought of that. Sinn Fein gathered wide public support in the national campaign to resist the introduction of conscription to Ireland in 1918. This threat, which would have sent the accumulated surplus of young men off to die on the Western Front, provided the stimulus needed to unite the nationalists of all shades. Many took the line that if they were going to die, they would die at home. In the General Election of December 1918 an overwhelming majority of Sinn Fein candidates were returned (73 out of 105 seats went Sinn Fein). The old Irish Parliamentary Party won only 6 seats, and passed into history in the same year that John Redmond died. The country's new representatives, except for 26 Unionists (all but three elected from Ulster), withdrew from Westminster. They decided to sit in Dublin and there constitute the elected assembly of the Irish people, and to form a government.

Those members of the Dail (as the new parliament called itself) who were at liberty met in the Mansion House, Dublin, in January 1919. They declared the independence of the new Ireland, and formed a government dedicated to taking over the running of the country. They passed a Democratic Programme based on the ideals of Pearse and Connolly. (Drafted by the Labour Party leader Thomas Johnston, passages promising the elimination of capitalism were eliminated: the final version was vague but nationalist in tone.) Other high-sounding statements were issued to a largely inattentive world. The new government set up its own ministries, and its own courts and judges. As time passed these courts became more acceptable, but it was the municipal and country council elections in 1920 which allowed Sinn Fein to gain real control over local affairs. De Valera, trailing the glory of a surviving leader of the Rising, was elected President. The government had its own army in the IRA, even though that armed body was virtually independent and was still under the control of Collins as chief of the IRB, rather than Cathal Brugha as Minister of Defence.

On 21 January 1919, as the Dail met in Dublin for the first time, a party of eight men from the South Tipperary Brigade of the IRA led by Sean Treacy ambushed a load of gelignite at a small place called Soloheadbeg. Two local policemen were murdered by Sean Treacy firing from cover: a war had begun in earnest.

'There can be no doubt,' Charles Townshend observes, 'from the account written by Treacy's companion in arms, Dan Breen, that the attack was a conscious self-assertion by the "physical force" wing.' Breen was convinced that 'some sort of action was absolutely necessary' to prevent the Volunteers becoming 'merely a political adjunct to the Sinn Fein organisation'. They felt that power and authority were slipping away from them into the hands of the elected members of the Dail.[13]

The Republic of the Dail was not the Republic of the IRA. The heirs of a long democratic tradition had different ideas on the source and use of authority from those of the heirs of a secret movement dedicated to revolutionary action. The Dail was determined to rule the country, while the IRA struggled to control it. One side or the other would have to give way. So even at the very beginning of the struggle in Ireland there was a basic division between the fighters and the politicians. As the only settlement could be a political one, the IRA's choice of military action at Soloheadbeg meant that when the political settlement was reached the physical force wing would become isolated, fighting to the end.

In September 1919 the British government attempted to suppress the Dail, which then went underground. De Valera had gone to America, where he remained until December 1920. In Ireland a sordid war of murder and reprisal built up over the next two years—the horrors of the Great War had inured many people to the use of violence. To reinforce a depressed and depleted police force and army, the British government in May 1920 introduced an auxiliary and quasi-terrorist force soon known as the Black and Tans (after a Limerick hunt) on account of their uniforms. These forces (for which recruiting had begun in the autumn of 1919) were used to coerce the civilian population by murder, torture and the indiscriminate burning of farms, houses, villages, parts of towns and on one mad night in December 1920, the centre of Cork city.

The now all too familiar vocabulary of 'terrorism', 'vicious gunmen', 'murder gangs', 'criminal elements', 'the need to restore law and order' was heard from official sources. The British government said it would never negotiate with gunmen, but tried to keep open its contacts with the politicians. In the end the Army said it could go on no longer, unless the government were ready to support a far more intensive anti-terrorist campaign. The British government decided to negotiate with the politicians. The gunmen, who were themselves nearly at the end of their tether, were relieved. A truce was declared in June 1920.

The course of Irish history had been set by the Easter Rising. The old order with its landlords, great houses and quiet lawns gave way before the armed agents of a new democracy dressed in trenchcoats. The struggle was long and bitter, and politically confused. What it meant to Irish life and literature we shall explore in the next six chapters. What began with visionary idealism was to end in political disaster.

The Shape of Life

WRITERS AND THE IDEAL OF IRELAND

BETWEEN 1916 and 1918 Ireland passed through the first stages of a complete revolution in thought and feeling such that by 1919 the country was overwhelmingly in favour of Sinn Fein. Even the resurgence of armed republican resistance had the tacit, often even the active support of the people. But what did Sinn Fein stand for? Beyond their common demand for Irish independence, the actual political objectives of Sinn Fein, the Dail and the IRA were left vague and ill defined. This lack of definition reflected the confused hopes of the people which, as we shall see them reflected by Irish writers, were vague, hopeful and protean.

This current of change and the new national state of mind can be traced through the work and memories of those writers who took part in the movement and have recorded their impressions of it. Our account of this period had best begin with the imaginative re-creation of those years by Michael Farrell in *Thy Tears Might Cease*. This novel will provide some kind of context in which the fragmented memories of other writers can be set. The search for some new shape to life which Farrell ascribes to his central character Martin Reilly, we can also find in the lives of the other writers of the period such as Daniel Corkery and his protégés Sean O'Faolain and Frank O'Connor.

In trying to know what the country was like during this period of transition, the novelist gives us the most penetrating view. Farrell divides his narrative into sections which more or less correspond with the actual movements of history. The first two parts, which we have already looked at in chapter five, deal with 1910 and the period before 1916. The next three sections cover the period between 1916 and 1920, when Martin falls in love, becomes a nationalist and joins a Flying Column (the name given the mobile units of the IRA operating on a local basis). The final sections deal with what Farrell sees as Martin's return, after the disillusioning effects of war, to more humane concerns.

Appropriately the section dealing with the aftermath of the Rising is called 'Initiation in Love', at once the love of his girl friend Millie and love of his harassed country. That these two affections are conflicting emotions is slowly developed as Farrell's main theme.

Farrell faces the difficulty of writing about the Rising at all. Reviewing O'Flaherty's *Insurrection* the American critic Walter Kerr wrote that the novel 'seems to me to be a piece of a novel . . . in the final effect oblique and fragmentary. There is a big book to be made out of these events, a book that will organise and relate every side of the experience'. This is a very just estimate of O'Flaherty's novel, but I believe that the experience Irish writers had of their material *was* oblique and fragmentary. The novel nearest to Kerr's big book (though Irish writers do not have the obsession of the Americans with sheer bulk) in organising and relating many sides of the period, and not just of the Rising, is *Thy Tears Might Cease*.

In Farrell's novel, significantly, our view of the Rising is indeed oblique and fragmentary, the impressions of a schoolboy for whom it comes as the climax of a day out with a new girl he has just met. Martin is now seventeen and living in lodgings in Kingstown with a Miss Peters and her brother. Anxious for his health, she insists he go out for a swim that Easter Monday and get some fresh air. On his way into town he meets Conroy, the Sinn Fein friend he had known at his old school, who is leading a group of Volunteers down into the city centre. After a brief conversation where Conroy speaks with a flash of excitement about the importance of men like Martin to their country's future, they part with a joke about blowing up the Castle.

On his excursion Martin picks up Millie, a girl from a poor part of the city, and with difficulty they return to Dublin after hearing news of the Rising, to find everything in the city altered. They wander the streets, watching the disturbances, reading the Proclamation, witnessing the release of tension in singing and dancing in the streets. Martin slowly realises just what it is that is happening : this is the beginning of a revolution.

At first Martin's reaction to the rebellion is that of his class, one of deep shock. How could Sinn Fein stab England in the back after the promise of Home Rule? But after the executions his opinion alters. His nationalism, latent since his childhood at Glenkilly, emerges again. He begins to sign his letters, 'Yours in the Cause of Freedom'. He becomes even more deeply involved : the next section of the novel is to describe his 'Initiation in Hate' as a member of a flying column.

How Martin travels from love to hate, from 1916 to 1919, the changes in his mind and in the country, are perhaps not quite representative, at least not in the same way that the growth of Sean O'Faolain and Frank O'Connor was.

Martin is not typical of his time in Ireland, however familiar he may later become as the disenchanted intellectual. The shy, bookish, almost girlish child of the early parts of the novel, the tormented schoolboy, the pruned sapling, are an artist's creation. These pages contain some excellent and moving writing. The clash of the excessively sensitive boy with the people of the small town and the schools' priests is described with great feeling. Social and emotional pressures are brought to bear on him which almost overwhelm his slight frame. There are few more vindictive passages in modern Irish writing than that in which the school prefect gloats over the innocent affections for his cousin Sally and his friend Norman which are revealed by Martin in his private diary.

Meeting his old school friend Conroy that fateful Easter Monday, Martin says to him, in reply to the Sinn Feiner's notion that 'ten men with the right gifts will be enough to awaken Ireland,' that 'the things I'd like to waken people to are not your things, Seamus.' This is the perennial clash between the patriot and the intellectual.

The things which affect Martin are the wider realms of culture and personal freedom, concepts with little meaning for many nationalists. His fight for Irish freedom becomes inexorably involved with his personal relationships. He is in revolt against the narrow puritanism of his people, as well as the strong hand of British rule. Wishing, for instance, to protect Millie against the risks of their love, Martin is forced into a grubby and degrading search for contraceptives. He realises from this situation how unprepared for life he has been left.

Knockester had soiled everything, and now his own imagination had turned into the same paths. Pulling aside the bandagings which pride had wrapped around his mind, he looked at himself on his knees before priests while they begged him to see the sin of his love for Sally, the worse sin of his love for Norman, and he renewed his vows that one day he would make it impossible that such things should be said and done to other boys after him. In a free Ireland ![1]

He is forced to 'go like a thief to his love'. In contrast to Martin, Conroy, idealistic about Irish freedom in a different way, cannot—as Martin discovers when they find some love letters while censoring the post—'even read about love-making without feeling your delicious sense of sin'. Their sullen contempt for each other after this incident is only dissipated in the heat of a shooting encounter with the military, Martin's first fight. The potential disagreements of other Reillys and Conroys must have been similarly put aside for the duration of the war.

Through her love Millie helps Martin maintain some sense of human decency and order, though their meetings are often disrupted by his journeys round the country for the IRA. 'When they did meet, the old rhythm of their intercourse was shaken by searing memories of the things from which he had just come and by her silent repressed horror of the bloody deeds done by both sides in a struggle which had once merely bored her but now dismayed her.'[2]

Later on, staying in London with Millie, he is surprised to find that though he wants to, he cannot feel like a foreigner in England. His nationalism is even more jarred by France where he goes intending to meet Norman at Carcassone. He is taken to see the battlefields of the Great War and returns

filled with a wonder and fear before the implications of those unending graveyards of men who died for the names of nations, unlike the Greeks and Trojans, who had fought only for Helen, who had looked so beautiful when she walked upon the wall; unlike the Crusaders, who had died for the birthplace of a God. Doubtfully, he looked up at Norman's photograph—what would Norman [then fighting with the IRA] say to that.[3]

Yet in his diary he records the sobering thought that 'it is queer to think that there was a time when the world was without the idea of nationality. Without it for a longer age than it has had it.'

Such confused sentiments contrast with the simple beliefs of Conroy. He wonders what clever chaps like Martin will be able to do as a result of Ireland getting her freedom : 'I mean when we have a new Ireland with no middle-class snobbery'. He despises Norman for being a West Briton. This inverted snobbery of nationalism he shares with the priest at Knockester who comments on the 'English' accent with which Martin speaks Gaelic.

The priest spoke earnestly about 'the language', how noble it was, how cultured and, above all, how pure. 'Purity in a priest's meaning', thought Martin when Father Halloran said that if Irish were spoken by all it would 'keep bad ideas from coming in from other countries of the world'. Martin should go and live in a cottage in an Irish-speaking district, go out planting potatoes with the cottagers, and thus get the 'blas'. Only then could one get the true accent. 'Indeed, more than the "blas", O Mairtin, the true Irish life which continues there for all to copy'.[4]

That phrase, *the true Irish life*, sums up the desire at the heart of the idea of Irish nationality. It is the key to what much of the revolution was about, the goal towards which the revolution in thought and feeling was tending. The conflict between the nationalist and the individualist, between the patriot and the intellectual, here represented by Conroy and Martin Reilly, was irreconcilable. They might find common cause against a common enemy, but never the completeness of unity. The fateful and fatal divisions already existed at the same time as the first confident gestures were made towards the creation of a new country in 1919.

Some of the elements illustrated in *Thy Tears Might Cease* as affecting Martin, such as the fragmented nature of political experience, the desire for personal freedom, the contrast between patriot and intellectual, the idea of rural life and Gaelic as the key to the true Irish life, can also be found in the lives of political people such as Collins and de Valera, as well as in the experiences of other writers. Political activists will be discussed in chapter ten; at the moment only the writers concern us.

One writer who took part in the resurgence, Ernie O'Malley, describes the alterations of feeling which people went through during this period as they impinged on his own life. O'Malley, who was to become in time the Commandant-General of the IRA, and later a close friend and admirer of Jack Yeats, was an exceptional man as a soldier. As a writer of great talent he was able to record vividly the experiences of the period. His book *On Another Man's Wound* is one of the few memoirs of the period, and the only one which can be read as a piece of fine writing. There is one story every man can tell, his own. O'Malley was lucky with his life in the living and the writing; one regrets only that he never brought himself to publish the chapters he wrote about the Civil War.

On the war of independence he is an indispensable witness; a keen fighter with the ability to record his experiences and moreover to understand their meaning. In his introduction to the book he writes:

> My attitude towards the fight is that of a sheltered individual drawn from the secure seclusion of Irish life to the responsibility of action. It is essentially a narrative against the backgrounds of the lives of the people. The tempo of the struggle was intermittent, life went on as usual in the midst of tragedy, and we were intimately related to the life of our people. The people's effort can be seen only by knowing something of their lives and their relationship to our underground movement and armed resistance. We who fought effected a small part of the energy induced, and our individual effort as personalities was subordinated by the impersonality of the movement, not impaired by it.[5]

Yet personality was important to the movement. When he came to write his book in the early thirties, he saw that he could not write a purely factual history. The perception of those years was often more important than the events themselves warranted, the man of the moment turned all too easily into a hero or a traitor. 'Our people seized imaginatively on certain events, exalted them through their own folk quality of expression in song and story. Anonymous songs of that period, at the end of some chapters, express what the people thought, and amplify, in so far as they are concerned, the situation described.'[6]

The hero of Kevin Barry, for instance, the one song most people remember from the period, was a young medical student (a martyred schoolboy according to legend however) captured by the police after an abortive raid. Rumours of his torture and his final execution in November 1920, the first in a series of twenty-four, turned him overnight into a national figure. 'Another martyr for old Ireland/Another murder for the Crown'. Such songs as this appeared almost at once. In Sean O'Faolain's short novel *The Small Lady*, Mrs Sydney Browne lives long enough to hear her treason denounced in song as she travels through West Cork with a flying column to her death by shooting.*

O'Malley's emphasis on the folk element is important, for that quality had been a major source of both the revival and the revolution. Though he was born into a comfortable middle-class family, later when he was working in Clare organising the IRA there, he came in contact with real country people, such as he had not known since his childhood holidays in Sligo. He was impressed by their qualities.

> They were starkly real like chunks of their own earth when they spoke of the land, its irritable uncertainty and its aching sweat, but a feeling for words and poetry would lift talk above manure. . . . These were the obvious signs of outward realism and the harsh background of their lives; but there was a deep content, an ease in life and a depth in themselves that could well up nourishment. . . . Gentleness and fierceness, lack of sentimentality and a definite concreteness merged with poetry and sharp realism in speech, kind towards suffering and callous towards cattle and dogs and their burden bearer the skinny ass.[7]

Among these people he found that 'song was a definite expression as natural as talk'. Poetry too came naturally to them, and the old men would recite at length from well-stored memories with casual ease.

> Their sense of literature was on their lips and in their faultless memories. In craggy Carren an old man recited the whole of *The Midnight Court* for me. They were not literary nor had

---

*This story is based on the murder of Mrs Maire Lindsay, which has been described in a recent book *Execution* by Sean O'Callaghan.

they any pretence to learning. The extension of their knowledge made them simple; they were not conscious of it, but they knew more of poetry as a living feeling than anybody else I had met save poets themselves. They could curse hard and long mostly for emphasis and the sounds of words, but also in anger.[8]

One senses here the feeling of a real culture and community, the very qualities that Synge and Yeats so much admired.

But what of the poets themselves? At this time (early in 1918) O'Malley knew only one poet involved with the IRA, the bearded Darrell Figgis. His impression of Figgis from the outside is worth quoting here as an example of the impression a writer made on the men of action, men like Collins, Mulcahy and O'Malley. Collins is said to have disliked Figgis, and from such personal reactions sprang some of the later opinions of poets in general, such as General Mulcahy's denunciation of Irish writers from the Abbey stage in 1921. O'Malley, however, was more balanced :

Figgis was not popular; it was thought he was too vain. Stories were told about his Christlike beard. His manner, his insistent focus of attention on his words, was the porcupine quill effect of an artist amongst those who thought of nationality alone. He was egotistical; it could be seen in his face and mannerisms; his image was reflected in the half-suppressed smiles of his listeners. He had come from another life; he would find it hard now, I felt. I had read his novels; *Children of Earth* was the best book I had read about the West of Ireland. He was pleasant when he talked to me of his books; but he had the unfortunate habit of making enemies.[9]

O'Malley must have been one of the few people in the IRA at that time capable of admiring both the unconscious poets of west Clare and the ever so self-conscious literary artist. The example of Martin Reilly and Conroy in *Thy Tears Might Cease* suggests that for many others there was no bridging this gap. But, in searching for an ideal of Ireland, that did not stop others trying.

The passages above are from O'Malley's account of the limbo period between 1916 and 1919, when the war began in earnest.

He attempts to describe the difficult transition of a young man from a sheltered middle-class home, much like the one described in *Thy Tears Might Cease*, into the soldier of daring and initiative who commanded in Kilkenny, Tipperary and Limerick during the war. This was a time when other young men such as Frank O'Connor and Sean O'Faolain were becoming aware of Ireland in a new way (much as boys in peacetime might become aware of girls), and of their vocations as writers. For them revolution was a kind of sentimental education.

The differing reactions of the fighters and writers which are clear in O'Malley's vignette of Darrell Figgis, were the result of very different experiences which seem to have coincided only over the matter of Irish independence. Their differing attitudes on matters of literature and life, which is what concerns us, can be illustrated by the reactions of the young Michael Collins and the younger Sean O'Faolain to a play by Lennox Robinson. His comedy *Patriots* (1912) was a mild little satire on an old Fenian who returns to his Cork village from exile and attempts to inspire the young men to revolution, only to find them far more interested in the latest thing, the cinema. Robinson presents the view of the Fenians as a spent force in Irish life, but it was just such attempts at converting the youth of Ireland to violence that led to 1916. Collins owed much of his early enthusiasm to the example of another old Fenian, Thomas Clarke. When Robinson wrote the play it might have seemed amusing, but history has a way of treating such laughter with strange irony.

As for its immediate effects, these were also ironic. Michael Collins went to see the play in London; he came away unchanged, merely confirmed in his faith. He and his London friends had gone to boo its London production because of the outrageous idea that their own Cork people, their own flesh and blood, might prefer the cinema to revolution, Charlie Chaplin to Robert Emmet.

Collins was an enthusiast, not a fanatic. He was widely but not deeply read. He was a worker and planner, not an intellectual or dreamer. He absorbed a great deal of economics and poetry in his early diligent efforts to improve himself. The economics stood him in good stead; indeed sound business practice was the only model he ever had for conducting the nation's affairs. But, as Frank O'Connor puts it in his perceptive biography of Collins, 'culture remained a mysterious and all powerful magic, though not one for everyday use'.

> To literature and art the real Michael Collins brings the standards of the country fireside of a winter night, emotion and intimacy, and the boyish enthusiasm which makes magic of old legends and can weep over the sorrowful fate of some obscure blacksmith or farmer.[10]

That is almost exactly the Yeatsian formula for the literary revival and its magic : the magic of old legends and the obscure fates of blacksmiths were its stock in trade. Collins warmed to such an ideal; as a young man he read a great deal of the early Yeats. So that when he saw *Patriots*, he saw only an attack on the ideals of his youth. Actually it is curious to note that his favourite play was *Peter Pan*; and that when he met Barrie in 1921, he liked him as well. This is not only the sentimentality of an essentially hard man, but also a hankering in him after some kind of eternal youth.

Yet, on someone different *Patriots* had quite different effects. One wet night in January 1915, Sean O'Faolain crossed the road from his policeman father's house, where his mother let rooms to theatricals, to climb the stairs to the gods of Cork Opera House. That night the theatre was half empty; but young Whelan, as he was then, was a theatre enthusiast. When the curtain rose he saw on the stage below him, not some English mansion, but 'with an astonishment never before or since equalled for me by any theatrical experience, the parlour of a house in an Irish country town and my uncle Owen Boylan'.

It was the shock of recognition : this is what we are. Rather than the expected English family with its attendant butler and maid, a sort of *Boy's Own* vision of the good life, here instead was reality itself. It was an Irish reality : 'a geranium pot in the window, a chenille cloth covering the table, pictures of Robert Emmet and Pius X on the walls, old lace curtains, old padded furniture'. And this old Fenian talking always of revolution was the very revolutionary of romance, a figure he had always thought of till then as of Robert Emmet in a cocked hat; but which he saw was really his own country uncle. 'The fantastic thought burst upon me that in Rathkeale, even in Cork that night, there might be other real, living, exhaling-inhaling, dusty, scruffy, angry old men with the same gallant, hopeless ideas.'[11] And more than that there was the realisation of what this meant to him personally : it was a revelation on the road to Damascus, sudden and profound.

> The sight of them on stage brought me strange and wonderful news—that the streets of my native Cork might also be full of unsuspected drama. When the final curtain fell in the Cork Opera House, that wet night in 1915, I was ready to explore, to respond to, for the first time to see the actuality of life in Ireland.[12]

A couple of hours at an Abbey play and (by his own admission) one young man came away confirmed as a writer. For O'Faolain the experience brought together the strands of his life and experience and twisted them to a purpose, that of a writer of realistic prose. How different from the reaction of the slightly older Collins.

Can there, however, be any doubt as to which of these men was living in 'the real world'? Which of them sees more clearly the ambiguities of life rather than the simple solutions of politics? When Collins denounces *Patriots* as unworthy of Ireland, when he denounces GAA members who played rugby, or when he drives an Irish soldier in a British uniform from a hurling field, we realise that he has not escaped the tendrils of childhood, that under the sentiments there is perhaps a heart of stone.

Collins was from the country around Clonakilty; but the realist O'Faolain also loved such rain-soaked acres, for him his cousin's farm near Limerick. As an artist he was nourished by the same sources as was Michael Collins as a politician. But the artist's loyalty is to the truth of reality, a harsher mistress than the ideals of politics. The politician wanted to maintain tender thoughts about his childhood, which the writers despite their love of the country found faulted. O'Faolain had his own Fenian, the relative described with loving care in *A Nest of Simple Folk*—the title is lifted straight from Turgenev, though the nuance has been changed. Collins's contact with that life, with what Yeats called 'that dream nourished amid little shops and little farms', was through the remarkable Tom Clarke. That old patriot had gathered round him young men who preferred revolution to the cinema; there were few jobs for them anyway, so a change would be welcome. Collins was always to remember the last hours of that brave old man, when he was beaten and humiliated by British soldiers after the Rising and then taken out and shot. The Fenian tradition for both of them was a way towards creating the new shape of life for Ireland, both in literature and politics.

The search for a new way may be made clearer by looking at Daniel Corkery, another Cork writer turned revolutionary, and his relationship with O'Faolain and O'Connor. This little nest in Cork city comes closer to the heart of the motives behind the revolution even than Collins or O'Malley.

When O'Connor and O'Faolain were young men in Cork, Daniel Corkery was perhaps the greatest influence in their young lives. For both of them he filled the role of an old Fenian, though he preached literature rather than revolution. A character in Corkery's own book of short stories, *The Hounds of Banba*, says of those old Fenians, those 'Osians dreaming of the heroic dead they have so long outlived' :

> I saw that every extreme movement in Ireland leaves behind it a remnant of its broken army—an old workman in a factory in a city, a cobbler in a little shop in a village, or a shepherd in a hut on a mountainside—great old hearts that preserve to the next generation, even to the second next, the spark of fire that they themselves had received in the self-same manner from those that long since were gone home into silence.[13]

That indeed is how revolution smouldered on in Ireland. But the interest of Corkery's own life lies in what revolution does to the artist. There is no line quite so poignant to describe what later happened to the artist in Corkery as 'gone home into silence'.

It was about this time, when the real fight against the British was beginning in Ireland, that Corkery remarked to Frank O'Connor, 'You must remember that there are things more important than literature.' O'Connor did not believe that, at least not in the sense that Corkery meant it. This was the beginning of the final phase of Corkery's life, when the passionate defender of Gaelic culture displaced the excellent writer of short stories in English. But however curious and sterile his later work would be, at this point of time he is important for the example he set his two young friends, then named Michael O'Donovan and John Whelan.

The search for the Gaelic sources of the true Irish life are well illustrated by the life and character of Daniel Corkery. He was born in 1878 in Cork city where he spent the whole of his life. He was an urban provincial. He was as much a stranger to the 'fair, the hurling match, the land-grabbing, the priesting, the mission, the Mass'—to all indeed that he characterises—as he was truly Irish in his critique of Synge. After learning Gaelic he became an enthusiastic member of the Gaelic League. The local branch, the Lee Branch it was called then, also had Daniel Bergin among its members. Because of their political enthusiasms they were expelled from the League for a short while. Corkery's devotion to the Irish language became the dominating passion of his celibate life. In 1904 he and some friends set up a small theatre where his Cork Dramatic Society could perform; he even wrote their first play. In his spare time from his teaching job he began to work on scenes for a novel. A collection of short stories —we are reminded again of the example of George Moore at work—was published in 1916, followed the next year by a novel : *A Munster Twilight* and *The Threshold of Quiet* contain his best work.

A halt leg prevented him from taking an active part in the fighting during the next few years. Another volume of stories, *The Hounds of Banba*, was his contribution to the Irish cause. In these the dogs of war are let slip among the people whose quiet sober lives he so admired.

He went on writing stories and plays of varied quality—*The Labour Leader* was presented at the Abbey in 1919—but more and more he concerned himself with public issues. As Dail deputy for North Cork in 1925 he signed with de Valera and other Republicans a declaration of their opposition to the partitioning of Ireland. His great claim to attention lies in his two critical books *The Hidden Ireland* (1925) and *Synge and Anglo-Irish Literature* (1931), where he sets off a lyrical account of the Gaelic Munster poets of the eighteenth century with a virulent critique of Irish writing in English. He became the cultural theorist of those such as de Valera, who were satisfied with the frugal comforts of Ireland's impoverished past. Synge was selected for attack rather than Yeats, because Synge's view of the Irish peasant as wild and earthy was the real enemy of the ethereal creature of high virtue beloved by the nationalist imagination.

Corkery was one of Frank O'Connor's earliest teachers and he made a great impression on the small boy, with his shuffled gait and his strangely clipped and unvaried speech. This, O'Connor later learnt, was due to an early stammer which Corkery had cured by sheer discipline. 'This sounds probable enough,' O'Connor later wrote, 'for though I did not realise it until much later, the most striking thing about the Daniel Corkery of those years was his self-control.' It was through Corkery that O'Connor later came to learn Irish. His emotional and intellectual faculties were knitted up in this father-figure (so different from his own rather feckless parent), the older man and Irish being his first loves. For both O'Connor and O'Faolain (three years older than him) Corkery's house on Gardiner's Hill where he lived his cosy bachelor life with a sister and his mother, was a safe haven from the poverty of their own homes, a place where many aimless evenings ended. Corkery provided them with books, music and conversation. He took O'Connor on sketching trips, went to devotions with O'Faolain. He encouraged them in their interests, which was a great deal to do for young men in an Irish provincial town.*

Looking back on Corkery from their own sixties, both writers were to see in him aspects of themselves. O'Connor, so dreamy and scatterbrained, came to admire Corkery's self-discipline, so different from his own way of life. O'Faolain noted the discipline as well, but so eagerly has he cultivated his European interests that it is the dire effects of provincialism that strike him most now. Stendhal was one of O'Faolain's touchstones. The epigraph for *The Threshold of Quiet* is taken from Thoreau: 'The mass of men lead lives of quiet desperation'. Stendhal or Thoreau? That choice is perhaps one which every Irish writer must face. Despite its quietistic resignation, that novel remains the best one that Corkery ever wrote. But it is not *The Charterhouse of Parma* or *The Red and the Black*. Its puritanism of feeling and local self-

---

*They were not the only Cork talents we have to thank for his early encouragement: he arranged for Seamus Murphy to enter a stone mason's yard and so begin his career as a sculptor, and gave a first commission to Joseph Higgins—a bust of himself.

satisfaction were elements that both O'Connor and O'Faolain later reacted against.

Corkery's views and his admiration for the traditional rural life of Ireland with its Catholic roots gave him the outlook of a cultivated and talented writer. This ideal which his young friends were to react against and yet in the end return to, became in different hands the dogma of a narrow puritan establishment whose members would not have cared to recall what Frank O'Connor came to remember vividly, an authentic voice of the real hidden Ireland, the voice of Brian Merriman.

The search for that voice, the tone of Merriman which Synge speaks in, was part of the quest for identity undertaken by the young men Corkery encouraged.

For Corkery the Easter Rising and what followed from it was the climax of all he had ever hoped for. Sean O'Faolain admits, however, that 'my heart did not burst with excitement and joy when I heard that a Rising had broken out in Dublin that Easter morning in 1916'. He was to become politically involved only slowly, however sudden he claims his literary awakening may have been.

As we have seen, O'Faolain claims to have awoken to the reality of Ireland on seeing his first Abbey play. Previously his young imagination had fed on other sources. His father was an old soldier and former member of the Royal Irish Constabulary; a man proud of his past. O'Faolain's childhood dreams were filled with stories by Henty glorifying the exploits of British Imperialism. The 1916 executions shook him out of this dream world. Under the influence of a friendly teacher he began to learn Irish and his experience of new feeling about his country became entwined with his love for his future wife Eileen Gould, whom he met at an Irish summer school.

In his memoirs he provides a vivid vignette of this imaginative awakening. One of his new Irish texts was a volume of songs by a nineteenth-century Kerry postman, which he kept for years afterwards.

I cherished it solely for its frontispiece—a smudgy photograph showing a rocky promontory on the Atlantic, a ruined chapel, an old graveyard, a few small fields. Time out of mind I used to open the book at this photograph and gaze and gaze at it. Sea, chapel, graveyard, lonely rock, poor fields—they became my new symbols transfigured by my longing for that liberty from the body in a nobly patterned world which I now equated with remoteness, hardness, age and a traditional life whose pieties they rounded. It was not the place in the photograph I revered or wished to possess but the absoluteness or essence of the entire life that made it, so that what I was really shaping in my mind whenever I looked at the photograph was a myth of life for which, so far, the only bodily vessel I knew was the wet warm plain of West Limerick, with its lichened limestone walls, its distant sea, its battered Norman ruins, its dead, my dead. Gazing at that picture, I was creating a new legend, a new myth. I was unconsciously writing it, peopling it. I was engaged on every writer's first task—hypothesising life, imagining himself in it, as another Adam, self-created, fecund.[14]

His search for a new myth involved other changes as well. While in flight from the unfree city and its provincial ties into the freedom of the countryside and its traditions, he changed his name from John Whelan to Sean O'Faolain. Such a change, he notes, dates a whole generation, and marks a profound alteration of identity. Normally a man does not easily change his name which is so intimately associated with his very self, and change it moreover for an alternative which was barely pronounceable to many of his countrymen.

Going back with Eileen into the country—a passage notably described at the beginning of his story 'Midsummer Night Madness'—was not merely to cycle up the valley of the Lee from Cork into the Muskerry Mountains. It was to alter one's consciousness completely. This was the importance of the whole endeavour. Gaelic gave one a whole new world to live in, not merely a new world of mountains and lakes and farming people, but a whole new mental world. A *grocer*, O'Faolain points out, is not the same person as an *epicier*. *Girl* does not evoke the same possibilities as *fanciulla* or *cailin*. Loch is not a lake, nor is a lane a boreen.

So, when we spoke Irish we simply evoked another country, another life, another people. *Mountains* were mountains, *roads* were roads, and glens *glens* (always Scottish); but when, for those things, we uttered the Irish words *sléibhthe, bóithre* and *gleannta* we spoke passwords to another world. Irish became our runic language. It made us comrades in a secret society. We sought and made friendships, some of them to last forever, like conspirators in a state of high exaltation, merely by using Irish words.[15]

The old language of Ireland became the 'symbol of the larger freedom towards which we were groping'. They foresaw 'the new Ireland as a rich flowering of the old Ireland, with all its old simple ways, pieties and native traditions'.

Why the Irish language should have had this effect is illuminated for us by a modern Gaelic poet Maire Mac Entee, who writes in a most stimulating essay on the two languages of Ireland about the 'radical' nature of Gaelic. The learning and using of the language involved far more than a mere return to one's roots. It was also a political choice.

For, no mistake about it, the culture to which Irish is a key is, in our time, a revolutionary culture. It is a culture of the oppressed, the almost legendary dispossessed. It is impossible to know it without being caught up in the great wave of historical indignation that informs the world-wide social revolution of today. No man reared in this tradition can feel any confidence in great-power virtue, or in the benevolence of the Right. No adult in the Irish-speaking districts has any doubts who killed President Kennedy : 'Na bosses—cad eile?' *Il eterno presente nemico dell Umanita*. No realist need be astonished at the politics of Peadar O Donnell or for that matter of Kickham or Davitt.[16]

And, she might well have added, of Liam O'Flaherty or Mairtin O Caidhin. A whole generation was inspired to revolution by the same tradition.

The objective correlative of much of O'Faolain's longings and dreams was Gougane Barra, that small, astonishing mountain lake at the source of the river Lee. 'We loved this valley, lake, ruined chapel and rude cloister because of their enclosure, their memories, and their silence.' Around this silent remote scene he and Eileen built up 'a juvenile fantasy of grown desire'.

Such then was the countryside : an epitome of freedom. Cork

city was to come to mean much to him as well through Eileen's father, an almost Dickensian character who must have been something like Simon Dedalus. But on the whole Cork remained deadeningly provincial. The journal of a small literary group he joined about this time, reread for his autobiography, revealed all the crushing narrowness of his contemporaries. For the older O'Faolain, Corkery himself symbolised much of this atmosphere. Ever since those early days, in his studies in America, teaching in England, travels in Italy, admiration of Stendhal, he had been in flight from Corkery's fate. But this flight was caused by his reaction to experiences caused by other men in Cork at that time, with other ideas.

In a shop opposite the house where the little literary group met, some 'rather more realistic men' were organising the IRA in Cork. He was soon approached to join, which he did. Not that this made him 'realistic'. More revealing of the time is a paper on Tolstoy he read to the group, composed out of an almost complete ignorance of the writer. Just as the nationalists conjured up a country out of almost nothing, these young writers were inventing literary attitudes for it, and in time a literature.

Frank O'Connor's reaction to Easter Week was also one of horror that Irishmen could do such a thing to England. His head, too, was full of dreams inspired by boys' books. 'It was a difficult situation,' he remembers, 'for a boy of twelve with no spiritual homeland but that of the English public schools, and no real friends but those imaginary friends he knew there.' The executions, however, were a worse shock. These men were poets after all, and he was in favour of poets. Moreover they wrote in Irish, which was of great importance to him.

It was through Corkery that O'Connor had been introduced to Irish—or as his mentor called it in the clipped accents the boy tried to imitate, *eye rish*. At first this was nothing more than Corkery writing on the blackboard 'Waken your courage Ireland', and giving unfamiliar names to familiar objects. He used the set English texts, such as Scott's 'Breathes there a man. . . .' to promote disaffection among his pupils under the eyes of the school authorities. One day he produced two of his own paintings. One showed Shandon church shimmering in the sunlight; the other a man playing a fiddle to a crowded cottage, his face turned to the wall. These were two images O'Connor never escaped from : his Cork scene made new, and the haunting presence of Irish poetry.

O'Connor copied down the poem from below the second painting and took it home to his grandmother. He had found a use at last for that extraordinary and irritating old woman, for Irish not English was her native tongue. She didn't think much of the poem—it was, of course, Raftery's lament on his sad plight playing music to empty pockets—and others she knew well were too hard for the boy to understand. But nevertheless she taught him his first Irish sentence : 'A cailín óg tabhair dom póg agus posfaidh mé thu'—give me a kiss young girl and I'll marry you. This was the authentic voice of Gaelic Ireland; very different in tone, he realised at once, from Henty and the *Boy's Own Paper*.

In 1916 he learnt that Pearse's poetry was written in Irish, and this stimulated him to take out again the old grammar and try to learn the language Corkery had failed to instil in him. 'A revolution had begun in Ireland, but it was nothing to the revolution that had begun in me. It is only in the imagination that great tragedies take place, and I had only my imagination to live in.'[17] So to escape from those invisible presences, the friends he had made in the public school stories, he deliberately Celticised himself. He nagged his kindhearted mother into making him a kilt to play the part in; and he even found a substitute for Henty's Imperial heroes.

> Somewhere or other I had picked up Eleanor Hull's *Cuchulain*, a retelling of the Ulster sagas for children, and that became a new ideal. Nobody in any English school story I had read had done things as remarkable as that child had done at the age of seven. But for me, even his deeds were small compared with what he said when actually seven and some druid prophesised a short life for him. 'Little I care though I were to live but a day and a night if only my fame and adventures lived after me.' No one had ever better expressed my own view of life.[18]

He also began reading Eugene O'Curry and other scholars, and borrowed from the library books on Irish art and music. He had also discovered the freedom of the country that O'Faolain speaks of.

In October 1916 he was astonished to see in a shop window a

book called *A Munster Twilight*, and to discover that the author
was indeed his old teacher Daniel Corkery. He was now growing
out of the need for those invisible presences, 'a child's vision of a
world complete and glorified', and this novel about the real life
of local Cork people was another step on the way to freedom.

He had to work hard at educating himself, harder than at his
real job, though a post on the railway provided the security in
which to continue his reading. An English visitor in a kilt who
insisted on speaking Irish found to his surprise that only this
scruffy office boy could understand him. This incident, O'Connor
surmised, was 'a small indication of the revolution taking place
without the smart boys being aware of it'. He was in on the
start of something new and exciting. When his first piece of
writing was published in a boys' paper there was general amaze-
ment at the depot; his boss told him, 'for God's sake stick to
writing. You'll never be any good on the Great Southern and
Western Railway'.

And he wasn't. He was soon fired. The same night as he lost
his job he read a paper on Goethe in Irish to a local literary
group, an author he knew nothing about in a language he could
hardly speak. Goethe he reconstructed in his own image 'as a
patriotic young man who wished to revive the German language,
which I considered gravely threatened by the use of French'.

This peculiarly Irish Goethe was a symptom of his growing
nationalism. Concerts, songs, meetings in public parks gave way
eventually to war, to shootings, bombings and murders. Yet 'I
suspect that in those few years more books were published in
Ireland than in any succeeding twenty years. Not good books,
God knows, any more than the little papers that kept appearing
and being suppressed were good papers. But they expressed the
mind of the time. . . . The impossible, and only the impossible,
was law. It was in one way a perfect background for someone
like myself who had only the impossible to live for.'[19] But behind
the dreams there was also a reality. While he was working on the
railway O'Connor became friendly with one of the checkers, who
like him did not believe in a world of 'dockets and bales of pelts'.
One day, in a conspiratorial fashion, he drew the boy aside and
produced a book from under his jacket. 'Read that, boy,' he
whispered. 'That'll show you what the country is really like.'

The book was *Waiting* by Gerald O'Donovan. He read it with

great care, 'though a boy who didn't know what a foreskin was' could hardly expect to understand what the country was like. The episode is a curious one, showing perhaps why the Irish novelists were so feared once by the censor : they showed people what the country was really like. The Irish novel is a conspiracy against the smart boys, the stake-in-the-country men, the dockets and bales of pelts for export. Not surprisingly O'Connor, immersed in the idealism of the period, did not understand the checker's admiration of O'Donovan. Yet through O'Donovan we can see here the tradition of the realistic novel passing into another generation.

I have tried to give in this chapter some impression of the flux of emotions, loyalties and ideas in Ireland between 1916 and 1919. Perhaps some summary composite of the national mind can now be sketched out.

The desire to see what the country is really like is the desire of the realist; the desire for the true Irish life the dream of the idealist. During this period it was a search for that ideal dream country that dominated the national imagination. From Collins and de Valera down to O'Connor and O'Faolain, the countryside was imagined as the place of true freedom as against the political and social slavery of the city. By instinct these were all country men. The city was a British invention in Ireland. But by rejecting the city there was also the danger of rejecting the values of the city, of urbanity and civilisation. Whether the values of the countryside, of simplicity and tradition, would be enough to live with in this century was not a problem that presented itself to many at that time. These men were all drawn from the lower classes : what were they planning to do with the middle classes, and with the urban working class? They had no idea. They had their dreams, and it was enough for them to dream. But from the very exclusiveness of the dream would arise many later divisive troubles.

The elements of the ideal were few enough. There was a rejection of British values, essentially urban, rational and liberal values, in favour of traditional Irish pieties, essentially rural, religious and puritan. There was the revival of Irish, not as the real language of the depressed peasantry as Synge had seen it, but as an emotional outlet for the urban lower classes from which most of the revolutionaries were drawn. There was an element of perverse snobbery, which began to see the limited and depressed conditions of the countryside of Kerry, Cork and Connaught as superior to what were described as West British, or merely middle-class, ways. But above all, the ideal was a new thing. Into Irish lives there suddenly came this dream, with its promises of improvement, of conviviality, comradeship, even of love; with its great promise of social mobility and of increased personal freedom. Young men suddenly saw the chance of something different and, like most young men anywhere, they seized it. Freedom for Ireland may have been their avowed cause, but the real cause of both the Conroys and the Martin Reillys was inner freedom.

The true Irish life : that is the key phrase, and it was what much of the revolution was about. Yet the conflicting ideals represented here by Ernest O'Malley and Darrell Figgis, by Daniel Corkery and his protégés, by Martin Reilly and his friend Conroy, were exclusive. They might all find common cause against a common enemy, but never the completeness of unity. Fatal division already existed in the country, even as the first confident gestures were made towards the creation of a new nation in 1919.

Life itself was what, in their differing ways, both the artist and the politician attempted to give shape to. In Ireland the political leaders and their fighting men had taken their vision of the ideal Ireland largely from the beliefs of the literary revival. The writers of that revival encountering the revolution they had helped to create, drawing back to the realistic tradition of George Moore, created a different vision, eventually parting company with the patriots.

We have now some clear idea of the ideal for which the nationalists fought, of the shape of Irish life they envisaged for a free Ireland. As often as not this ideal was seen as conflicting with the British way of life, in Ireland represented by the Anglo-Irish and the landed life of the gentry. We shall now turn to look at what the situation of the Anglo-Irish was, how they saw themselves and what they thought in the gathering darkness of their last days.

8

On a Darkling Plain
THE ANGLO-IRISH SITUATION

THE revolution impinged only gradually on the lives of the Anglo-Irish. Bereft of their land, they now faced the complete loss of their position. For the war being fought around them was not merely to throw out the British, but to topple a dominant class, to replace the feudal with the democratic. For Anglo-Irish writers the war was one of torn loyalties, of fears and conflicts not easily resolved even in the perfections of art. From high imaginative visions to the difficulties of daily life and common terror, these writers attempted to control and understand their fate by writing about it.

For Yeats, at least, the revolution came at an opportune and exciting moment in his life, as he writes in the introduction to *A Vision*:

> On the afternoon of October 24th, 1917, four days after my marriage, my wife surprised me by attempting automatic writing. What came in disjointed sentences, in almost illegible writing was so exciting, sometimes so profound, that I persuaded her to give an hour or so a day to the unknown writer, and after some half-dozen such hours offered to spend what remained of life explaining and piecing together those scattered sentences. 'No,' was the answer, 'we have come to give you metaphors for poetry.'[1]

The occult advisers provided, as Yeats relates, the outline of the philosophy of history that informs his later poetry. His critics have found the occult Yeats of this system, which lends itself to exposition by initiates, of most interest to them. So much so, that the sense of a poet working in the midst of a profound revolution, of a dramatic alteration in a literary movement which he had founded and with which his whole imagination was bound up, is often lost. Yet if anything gave Yeats 'metaphors for poetry' it was the scenes, personalities and images of that revolution, which nourish in some mysterious way the great and overwhelming poems of his final decades.

The last of his poems on 1916 had been finished in October 1917. Maud Gonne had refused again his offer of marriage when he hurried over to see her in Normandy after MacBride's execution. He was much taken with her children Iseult and Sean. The boy had a sharp independence of mind, and the girl he thought would civilise Dublin with her enthusiasm for Péguy, Claudel and Jammés. Smitten with Iseult—she is the girl dancing on the beach in the exquisite little poem 'To a Child Dancing in the Wind' written at the time—he proposed to her as well, but she also refused. So he went ahead with his intention to marry George Hyde-Lees. Her spirit writing was only one of a number of new themes and ideas taken up at this time.

First there was an interest with Noh, to which he had been introduced by Ezra Pound who was editing for publication the translations of the late Ernest Fenollosa. In the conventions of Japanese drama Yeats found a theatre that was at once noble, remote and peculiarly effective. The effect of the past on the present—Noh is mostly concerned with revenant spirits and their influence on the living—provided a form into which he could cast his complex feelings about the matter of Ireland. *The Only Jealousy of Emer* written at this time, put the Cuchulain legend under the sway of his new system, but the theme of reincarnation and the competition of the living and the dead are not dependent on it. They speak for themselves:

> How many centuries spent
> The sedentary soul
> In toils of measurement
> Beyond eagle or mole,
> Beyond hearing or seeing,
> Or Archimedes' guess,
> To raise into being
> That loveliness?[2]

It was the memory of 'that loveliness' that brought him to buy as a home in Ireland Ballylee Castle near Coole. Mary Hynes, whom Raftery had celebrated in one of his poems, had lived

1. The heroic peasant, as seen by Jack Yeats.

ambush, the reality of revolution, recreated for *The Dawn*.

3. Idealism: Maud Gonne impersonating Ireland in *Cathleen ni Houlihan*.

ᴀɴ ᴍᴀɪɴɪꜱᴄɪʀ: **THE MONASTERY,**
The Burial Place of Tomas Ruadh O'Sullivan

4. The ideal landscape admired by Sean O'Faolain: untilled fields in West Cork.

5. Idealism personified: Daniel Corkery in 1909.

Altar piece of the Risen Christ from Loughrea, commissioned by Fr O'Donovan, executed by John Hughes.

Fr Jerry O'Donovan, the priest who became Gerald O'Donovan.

8. Title page of the original Gaelic edition of *The Untilled Field*.

9. Orpen the painter in a happy mood celebrating 'the spirit of Sinn Fein'.

10. By contrast, the more common spirit of the country, the memory of the dead, in Yeats's *Bachelor's Walk*.

11. 'The images of thirty years' (Yeats): 'an ambush' (Keating's) *Men of the South.*

12. 'Pilgrims at the waterside' (Yeats): the deep religious feeling of the race.

13. A great house 'flames upon the night': Sir Horace Plunkett's house *Kilteragh*.

14. Sato's gift, 'a changeless sword' (Yeats).

15. Hearts grown brutal? Women scouts of the Republican Army.

16. 'Sex as God intended it to be' (Frank O'Connor): women calling to Republican prisoners in Kilmainham Jail.

17. 'A grave deep face': John Synge.

18. 'A great ebullient portrait': Lady Gregory.

19. 'Griffith staring in hysterical pride'.

20. Kevin O'Higgins: 'a gentle questioning look that cannot hide/A soul incapable of remorse or rest'.

nearby, and in *The Celtic Twilight* Yeats had written that 'our feet would wander where beauty lived its hour'. This old Norman tower was to become one of his dominating symbols. In its winding stair he saw the historical gyres of his system, where his old friends and the great men of the Anglo-Irish tradition walked, Berkeley, Swift and Burke. It was also for him a symbol of the permanence and tradition he associated with the Big House.

His sense of *pietas* to the tradition of the gentry, as he imagined it, found another symbol in Robert Gregory, Lady Gregory's only son, who died while flying in Italy during the last year of the Great War. 'In Memory of Major Robert Gregory' was completed in June 1918. He is among those friends summoned up who cannot dine with them in their new home : Lionel Johnston, John Synge and George Pollexfen are followed by 'our Sidney and our perfect man'.

> We dreamed that a great painter had been born
> To cold Clare rock and Galway rock and thorn,
> To that stern colour and that delicate line
> That are our secret discipline
> Wherein the gazing heart doubles her might.
> Soldier, scholar, horseman, he,
> And yet he had the intensity
> To have published all to be a world's delight.[3]

In another poem, 'An Irish Airman Foresees His Death', the flier is seen as driven to his death not by any sense of compulsion or duty, but by 'a lonely impulse of delight', as though the artist in him chose also a fitting death.

At this time Yeats and his wife were living in Oxford, while work went ahead on the tower supervised by the architect William Scott. However, they came across to Dublin so that their first child might be born in Ireland : Anne Butler Yeats was born on 24 February 1919. He began to write 'A Prayer for My Daughter' a few weeks later, completing it in June at Ballylee. It begins magnificently and is one of his few poems to remain unaltered from the first draft.

Five years before he had called on the pardon of his father's people :

> Merchant and scholar who have left me blood
> That has not passed through any huckster's loins,

F

and on his grandfather especially, that 'silent and fierce old man' who had told him as a boy that 'Only the wasteful virtues earn the sun'.[4] He was then nearly fifty years old and had no child, nothing but his poetry to prove his blood. Well: here was a daughter, and he was not disappointed: her horoscope, cast by her mother, showed she would be good-looking and lucky.

The poem opens with the screaming of the Atlantic wind, but that storm is only the image of another, very different storm coming on the country. The poet, in great gloom, prays for her,

> Imagining in excited reverie
> That the future years had come,
> Dancing to a frenzied drum,
> Out of the murderous innocence of the sea.[5]

It was not now the question of conviction that had concerned him in the 1916 poems, but the effects of this rising tide of violence. Civility was threatened, the civility which belonged, in his imagination, to the cultivated leisure of the Ascendancy. If his daughter had beauty, courtesy and those other virtues born of manners

> She can, though every face should scowl
> And every windy quarter howl
> Or every bellows burst, be happy still.[6]

He wishes that she may be brought in marriage to one of those great houses, like Coole or Lissadell, 'where all's accustomed, ceremonious' for

> How but in custom and in ceremony
> Are innocence and beauty born?
> Ceremony's a name for the rich horn,
> And custom for the spreading laurel tree.[7]

Now both were threatened, by those politics he so solemnly warns his daughter against—politics which he had seen wither up Constance Markievicz, the daughter of Lissadell, once so beautiful herself when she rode to hounds.

In January 1919, that most significant month of the Dail's first meeting and of the shooting at Soloheadbeg, he wrote 'The Second Coming'. The revolution in Ireland was only a small part of the generally disturbed state of Europe, where that year there seemed to be few countries without some fighting—the Soviets fighting for their life in Russia, the Sparticists and Frei Korps battling in Berlin—the hawk had escaped from the falconer's controlling cry.

> Things fall apart; the centre cannot hold;
> Mere anarchy is loosed upon the world,
> The blood-dimmed tide is loosed, and everywhere
> The ceremony of innocence is drowned;
> The best lack all conviction, while the worst
> Are full of passionate intensity.[8]

These lines that are now so familiar, are often quoted as foreseeing the rise of Fascism. Today they echo with increasing resonance in memories stocked with images of daily violence in Irish streets. But writing in 1919 Yeats was afraid,

> Surely some revelation is at hand;
> Surely the Second Coming is at hand.[9]

Richard Ellmann has pointed out the influence of the image of the Returning God which Yeats had read about in *The Golden Bough,* and the cyclic deities of the Theosophists. His poems, however, had always been strewn with such references, the desire for some inhuman intervention to change the course of history. His invocation of Manannan in the New York speech in 1904 is an instance. The instructors who spoke to him through his wife had recently impressed upon him the word 'terror'. For the orthodox Christian the Second Coming means the redemption of man by Christ as well as the horror of Saint John's Apocalyptic Beast. Here there seems to be no redemption at all, not even that of the rocking cradle. Christianity had vexed twenty centuries to nightmare. Now this vision out of *spiritus mundi* disturbs him:

> And what rough beast, its hour come round at last,
> Slouches towards Bethlehem to be born?[10]

That was a question he waited in fear for history to answer.

Among his wishes for his daughter Yeats included his desire:

O may she live like some green laurel
Rooted in one dear perpetual place.[11]

Just such a place his tower might be, yet we can guess that he has in mind some great country house. The life of such a place has been described for us by Elizabeth Bowen in her account of her family home, Bowen's Court in County Cork. In that book, and in her first novel, *The Last September,* she gives an impression of just what it was like in those houses with war rising round them in the early autumn of 1920.

She was fifteen when Great Britain declared war on Germany, and remembered going to Mitchelstown Castle garden party, where all the local families turned out for what was to be the last time. They discussed the war with trepidation while a wind from the Galtee Mountains tossed everything about, harassed the band, and blew grit into the ices.

The novel gives a similar sense of finality and hopeful youth. Lois, the young girl of the novel, sits through a dinner one evening, her thoughts running on herself, while the others discuss 'the situation'.

Lady Naylor spoke of the way things were, with her pointed spoon poised over her plate. She noticed the others were waiting, and with a last bright emphatic look in Hugo's direction bent to finish her soup. [Mr Montmorency] said at once to Laurence : 'And what do *you* think of things?'

'Things? Over here?'

'Yes-yes.'

'Seem to be closing in,' said Laurence, crumbling his bread detachedly; 'rolling up rather.'

'Ssh!' exclaimed Lady Naylor, running out a hand at both of them over the cloth. She frowned, with a glance at the parlour-maid. 'Now you mustn't make Laurence exaggerate. All young men from Oxford exaggerate. All Laurence's friends exaggerate : I have met them.'[12]

After dinner, sitting on the steps, they hear a patrol passing the demesne wall, and 'the jarring down the spines of the listeners'. Laurence remarks, much to Lady Naylor's annoyance, that 'A furtive lorry is a sinister thing'. These are undertones of war which cannot be kept even from the parlour-maid.

The others go in; Lois walks out towards the wood where it is rumoured that someone has been seen burying guns. No one wishes to investigate, to get involved, so she goes alone.

First, she did not hear footsteps coming, and as she began to notice the displaced darkness thought what she dreaded was coming, was there within her—she was indeed clairvoyant, exposed to horror and going to see a ghost. Then steps, hard on the smooth earth; branches slipping against a trench-coat. The trench-coat rustled across the path ahead, to the swing of a steady walker. She stood by the holly immovable, blotted out in her black, and there passed within reach of her hand, with the rise and fall of the stride, a resolute profile, powerful as a thought. In gratitude for its fleshiness, she felt prompted to make some contact : not to be known seemed like a doom : extinction....

It must be because of Ireland he was in a hurry; down from the mountains, making a short cut through their demesne. Here was something else she could not share. She could not conceive of her country emotionally : it was a way of living, an abstract of several landscapes, or an oblique frayed island, moored at the north but with an air of being detached and washed out west from the British coast.[13]

She thinks he 'might have been a murderer he seemed so inspired'; but 'a man in a trench-coat had passed without seeing her : that was what it amounted to'. Running back to tell the others, she realises she cannot tell them for they would not want to listen. Though it was impossible for her to speak of, 'conceivably, she had just surprised life at a significant angle in the shrubbery'.

For Miss Bowen herself there was a significant angle on the war. As the fighting grew worse, with reprisals and counter-reprisals, Sinn Fein farms being burned down for the destruction of such houses as Rockmills, Ballywater and Convamore, her father wrote to her abroad warning her that their home might be next. If it were burned he would write at once.

I read his letter beside Lake Como, and, looking down at the blue water, taught myself to imagine Bowen's Court in flames. Perhaps that moment disinfected the future : realities of war

I have seen since have been frightful; none of them has taken me by surprise.[14]

But the realities of the Irish war which her young character had surprised at a significant angle in the shrubbery were not so easily absorbed by others.

Though a mood of romantic involvement with the Rising can be seen in Yeats's poetry, it was not an attitude generally shared by his class. Something of their feelings can be found in the novels of Somerville and Ross, the more authentic voice of hard-riding Anglo-Ireland.

Early in 1915 *In Mr Knox's Country* appeared; this was the last volume of the stories of Major Yeates the RM and his west Cork friends and neighbours, the saga of the foxhunters which had amused so many readers and made the authors' names synonymous with Irish humour. But there had always been a darker side to their writing, as in the early novel *The Real Charlotte*, and even darker concerns were on the horizon.

In May 1915 the *Lusitania* sank off the Cork coast, drowning Hugh Lane. Martin Ross sent a copy of the new book to her cousin, his aunt Augusta Gregory. Lady Gregory read the book aloud in the evening to amuse W.B. Yeats, who had to be reassured that the Major's name was spelt with an 'e' before he gave himself up to uninterrupted enjoyment. During that summer Martin fell ill. She had never really been well since an early hunting accident, but when she entered Cork hospital she was found to have an inoperable tumour on the brain. She died on 15 December.

The partnership of a lifetime was dissolved. The death of so close a love could have shattered Edith, for their marriage of feeling was a deep one. She never came to admit the final end of death. How she recovered from her grief, and through seances continued their association has been told with tact by Maurice Collis. The effect of Martin's death on the books still signed 'Somerville and Ross' is marked. The knockabout humour has gone, replaced by a more melancholic, a more sombre feeling.

Perhaps inevitably the next book in 1917 was a collection of essays called *Irish Memories*, in some of which Edith recalls her past, while others are by Martin herself. Soon, however, she took up an unfinished novel begun jointly and used parts of it in a long ambitious novel published in 1919, called *Mount Music*. This is an ambitious book because, in spanning the years 1890 to 1907, she has to deal with Catholicism and what she sees as its effects on ordinary life in Ireland. With the troubles rising round her in those uncertain years, she chose bravely to explore a subject they had never attempted during Martin's life.

The novel records the decline of the Talbot-Lowerys of Mount Music, and how their land passes into the hands of the Catholic bourgeois, Dr Mangin. A cousin of the Lowerys, Larry Coppinger, finds himself caught between his relationship with the old family, whose daughter Christian he falls in love with, and the religion he shares with Dr Mangin. Religious intolerance—the Spirit of the Nation, as the authors lightly call it—separates him from Christian. Mangin persuades him that his nationalism places him with the country people and not with the gentry. Mangin, of course, despises the Talbot-Lowerys but lays his hands on their land, reaching for their status himself. He intends Tisley his daughter for Larry, and his son Barty for Christian. But as these plans move to their conclusion, Mangin, while driving out to a childbirth, is drowned in the flooded river. The body is washed ashore below Mount Music, to which it is carried up on a hurdle. 'Well, ye wanted Mount Music,' the Protestant Butler sourly observes, 'How d'ye like it now ye've got it?'

What is of interest here is that Larry, who as a boy led a gang called the Companions of Finn (such was the insinuating influence of Irish myth), sworn to drive out the Saxons, has a hazy romantic nationalism of a type exceedingly widespread in the years after Parnell's death. (See for instance, the row with the English boy in an early chapter of Michael Farrell's novel.) He believes in Irish freedom, a certain populist bias, but nothing more. Nothing comparable with the old dignity of the Talbot-Lowerys or the conniving energy of Mangin. The love interest is of small concern to Edith Somerville, and is treated quite perfunctorily: Larry and Christian come happily together in the final page over the dead body of Mangin. Nothing here of sex as a driving force against economic and social arrangements such as is found in the novels of Moore, Joyce or O'Donovan. The treatment of religion as an emotional feeling is rather superficial, as if the author has no real appreciation of Catholic feeling. The ending is also a little novelettish; as if the author cannot bring herself to countenance the real threat of Mangin's victory, fate removes him just in time to save the Big House. But history is not written half as well as fiction, and the real-life Mangins were a threat not so easily resisted.

Yet one cannot but feel that Edith Somerville's sketch of how religion works socially, in advancing Mangin, closely reports the actual. The Catholic Church in Ireland had since 1795 been an instrument of British and Vatican policy dedicated to the maintenance of a suitable status quo, peace in Ireland being exchanged for English conversions. The Church had no objections to her sons rising to prosperity as Mangin does; it did object to Young Ireland, Davitt, Parnell and the Republicans. What such radical elements threatened was not religious belief—the notion of Ireland ceasing to be religious was absurd—but rather the social influence of the hierarchy. 'Make no mistake about it,' Davitt once told the Bishop of Limerick, 'democracy is going to rule in these countries.' That was a fact of life which neither the Church nor the Mangins and Talbot-Lowerys could fully accept. *Mount Music*, however flawed as a novel, is important in showing us the realities of Irish life as they appeared on the eve of revolution to the shrewd eyes of an Ascendancy lady.

Coming to terms with the revolution was a more difficult matter. Edith Somerville, living through these years in West Cork, looked out on what seemed dreadful madness to her. Martin's death had left her emotionally shaken, and though she managed to finish *Mount Music*, she fell back again on memories and reminiscences for her next books. *Strayaways* (1919) includes a critique of several nineteenth-century Irish novelists such as Carleton, Lover and Lever, the very writers with whom Daniel Corkery would have placed her. Yet she herself berates them for their failure to write down the language of the Irish country people as actually spoken. She is just and harsh for, as we have seen, it is just this question of language that vitiates the work of so many Irish writers before the Revival. But *Castle Rackrent* she says might 'have been written by any realist of today'.

Its effortless composure, its tranquil reliance on idiom and mental outlook, rather than on misspellings and expletives, might have been a lesson to its successors, had they had the intelligence to perceive and the wisdom to accept the example it offered.[15]

In another essay she explores with great finesse the actual nature of English as spoken in Ireland. We can take it that this exactness, this sensitivity, of ear and intellect was her own standard. In the same way as Maria Edgeworth, Somerville and Ross are uniquely Irish.

But it was a peculiar Irishness, one not widely accepted in a country where families such as hers would be referred to as 'English', no matter how long they had lived there. In 1920 she began, with Martin's spiritual assistance, to write a new novel which would deal with this very situation. A new friend, Dame Ethel Smyth now provided some of the emotional affection which Martin's death had deprived her of. Dame Ethel widened her horizons, introduced her to London writers and to James Joyce's work (which Edith was to defend by adding her name to the protest against the American piracy of *Ulysses*). But Edith, grateful for all this, resisted efforts to place their relationship on a more physical level. She wanted only what she had got from Martin, love not sex. Returning from London to a troubled Cork, suffering from rheumatism, she worked on *An Enthusiast* which took those events for its background.

The enthusiast of the title is Dan Palliser who inherits the big house on the death of Colonel Palliser. The novel opens with the set piece of the old soldier's funeral : a coffin draped with a Union Jack, a sabre and shako on top, carried to the grave past keening country women and an honour guard of a hundred horsemen. The author could almost be describing the burial of Anglo-Ireland.

Dan Palliser has all the new ideas for improving the land, the new techniques of farming and co-operation such as Horace Plunkett advocated. He finds resistance to these innovations, especially when he introduces a tractor. He fails in his schemes and in his love for Car Ducarriag, the wife of a retired governor. The whole decayed ambiance of Anglo-Ireland is captured when the author describes the bloodthirsty proposals of Dan's uncle Admiral Caulfield and his fellow unionists for dealing with Sinn Fein. They have lost touch with reality, and reality will destroy them.

The climax of the novel is a raid on the admiral's house. Dan manages to drive off the raiders using his father's Crimean sword, but the admiral accidentally shoots him. Dan Palliser dies, moreover, just as the woman he loved has gone back to the husband she had loathed. The symbolic death of the enthusiast suggests that the failure of Unionist Ireland was not only a political failure, but a failure of the heart.

The Enthusiast, which appeared under Edith Somerville's name alone, was finished early in 1921 at the height of the Tan war. In a letter to Ethel Smyth (16 Feb 1921) Edith writes of the novel and the current situation : 'Sinn Fein make all communication between Skibbereen and the outer world very difficult. All bridges round the town have been blown up. We are cut off. The post has just come out by a man on a bike who scrambled over a gulf in the road.'[16] In a later letter she says that the Tans are worse than the Republicans. 'They are as despicable as ever in most places. Here and there one hears less shame-inspiring accounts of them.' It was this sort of feeling, that the price was too awful to pay, that soon brought the war to an end.

Edith's letters are almost dispatches from the front, and give some feeling of what the war was like in rural Ireland. At the beginning of March 1921 a party of Republicans commandeered one of her best horses. 'Why must I do that?' her groom asked, when told to give up the animal, and the IRA officer tapped the pocket where his pistol was. The police warned Edith that the Tans could do nothing to trace the horse, and that a visit from them would be worse than the robbery.

In April she writes 'that we have been assured that we will be unmolested. I have been told that I was a nice lady always with many allusions made to hounds and the sport'. She was, of course, Master of the local hunt which provided much colourful amusement for everyone. She was resolved not to leave her home in Castle Townshend. Though 'some people say the Republicans get £500 for killing a policeman', she admits that 'the Crown outrages are appalling'. When the British lost the support of Irish people like Edith Somerville there was nothing left to fight for.

Like Edith Somerville's letters, Lady Gregory's journal also records impressions of the Anglo-Irish war. Through the good offices of its editor she was contributing to *The Nation* accounts of the Tan outrages from October 1920 through to January 1921. These had a great effect on liberal opinion in England. She was also left unmolested, a fact which annoyed her more conservative relatives. 'Your aunt Augusta is hand in glove with the rebels' her nephews were told and forbidden to visit her. One of them, Frank Shaw-Taylor, was actually murdered near his Athenry home, and her daughter-in-law was the only survivor when a car was ambushed on the Baggot estate at Ballyturin. Lady Gregory and Mrs Baggot refused to leave and stuck it out. Coole, Lady Gregory heard, was 'always on the side of the people'.

However it was through Yeats's poetry that Lady Gregory's experiences were transformed into literature.

After the summer of 1919, aside from a brief visit to have his tonsils removed by Oliver Gogarty, Yeats spent little time in Ireland, during the Tan war. It was not a safe country for his English wife. His one visit to Glenmalure (where Maud Gonne had a cottage where he stayed), produced 'The Black Centaur', inspired by a painting by Cecil Salkeld, one of her protégés. Yeats had been living in Oxford, but in October 1919 he went on a lecture tour in America in order to raise money to put a roof on his tower. But he kept in touch with events in Ireland and was shocked by the increasing violence there.

The Black and Tans were roaming the countryside in lorries netted against bombs. Their swaggering violence was for the daylight only, but where there was light they rampaged. They would spray likely ambush places with bursts of machine-gun fire, little caring what they hit. At Kiltartan they fired a Lewis gun across the main street, killing a woman.[17] This was the incident that inspired Yeats to write 'Nineteen Hundred and Nineteen', begun that year but only completed in 1922.

> Now days are dragon-ridden, the nightmare
> Rides upon sleep : a drunken soldiery
> Can leave the mother, murdered at her door,
> To crawl in her own blood, and go scot-free;
> The night can sweat with terror as before
> We pieced our thoughts into philosophy,
> And planned to bring the world under a rule,
> Who are but weasels fighting in a hole.[18]

In this way the news from home, for this was nearly his own chosen parish, was translated into poetry.

Some events, though they might have suggested to his imagination mythical parallels to save them from their mere sordidness, never became poems. In a letter Yeats describes one such incident.

We have had years now of murder and arson in which both nations have shared impartially. In my own neighbourhood the Black and Tans dragged two men, tied alive to a lorry by their heels, till their bodies were rent in pieces. 'There was nothing for the mother but the head' said a countryman and the head, he stated, was found on the roadside. The one enlivening truth that starts out of it all is that we may learn charity after mutual contempt. There is no longer a virtuous nation and the best of us live by candlelight.[19]

These murders at Kiltartan rendered futile the disinterested and heroic sacrifice of Robert Gregory. Those who had gone to fight in Europe from the loyalist classes were mocked by them. Fittingly Yeats swung more and more to the nationalist side. At the Oxford Union in the winter term of 1920–21, prompted by Lady Gregory's letters, he made an impassioned defence of the Irish cause which brought a hostile meeting to his side.

In his poetry he returned again to the figure of the Irish airman :

> Some nineteen German planes, they say,
> You had brought down before you died.
> We called it a good death. Today
> Can ghost or man be satisfied?
> Although your last exciting year
> Outweighed all other years, you said,
> Though battle joy may be so dear
> A memory, even to the dead,
> It chases common thoughts away,
> Yet rise from your Italian tomb,
> Flit to Kiltartan Cross and stay
> Till certain second thoughts have come
> Upon the cause you served, that we

Imagined such a fine affair :
Half-drunk or whole-mad soldiery
Are murdering your tenants there.
Men that revere your father yet
Are shot at on the open plain.
Where may new-married women sit
And suckle children now? Armed men
May murder them in passing by
Nor parliament nor laws take heed.
Then close your ears with dust and lie
Among the other cheated dead.[20]

This poem, called 'Reprisals', was the third in a series of memorials to Robert Gregory. Yeats, however, at Lady Gregory's request, did not publish it : she could not live with the knowledge that her son's death had now been rendered completely pointless. 'A war for civilisation' the British had called the Great War, yet see what that civilisation had wrought on the quiet villages of Clare-Galway. This was war impinging on their lives at the most personal level.

In 'Nineteen Hundred and Nineteen', among the handful of Yeats's greatest poems, all his feelings about this war and its meaning find their most elevated expression. He had been able to see the Rising as a single event, dramatic and heroic like one of his own plays, something he could admire for its peculiar courage and conception. The long drawn out war of raid and ambush aroused quite different emotions. Events were obscured by rumour and doubt. Terrible beauty having been born again, was growing more terrible and less beautiful. He wondered in a letter if 'literature would be much changed by that momentous event, the return of evil'. A distinction is clear between the 1916 poems and these later ones. Not only were his attitudes changing, even contradicting themselves, but he was entering his major period as a poet. The occasion of high serious themes coincided to his benefit with his own startling maturity, a style capable of handling those themes with final certainty. If he had doubts about the effect of the return of evil on literature, his own poems were there to answer him. Literature was much changed, for the better.

'Nineteen Hundred and Nineteen', though completed later,

belongs in theme to the same period as 'A Prayer for My Daughter' and 'The Second Coming'. Like them, this is a complex poem, for which critical prose does little good. All the sense of foreboding, fear and violence which we have seen in Elizabeth Bowen, Edith Somerville and Lady Gregory, are summed up in this poem—or rather transformed, for there have been few who saw these Irish local events in such high imaginative terms.

The central images are those of cultivated civilisation being overcome by the destructive whirlwind of history. The poem is filled out with despair.

> Many ingenious lovely things are gone
> That seemed sheer miracle to the multitude,
> Protected from the circle of the moon
> That pitches common things about.[21]

The things he selects—an ancient image made of wood, Phidias' ivories and the golden grasshoppers and bees—are of classical perfection, Byzantine antiquity; all belong to art. When he was young it had seemed that society itself shared something of this tradition and perfection, 'that the worst rogues and rascals had died out', war and soldiers being reduced to fancy playthings.

Now, in these 'dragon-ridden days', scenes of casual violence deny that social order of a world brought under philosophic rule, deny the honour of art.

> But is there any comfort to be found?
> Man is in love and loves what vanishes,
> What more is there to say? That country round
> None dared admit, if such a thought were his,
> Incendiary or bigot could be found
> To burn that stump on the Acropolis,
> Or break in bits the famous ivories
> Or traffic in the grasshoppers or bees.[22]

'Incendiary or bigot' : those are images from the current political scene, of those weasels fighting in a hole. Those who had seemed to talk of honour and truth, now

> Shriek with pleasure if we show
> The weasel's twist, the weasel's tooth.[23]

The creative solitariness of the artist, symbolised by the swan in contrast to the weasels of war, finds no lasting perfection either, only the love of a creation which does not last.

> A man in his own secret meditation
> Is lost amid the labyrinth that he has made
> In art or politics...[24]

The contrast of art and destruction, civility and evil is brought to a climax by the central image of the dancer.

> When Loie Fuller's Chinese dancers enwound
> A shining web, a floating ribbon of cloth,
> It seemed that a dragon of air
> Had fallen among dancers, had whirled them round
> Or hurried them off on its own furious path...[25]

Loie Fuller, who had enjoyed a great vogue in the 1890s among poets and painters, was one of the pretty toys of Yeats's youth. One of her dances was done with a great sheet of cloth swirled round on sticks so that its fiery fluidity gave the swift impression of a dragon.

The image of the dancer was an important one for Yeats. As in the poem written to Iseult Gonne, he sees the dance as an image with no separable intellectual content. Manner and meaning become one: the earlier poem had celebrated the grace and unique beauty of youth; here the dancer appears as the image of the great Platonic year, the inevitable millennial progression in which all men are mindlessly bound up, whirling out new right and wrong, bringing back the older evil. The terrifying image is resolved in the last section of 'violence on the roads', with the garlanded horses and their handsome riders (a memory of how well Robert Gregory and Constance Markievicz rode when young), 'and gathers to a head'.

> Herodias' daughters have returned again,
> A sudden blast of dusty wind and after
> Thunder of feet, tumult of images,
> Their purpose in the labyrinth of the wind...

Salome like some decadent revenant haunts Yeats's work as the woman symbolising the cost of the artist's achievement by demanding the head of a saint. Here it is that goodness, excellence or achievement cannot withstand the whirlwind dance of history, and fall before the stupidity of evil. The true agent of the devil comes upon the scene:

> But now wind drops, dust settles; thereupon
> There lurches past, his great eyes without thought
> Under the shadow of stupid straw-pale locks,
> That insolent fiend Robert Artisson
> To whom the love-lorn Lady Kyteler brought
> Bronzed peacock feathers, red combs of her cocks.[26]

9

A Fellah in a Trenchcoat

THE GUNMAN AS FOLK HERO

THE figure of the martyr, whether Christ or Cuchulain, Connolly or Pearse, had dominated the imagination of the Rising in 1916. If there is such a symbolic figure for the years between 1919 and 1923, it is the figure we have already glimpsed slipping through the shrubbery, whom Lois in *The Last September* observes but fails to challenge. To many of her class, W.B. Yeats's 'infernal agent' Robert Artisson would have worn a green velour slouch hat and an old army trench-coat, and been armed with a Thompson machine gun.

Gabriel Fallon, a Dublin theatre critic, who played Captain Brennan in the first production of *The Plough and the Stars*, describes how this figure affected Irish people at that time.

The trench-coat, buff in colour, a three-quarter length garment made of rough water-proof cloth, first became fashionable in the Flanders mud of 1914–1918. It took on an added and unsuspected significance when it became what might be described as the battle-dress of the IRA in both our island wars. Many a peace-loving citizen—myself and Sean O'Casey included—affected a trench-coat, only to find oneself the object of suspicion from more than the forces of the British Crown. Whatever today's audiences may be like, the significance of Captain Boyle's line in *Juno and the Paycock* was never lost on those who first saw the play. After Boyle looks out the window cautiously, he says: 'It's a fellah in a trench-coat.' Early audiences always felt the desired frisson.[1]

This man in a trench coat was seen either ideally as the hero of a desperate struggle waged by 3,000 brave men in the IRA to wrest their country's liberty from an imperial tyrant;* or as a shabby, mindless threat to order and human decency. Views on the gunman were divided thus even in the first stories of the period, written as the events of ambush and reprisal were muttered in the streets outside, and remote country farms flamed upon the midnight.

In the dedication to *The Hounds of Banba*, written to celebrate the new national struggle, Daniel Corkery wrote:

> You stride in here, chant your wild songs and go;
> The chroniclers, with rushlights, stumble after;
> And oh! see them blot the sunrise glow
> Of your bright deeds and dreams, your tears and laughter.[2]

Corkery the quiet man believed in quiet people. But these young men, all action and enterprise, so it seemed to the cripple, stirred him to respect. But are his gunmen the real thing? That image from Corkery, of a band of singing men silent for a moment as they pass in the shadow of a convent wall: is that the war as it really was, or as it appeared it ought to be to Corkery's quiet contemplative mind?

It is arguable that at this time Corkery the artist was being replaced by Corkery the critic. For him there were now more important things in life than literature. 'He had a good deal of the harshness and puritanism of the provincial intellectual that I share,' Frank O'Connor wrote of him. It was this side of his character that was becoming dominant. In one story of *A Munster Twilight* a horse called Beauty pulls a poor farmer to death over a sea-cliff. The symbolism is obvious and final. Corkery was a close friend of Terence MacSweeney and Thomas MacCurtain, and their long slow lingering deaths moved him greatly, and led him to denigrate the role of the artist. When terrible things were being done, and brave men dying in such awful ways, to play at literature would have seemed sinful. This is the character of Corkery that we see portrayed by O'Faolain in his story 'The Patriot'.

In Corkery's stories the cause being fought for is justified through the lives of the quiet common people caught up into an approval of violence. There was no approval in the work of

---

*By contrast the Irish Volunteers in May 1914 had been numbered by the police at 70,000.

Brinsley MacNamara, a cynical young man from Delvin in Westmeath. He had already pilloried his neighbours in a bitter first novel of uncharity, *The Valley of the Squinting Windows*, a lurid and trivial book, not to be compared with Gerald O'Donovan or its first inspiration *The House with Green Shutters*.

His second novel, *The Clanking of Chains* (1919), deals with the nationalist cause as it came into being in one small midland town. The book appeared in 1920 and so can only have been inspired by events up to 1919. Yet already the cause is sour in the mouth. The heroic visions of the young man in the novel appear pointless when contrasted with the greed, lack of charity, envy and malice of his town. A certain personal bitterness must be allowed: the author's father had to resign from his national school after a law case following the first book. Yet it shows some lack of real understanding of what was going on around him for MacNamara to quote as his epigraph Yeats's lines from 'September 1913':

> Romantic Ireland's dead and gone.
> It's with O'Leary in the grave.[3]

When in actual fact Romantic Ireland had arisen from that grave to the turmoil of revolution.

Neither romantically indulgent nor cynically superficial are the novels of Peadar O'Donnell. Some remarks of his about MacNamara give an idea of his own approach to writing about his people:

> A novel that involves itself in its village, as this one does, will always create community excitement. Interestingly enough, Brinsley MacNamara did not choose to go into conflict with his own village. He did, however, set out to challenge the idealised view of themselves from which the Irish people seemed to him to suffer; or, more accurately, to challenge with a sharper sense of reality the great body of current writing at that period. He felt those were days when people might behave better if cut down to size.[4]

O'Donnell describes meeting a Polish author whose village was incensed at his portrayal of them. They came to a meeting with him on stilts and wearing masks: 'Really we are not like this', they said. The writer put on one of the masks and took it off:

'Really you are like that. Did you think that reared in poverty and grime, as we were, we could have realised our gifts to the full?' He was listened to.

That anecdote is far more relevant to O'Donnell's work than that of the author he was discussing. O'Donnell was born, 'in poverty and grime', in Donegal in February 1893, one of a family of eleven. A school monitor at fourteen—that is, an elder pupil who assists the teacher—he went on to a teachers' training college in Dublin from 1911 to 1913. He returned to Donegal as a National School teacher: one who obtained a new and better school by surreptitiously knocking down the old one overnight. In 1916 he was made principal of the school on the offshore island of Aranmore, to which he had the pleasure of sailing every morning.

In a rural community the schoolmaster was then often the only one with a proper education. The priests were merely trained, and a dose of anti-clericalism often gave the master some freedom of thought. O'Donnell was asked by the local people to go to Scotland and report on the strike there of Irish migratory workers harvesting the potatoes, as they did not want to be blackleg labour on their own people. The cruel conditions he saw in the potato boothies of Scotland made him give up teaching and join Larkin's Transport and General Worker's Union as an organiser. Agitation against conscription in 1918 got him into trouble with the British authorities. From that it was a short step to joining the IRA in 1920. He became Officer Commanding the Donegal Brigade in March 1921; he was wounded in action.

His novels are all set against this peasant, co-operative, militant background. *Storm* (1926) is set in the months following November 1919; *Islanders* (1927) describes the life of a family on Aranmore, and *Adrigoole* (1928) the decline to death of such a community. *The Knife* (1930), his most panoramic novel, describes the rise of nationalism in the Lagan of east Donegal and the struggle between the Republicans and Orangemen that led to the partitioning of the country.

Reading O'Donnell one is reminded again and again of Synge (O'Donnell's one play *Wrack* is very like *Riders to the Sea*). But he lacks that intensity of language and feeling which is peculiar to Synge. His pictures are realistic, playing on the commonalities of life rather than its outrages. On this point, Frank O'Connor remembers an interesting conversation with O'Donnell. He argued that the woman in one of his novels should have run away with the young co-operative organiser, as he felt the logic of the story called for such a resolution. O'Donnell disagreed. 'I was interested in his two characters as individuals, even if the community lost them. He, the more genuine novelist, was interested in the community and could take no decision that deprived it of the sort of men and women he admired. He preferred that life should go underground.'

What might seem merely a sexual choice for two literary characters was in fact a political choice : life in the largest sense went underground, love became a guerrilla. This was not just a matter of the different views of a novelist as against a short-story writer, as O'Connor suggests. This was the perennial choice between life and literature. Corkery chose politics and stopped writing. O'Connor himself abandoned politics in order to write. O'Donnell made a different choice, as we shall see, by trying to act politically and write as well. He is in a very special sense a true 'communist', a man for whom the community of his own people has been of the first importance. The way of life, the sort of men and women he admired, have indeed had to live much of their existence underground in Ireland.

Such were the divided views of three novelists in the early days of the war; all with different ideas of the gunman as hero. These were the ideas that O'Casey called into question in his first play.

In November 1921, in those months before the signing of the Treaty, Lady Gregory puzzled her way through an almost illegible play written in poor ink on worse paper called *The Crimson in the Tricolour*. When Yeats decided against producing the play, she wrote encouraging the author Sean O'Casey not to give up: 'Your strong point is characterisation'. He thought so himself, and they were friends at once. Their strong relationship grew out of mutual losses, her grief for Robert Gregory and his for his mother newly dead.

His mother's death, it would seem, liberated the artist in O'Casey. One cannot recognise in the maudlin ballads and the shrill invective of his earlier writing anything of his later genius. A deeply wounded and unhappy man, he went to live with his friend Micheál O Maolain (the original of Seamus Shields) in a room in Parnell Square. And it was there, living much like Donal Davoren, that he wrote his next play, which also deals with the choice between life and literature.

On 23 April 1923, while de Valera was beginning the negotiations of a cease-fire to end the Civil War, the Abbey Theatre presented *The Shadow of a Gunman*. The events portrayed had taken place only two years before, in May 1920. Yet the perennial first nighter of the Abbey, Joseph Holloway, could write in his theatre diary of 'that stirring period of our history', as if it were a decade past. Already, it seems, there was a tendency to look on the war with confused romantic indulgence—the very attitude that O'Casey pillories.

The play was a new departure for the Abbey. The events of history, however stirring, were to seem very different through the eyes of O'Casey, who knew no other life than the sordid existence of the tenements and the one he created out of his plays. Here the return of evil, which Yeats had dealt with in imaginative terms, is particularised.

The Shadow of a Gunman has several faults, notably the press announcement of the murder, but there is such a vitality in the drama that the audience is carried over these. The poet Donal Davoren is drawn from O'Casey himself; or rather, as Saros Cowasjee puts it, 'that part of himself that every great writer chooses to castigate'. The poet is discovered trying to write in his tenement room, but he is continually disturbed by his friends and neighbours.

First there is Sheamus Shields the pedlar, and then Shields's friend who leaves a parcel. After them is Minnie Powell, who drops in to borrow a cup of milk. Minnie, a clever independent girl who is quite fearless, is in love with Davoren. She believes, romantically, that he is a gunman on the run. For Minnie this poet becomes the 'fellah in a trench-coat', that figure of romance. Davoren is attracted to Minnie, and to please her and his own vanity, does not deny this identity. After all, he says, 'what harm can there be in being the shadow of a gunman?'

Such a pretence is no game in a country at war, where the lives of the real gunmen were lived in all seriousness. Shields realises the seriousness of the war and its effects, and when he denounces it, he does so in sentiments very close to O'Casey's own.

I wish to God it were all over. The country is gone mad. Instead of counting their beads now, they're counting bullets; their Hail Marys and Pater Nosters are burstin' bombs ... and their creed is, I believe in the gun almighty, maker of heaven and earth—an' it's all for the glory o' God an' the honour o' Ireland.[5]

In that passage, as well as catching the religious fervour behind the movement, O'Casey turns satirically on his own feelings. Like Davoren he had been a romantic idealist, but now ideals were lethal things, bombs in the street, a bullet in the back. 'Whatever the idealists may think,' he told his friend Tony Quinn, 'it is the poor who get it in the neck'. Or, as Shields puts it in the play itself : 'It's the civilians who suffer; when there's an ambush they don't know where to run. Shot in the back to save the British Empire, and shot in the breast to save the soul of Ireland.'[6]

Davoren is described by O'Casey as divided by weaknesses and strengths, torn by a desire for activity yet with a tendency to rest. In the sordid conditions of his life, he struggles to gain a little beauty by his poetry. Like O'Casey himself, he is a coward. O'Casey made no secret of his fear : during the raid on which the second act is based, he said nothing to the searching Tans.

In Shields (in the words of the stage directions) is 'frequently manifested the superstition, the fear and the malignity of primitive man'. Here is a slum dweller without any of Davoren's sensibilities and illusions, with a healthy sense of survival in troubled times. Wearied of war and killing, it is ironically Shields who brings about Minnie's death, for it is his friend who leaves the bomb that she hides.

Minnie is the first of O'Casey's heroic women. Saros Cowasjee believes she was suggested to the author by a woman arrested for carrying ammunition, who got ten years in gaol. But Minnie is not a Maud Gonne or a Countess Markievicz. What she does in hiding the bombs is not done for the sake of Ireland but out of love for the useless Davoren. Like Nora in *The Plough and the Stars*, she risks more for love than some men will risk for hate. Arrested by the Auxiliaries, the lorry taking her away is ambushed and Minnie is shot dead 'while attempting to escape'. Shields's earlier lines echo ironically here, for it is doubtful whether the bullet that kills her is English or Irish.

Her death forces Davoren down from the Parnassian isolation of his poetry into the valley of desolate reality. He realises that his pretensions, his detachment and his cowardice have come home and killed. Shame is his portion.

> Violence upon the roads: violence of horses . . .
>
> Now days are dragon-ridden, the nightmare
> Rides upon sleep: a drunken soldiery
> Can leave the mother murdered at her door
> To crawl in her own blood . . .
>
> We are closed in, and the key is turned
> On our uncertainty; somewhere
> A man is killed, or a house is burned
> Yet no clear fact to be discerned . . .[7]

Yeats in his poetry reduces the turmoil of war to these vivid images, which still hold for us now the fear of that day, the terror of those nights. But for the events themselves—the shootings, murders, burnings—we have to turn to O'Donnell and O'Casey, and to the younger writers Frank O'Connor and Sean O'Faolain.

During the war Sean O'Casey took no part in any fighting. He had long parted from the Citizen Army, and his communism did not see anything of value in mere nationalism. In his plays he presents Dubliners he knew, caught between the opposing forces of destruction. O'Donnell, also left-wing in his politics, found more purpose in the cause, even though the opening of *Storm* with the breaking of the gale presaging the coming war, might not suggest it.

Young men like O'Connor and O'Faolain did take part. For O'Casey and O'Donnell, both born in the previous century, poverty was the formative experience. For the younger men, born in the first years of the twentieth century, it was war. They were themselves the men in trench-coats: O'Faolain seems to have used his long-nosed Webley once only in battle, but O'Connor cryptically admits to having witnessed 'one or two' atrocities.

What follows then might be called 'A Portrait of the Artist as a Gunman'. A character in O'Connor's first collection of stories *Guests of the Nation* (1931) remarks:

One is glad to have been young in such a time, not too young
to miss being occupied with the mimic soldiering, yet not old
enough to have had one's fancy rubbed the wrong way by it—
just at the age when one's mind was ready for impressions and
without all of this would have found no more to brood upon
than books or games or a first love affair.[8]

Ben Kiely, quoting this in his critique of Irish fiction, finds a
dominant note of sheer fun in this collection: enjoyment of
fighting, pleasure and humour on the writer's part in his exciting
material. Sheer fun; if this is so, it is the fun of hysterical
laughter. The great influence on O'Connor while he was working
on these stories during the twenties was the Russian Jewish writer
Isaac Babel. O'Connor was doing for Ireland what Babel, not
Chekhov as Yeats imagined, did for Russia. O'Connor himself
devotes a chapter of his study of the short story *The Lonely
Voice* to the stories of Babel. The tone of *Red Cavalry*, in which
the best of Babel's stories appeared in 1926, is the same strange
mixture of humour and horror that is to be found in the early
O'Connor, who substitutes a Catholic conscience for a Jewish
imagination gone wild. What O'Connor finds in Babel, and sees
as the direct result of the violence he lived through, he calls 'the
romanticism of violence'. To romanticise violence was the only
way that Babel, a coward by nature, could live with it at all.

This gives some clue as to O'Connor's own attitudes to the
violence he had lived through. His autobiographies, being written
in that sort of *New Yorker* style that makes even the truth a lie,
are not the best guide to his life. There are blanks in O'Connor's
life which have yet to be written over. At present only the
stories provide the evidence of real horrors.

One of the stories that O'Connor chose to reprint from this
collection is 'The Procession of Life', dealing with a boy breaking
away from his father's house and the influence of his dead
mother, into the serious business of life. The theme of the
sheltered only child moving into maturity is one that O'Connor
returns to again and again. Sometimes he treats it sentimentally,
as in 'My Oedipus Complex'. Other stories, like 'A Man of the
World', have a truer feeling for the cruelty of human life, the
dimensions of loneliness that spread around the individual, and
how fragile innocence is.

In the well-known title story of the collection, O'Connor deals with a part of life's serious business. Here there is no sheer fun : only hard tragedy. And despite what his characters may say, there is no doubt that O'Connor's fancy was rubbed the wrong way by the experience of war.

O'Connor knew his gunmen—one wishes he had told us more in his memoirs of the 'atrocities' he witnessed. In another story Joe Kiely shoots an enemy off a bridge parapet and pauses to admire the pretty spread of the corpse on the railway track below. Here is the real danger of any war : the gunman who falls in love with killing. Derived from hatred, this perverse love calls itself patriotic duty.

In 'Guests of the Nation'* Belcher and Hawkins, the guests of the Irish nation, are the English prisoners of an IRA unit. One is easy-going, quiet and helpful; the other loud, friendly and kind-hearted. They and their guards, Noble and the narrator, become friends during the long captivity. The local commandant Jeremiah Donovan, who hates the English, is ready to shoot them as his duty. And this is done. As the narrator says after they have shot the Englishmen out on the bog :

> It was all mad lonely, with only a bit of lantern between our-
> selves and the pitch-blackness, and the birds hooting and
> screeching all round disturbed by the guns. . . . It is so strange
> what you feel at such moments, and not to be written after-
> wards. Noble says he felt he seen everything ten times as big,
> perceiving nothing around him but the little patch of black
> bog with two Englishmen stiffening into it; but with me it
> was the other way, as though the patch of bog with the two
> Englishmen were as a thousand miles away from me, and
> even Noble mumbling just behind me and the old woman
> and the birds and the bloody stars were all far away, and I
> was somehow very small and very lonely. And anything that
> ever happened to me after I never felt the same about again.[9]

*This story is based on the murder by Cork No. 1 Brigade IRA of a hostage Major Compton Smith for whom they had come to have 'a sincere regard' (Macardle, p. 407). Other details were suggested by the murder of three British officers and a private near Macroom in March 1922: they were killed and buried in a bog, where their bodies were found a year later. The shooting and burial by lamplight was suggested by the death of Mrs Lindsay. For details see *Macroom, People and Places* (1976) by James Cooney.

And there is the tragedy at its most final. But just as there are varieties of violence, there are varieties of tragedy.

Sean O'Faolain in his collected stories published in 1957, reprinted three stories from his first book called *Midsummer Night Madness* published in 1932. In the preface he writes of their background:

> When I was in my twenties I did not know from Adam what I wanted to say. I had no grasp at all on the real world, of real people. I had met and mingled with them, argued with them, lived with them, shared danger with them. They were mysteries to me. I could only try to convey my astonishment and delight at the strangeness of this bewildering thing called life. Besides when I wrote 'Fugue', my first successful story, in 1927, I had come out of an experience that left me dazed— the revolutionary period in Ireland. Not that it was really an experience as I now understand the word. It was too filled with dreams and ideals and a sense of dedication to be an experience in the meaning of things perceived, understood and remembered.[10]

The dreamy idealism of young men, such as O'Faolain was then, who fought the war is well described in that first story 'Fugue'.

A young IRA man is in flight across West Cork from the Tans. The theme of flight is indeed described in phrases repeated in variety at intervals, and counterpointed with the calm of the countryside and the peace of the cottage where he rests. Against the violence of war is set off his encounter with a girl: 'Smiling at me as a sick woman might smile upon a doctor who brought her ease from pain she slipped my hand beneath her blouse to where I felt the warmth of her skin and her warm protruding nipple, and I leaned to her for a kiss.' That is followed by: 'A rush of feet came to the door and the little girl from the roadside house flung it wide with a cry to me to run, to run, Rory was shot dead.'

Such a contrived structure and weighted style makes for a heavy romantic mood. O'Faolain (as Corkery remarked to O'Connor at the time) is 'a born literary man'. And this is the story of a young man trying to make literature rather than re-create experience. The details of this flight are derived from the author's experience of the Civil War rather than the Tan war, quite different experiences one would have thought.

The mood of a story written later, 'Midsummer Night Madness', is very different. Here the romantic style and diction suit the gothic nature of the story. Also by this time, O'Faolain had gained a little distance from his experiences; the dreams and ideals of youth have become the material of a hardened writer.

The narrator has escaped out into the Cork countryside—the opening catches that feeling of the passage into freedom which O'Faolain mentions in his account of these years in his autobiography—for what he hopes may be some quiet days while he looks into the activities of a local IRA commandant named Stevie Long. He intends to stay at Henn Hall in his mother's parish. But he soon realises that 'this hall and estate and countryside had an unpleasant real life of their own'.

Stevie Long is a Joe Kiely rather than a Jeremiah Donovan: he enjoys the violence he inflicts, the power he enjoys, while avoiding the duty of fighting the Tans. In another story O'Faolain describes the fate of this unsavoury character; here he is more concerned with Gypsy, a tinker girl pregnant by Stevie, and with Henn of Henn Hall, the old Mad Henn of his mother's childhood memories.

Henn Hall, like so many of the big houses in rural Ireland, is in decay and the owner heirless—though not it seems childless: in the district Henn, at eighty, still has the reputation of chasing young girls. Yet he retains the old Anglo-Irish confidence, remains arrogant and sure against these young agents of a new order. Gypsy, who lives in the gate lodge, has, like Henn, never found love. Stevie's 'other plots and plans' do not include marrying her, so he forces Henn to marry her, threatening to burn down the Hall as he has burnt down the house across the valley. Thus the political gesture against an alien culture, of destroying the Big House, as a symbol of the Ascendancy, is stripped of its political significance by Stevie, who makes it an instrument of personal power.

Marriage forced upon him, Henn hopes 'as if he were a Hapsburg or a Bourbon' that the child will be a boy: 'It will keep the old name alive.' Here is the clash between the insolent culture of the Big House, and the vengeful evil that finds expression in the acts of war, that very clash that informs much of Yeats's poetry. Yeats saw himself as part of that proud aristocracy which Henn represents and which withstood the levelling wind of modern democracy in Ireland with its puritan denials of life. The story ends when the narrator hears of Henn and his new wife going to Paris, and he imagines them there among the beautiful gaiety only for a moment, having more serious things to think of by then.

The ending is pathetic, but then tragedy often is to those outside it, and the personal tragedy of the story must not be overlooked. Earlier in the story the narrator sees Henn and Gypsy together in the gate lodge, the old man caressing her soft thigh with his slow hand : 'I could not bear those dog-like eyes of the old libertine, nor the sighs and sobs of the young girl. . . . Suddenly country and freedom seemed a small thing under this austere darkness with that pair, heavy with one another's sorrow, down in the weather-streaked decayed cottage.'[11] Here again is the same tone as at the end of O'Connor's story, the tone of simple human feeling.

Frank O'Connor claimed that the effect of a short story must be to make one feel the effect of Pascal's aphorism, 'Le silence éternel de ces espaces infinis m'effraie'. Since in a short story 'a whole life must be crowded into a few minutes, those minutes must be carefully chosen indeed and lit by an unearthly glow, one that enables us to distinguish past, present and future as though they were contemporaneous'. In his own stories and those of Sean O'Faolain it is the moment when their sense of that infinite loneliness breaks in upon characters so assured of their duty and their patriotism, that raises these vignettes of war in a small country into literature.

During a war, when those 'ceremonies of innocence' by which a society preserves itself are drowned, a man is forced to see the true reality of the human condition. As the characters in these plays and stories discover, love is our only salvation and

> A pity beyond all telling
> Is hid in the heart of love . . .[12]

Some fail to see this, as Denis in O'Faolain's novella *The Small Lady*, which ends with the two young men coming down the mountain to a stop with a girl 'in a gay mood, rejoicing in the loveliness of the night, and their own youth, and the promise of infinite days to come'. Here is an ending that chimes with the others in a sinister way.

Denis, who hates the small lady, Bella, not only for her betrayal of his comrades but for the passion she has aroused in his puritanical soul when they make love in the guesthouse of a monastery, is a weak man. He lets her die, kills his first man, is happy with his life in the end. Jeremiah Donovan and Stevie Long are the substantial gunmen, of which this Denis and Donal Davoren are the shadows. They are unromantic men, yet idealists. The moral dilemma of the soldier is that he must do evil for the cause of good. But so often, as with Donovan and Long, the evil overcomes conscience, they do evil for the good of the cause. Eventually they use their power for their own ends and pleasure. And finally the cause itself is forgotten in the confrontation of evil with human decency.

The experiences described in *Guests of the Nation* and *Midsummer Night Madness* are such that no conscience could any longer support them or these types of gunmen. They demonstrate how the cause is betrayed, when the regard for decency clashes with political necessity. O'Connor and O'Faolain were to find their ideals tainted by the presence of evil; the world they inherited was a broken world tainted by original sin.

The evil of Donovan and Long is an active, brutal one, and thus exceptional. In *Thy Tears Might Cease* Michael Farrell describes another species of evil, which was perhaps more common.

When the novel was published in 1963, the British critic Julian Moynihan compared it, with some justice, to *Dr Zhivago* and *The Leopard*. Like them, one ends by being unconcerned with the mere technique of the work, for these novels are more than works of art, they are great moral statements. They are concerned with revolution and its effect on the individual, as on a country. Martin Reilly has none of the aristocratic confidence, or the ability to compromise with the new order he dislikes, that distinguishes the Prince of Salina. Nor has he the poet's skill which enables Zhivago to turn his experiences of the Russian revolution and its aftermath, and of his love of Larissa, into those poems appended to the novel which run back through the memory of it like leaven.

Martin is perhaps a more typical figure, that of the disillusioned student. He is involved in events far greater than he can cope with, and so reacts against the pressures of conformity which bear upon him. He has no poetic talent, nor the intellectual discipline of astronomy to place these events in perspective. Where only death resolves the condition of a Salina or a Zhivago, for Martin there is one hope of resolution. As he is escorted by the British soldiers into Mountjoy Gaol at the close of the novel in February 1921, he is a changed man. 'He stepped on then, and his bearing was not without dignity, as he moved through the shade of his prison house, seeking at long last the old hammer of reality which yet might ring music from the anvil of a man.'[13] The echo of Wordsworth in these lines is deliberate, for this novel is at once realistic and romantic, and makes much of Martin's poetic perceptions.

Some lines of Milton's on the moon, a ballad of 1798, recurring minor characters: these serve as motifs running through the novel, which by their ironic counterpointing reveal the tragic discrepancy between hope and experience. The lines on the moon are from *Paradise Lost*:

> . . . with these in troops
> Came Astoreth, whom the Phoenicians called
> Astarte, Queen of Heaven, with crescent horns.

Returning to his memory during the fatal raid on Bannow, during which his friend Norman is killed, these lines first appear during a summer idyll of 1914. The sentiments of Wordsworth and Milton's title seem quite appropriate, for at the end of the novel Martin is lost both to the innocent vision of childhood and its hopes, and is cast out from the earthly paradise of the great house at Luracreen, lost to any hope of happiness in the life of the new Ireland he has helped to create. He has now only the artist's salvation in a re-creation of those hopes, that paradise, their loss.

Conroy, the Sinn Fein friend Martin had met marching off to the fight that glorious Easter Monday when he met Millie, is the Commandant of a flying column that Martin works with. Conroy is not a brutal man, but he is inspired by a narrow puritanical nationalism which disgusts Martin. For instance, Conroy asks Martin to take charge of the patrols to round up the prostitutes on the Dublin streets and pack them off to England.

Martin, astonished at such an activity, refuses but discovers that one of those prostitutes is Josie who had been the cook so many years before, down in Glenkilly. In that moment the temper of mind that would prevail in liberated Ireland is revealed, and all its subtle servility.

Martin's involvement with the flying column—his initiation in hate—causes a rift between Martin and Millie. The great set-piece of this part is the raid on Bannow, the large town near Martin's old home. It is told in odd flashes : the burning houses, the sleepy child looking over the banisters at the armed men sleeping in the kitchen. The total picture, like Fabriozo's Waterloo, is confusion. During this raid Norman, from whom Martin has also drifted away, is killed. Norman's parents are Unionists : his coffin with their brass plate is lowered into the grave with an IRA cardboard placard with his rank and service written on it, symbolic of the divided country.

For the class from which Martin and Norman come, the new Ireland will have little love. Martin finds his aunt Mary's house, where he had been so happy in the summers of his childhood, burnt out and the land sold for a new school to the Faithful Brothers, a deal from which Mr Tim Corbin has taken the only profit, 'and as though this brought home to him all the past elation of youth and the full realisation of his present deprivation, he leaned his head against a beech and allowed the tears to fall, pierced by the knowledge of what all mortality meant.'[14] On his return to Dublin he gets a letter from Millie in London : she is about to marry another man, a safe man in her family's eyes. The old mores have established themselves again.

The early chapters deal with Martin's childhood, but it is the later ones which are more directly concerned with the theme of literature in the revolution. It must be admitted, however, that these chapters are inferior to the glorious inevitability of the opening ones. (Some of the scrappy appearance of these final chapters may be due to rigorous editing by Monk Gibbon in preparing the novel for publication.) Much of Martin's experience as a boy at school and as a young man stands in contrast to the love and happiness of his childhood. When, after the Bannow raid, he returns to his aunt's house to find it burned out, he is 'pierced by the knowledge of what all mortality means'. The past elation of youth is lost in a Wordsworthian sense, but

for Martin there is as much lost with that house as there was for
Yeats thinking of Coole

> Where none has reigned that lacked a name or fame
> Or out of folly unto folly came.[15]

The burning down and sale of the house leave him bitter; this
is a poor end for the demesne of paradise.

Corbin is a character much like Don Calagero in *The Leopard*:
the lower-class tradesman who rides to wealth and power on the
tumbrils of the revolution. There is such a figure in nearly every
revolution, except those where the firing squads continue 'to
shoot the wrong people', as Patrick Pearse so delicately put it.
There is little the idealist ever seems to be able to do about it.
Tim Corbin and his kind will inherit the Ireland that Norman
Dempsey and his kind died to free. Martin realises when he loses
Millie that there is nothing to keep him in Ireland, where it is
clear his dreams will not be fulfilled. As many of his kind did,
Martin decides to get out. When he is arrested in February 1921
by the British he is preparing to leave for colonial service in
Indo-China.

Farrell himself was arrested for carrying messages (at his trial
his landlady, asked what her politics were, said 'she was all things
to all men'). Later he went out to work in the Belgian Congo,
after the failure of a love affair. On his return he settled down
to write his novel, but it was clear that the remembrance of
things past was too close to him. He could neither finish nor cut
the book, despite the pleadings of his friends. He brooded over
the past and, in the long years of writing, something of the mood
of many writers in the thirties filtered into the bitter flavour of
parts of the book. Only after his death in 1962 could it be published. His neighbour Sean O'Faolain used to argue with him
that the novel had no shape; the scenes were marvellous, especially the early ones, but the shape! the shape! Yet in the chaos of
experience Farrell had detected some small order.

Just as it is a minor character who expresses the novel's theme:
'It's queer what time will bring in its round', so another, Dan
the bargee, expresses the belief in the continuity underlying life.
Martin remarks to him, while they sail slowly down the navigable
canal which acts as an image of that continuity uniting the
present—Dublin and the war—with the past—Bannow and his

G

childhood—that 'the good shall suffer and the wicked prosper'. Dan answers eagerly: 'There ye are! Straight out of the Catechism itself! And isn't it reasonable when you look at it? If I was God Almighty—God forgive the blasphemy, for I don't mean any—I wouldn't arrange it any other way. It would be an awful world if everyone was taught to go out on the make for himself. 'Tis only the Catechism keeps a lot of us dacent. So, let others prosper, and the rest of us be dacent.'[16] No matter what the upheavals of history might bring, people like Dan, sailing his horse-drawn barge down the Barrow navigation, did not change. On them the imperturbable decency of life depended. Tim Corbin might prosper through evil, but the best hope of the future lay in common decency and humanity.

This tolerant belief in human decency informs the work not only of Farrell himself, but also Joyce and O'Donovan, O'Casey and the younger writers. It was the only standard they had by which they could gauge the true morality of their people. These writers, though their material is the harsh and brutal reality of revolution and suffering, are not completely realistic writers. They are romantic enough to be continually disillusioned by having their hopes shattered on the rock of politics. For

> Minute by minute they live:
> The stone's in the midst of all.[17]

Yeats, writing in 1919, expressed his own complexity of feelings:

> But is there any comfort to be found?
> Man is in love and loves what vanishes,
> What more is there to say?[18]

That is also what this novel presents. Martin Reilly is caught, both in love and war, in the flux of time. The author has insight into how time destroys what is most loved, in this case Martin's idyllic childhood, and presses him on into new things.

While the short stories reveal themselves in those epiphanies of insight into character, those moments of revelation under 'the bloody stars', the novel works through the development of characters through the course of time. We value O'Connor and O'Faolain for those captured moments, but it is Farrell who presents that movement of people through time, paralleling in fiction the events of history.

His novel is no mere superficial tale of Irish nationalism, but a great novel concerned in the classic manner with 'the knowledge of what all mortality means'. For Farrell, as much as for Yeats, the war meant the destruction of those cultivated houses which had created the distinctive character of the rural Ireland of their childhoods. Not that for every Bowen's Court there was not a Henn Hall, for every Coole a Castle Rackrent. What those houses represented was scorned by the new nationalism. The gunman—the fellah in a trench-coat—represented the return of evil into paradise, of social reality into Irish life. Under his scorn that old order crumbled to a broken world.

'It's queer what time will bring in its round,' remarks one of the minor characters. That could stand for Farrell's epigraph to the novel, which has been given two : some 'lines from a ladies album'—

> If thou and I could by a tale
> Some hours of wandering life beguile,
> Thy tears might cease, and we might fail
> To mind ourselves awhile.

Perhaps for fear of sentimentality, the other is from Falstaff :

> '. . . tush man, mortal men, mortal men.'

The Shape of the Sword

TOWARDS THE CIVIL WAR

LIFE went on, as life has a habit of doing. Many Irish people, like Brueghel's peasants in *Icarus*, turned quite leisurely away from the disaster. Though they may have heard strange cries, for them this was not an important failure. There were perhaps less than 5,000 men in the IRA: the rest of the population were largely an audience to acts of war. The atmosphere of that day, the fear and tension, the laughter and exhilaration, were peculiar: like picnicking in a thunderstorm.

Austin Clarke, in his memoirs, relates some anecdotes which capture this tension, and this indifference on the part of those not actually involved. Not all writers were on the run in those days; Clarke was trying to be a poet. Sitting in the Tower Bar one morning in 1921 with F.R. Higgins, correcting the proof of a poem (for literary life also went on, as literary life has a habit of doing), he felt a nudge in the ribs.

He ignored this till Higgins whispered to him to put up his hands. The bar was full of Auxiliaries, one of whom was sticking a large Colt revolver into his back. The soldiers searched the two poets, giving Clarke back his love letters but reading through the proofs for evidence of sedition. Leaving the pub ten minutes later, they found a large crowd had gathered, which divided to let them pass. Once around the corner into O'Connell street, they burst out laughing. 'For twenty seconds we had felt the thrill which Eamon de Valera, Sean Lemass and other heroes have known.'

Shortly afterwards Clarke found in his waistcoat pocket a revolver bullet, one of several he had brought back from Paris as a patriotic gesture. That was the sort of silly thing some people did then. He would have found it difficult to explain that away to the Auxiliaries. 'With a shiver, I remembered how many persons had been shot while trying to escape.'

How many did die between 1919 and the truce in June 1921? There do not seem to be any certain statistics. Official returns quoted in a recent study of the campaign in Ireland by Charles Townshend, are far lower than the figures given by Dorothy Macardle. She says that 752 people were killed on the Irish side and 866 wounded. The official returns show that 150 soldiers were killed (345 wounded) and 405 policemen were killed (682 wounded). Civilian casualties were 196 killed and 185 wounded. But other unofficial estimates from inquiries into deaths in lieu of inquests suggest that some 298 people were killed by Crown forces, and some 347 people were killed by the IRA. As a campaign of violence, the war was very bitter, but it would seem that the IRA did most of the killing, and most of those killed were Irish, either policemen or civilians.

Mixed with the fear of sudden shootings and surprise raids was a kind of mad gaiety, which is one way of responding to the sort of situation the figures above suggest. There was the occasion when Clarke was in a brothel down in Monto, Joyce's Nighttown, with the Gaelic writer Padraic O Conaire,* being entertained by the girls of the kips.

> Suddenly a pretty girl who had consumed, no doubt, too many half-pints, leaped into the middle of the floor and began to dance wildly. Faster and faster, she whirled around, her skirts flying higher and higher. Before we could avert our eyes in modesty, we saw the illegal tricolour of the Irish Republic for her petticoat, slip and knickers were a flag of green, white and gold. This was audacious lingerie, because the lorries of the Black-and-Tans rattled through the streets after Curfew and any moment armed men might rap with the butts of their Colt revolvers on the door.[1]

It was in these stews among these same handsome girls with their feckless ways and seditious underwear that many a member of the IRA is supposed to have passed the night while on the run. Phil Shanahan's pub at 134 Montgomery Street was a rendezvous for the IRA, especially Sean Treacy, Dan Breen and others of

*'Padraic O Conaire, whom I admired, borrowed a pound from me and I was surprised to learn some weeks later from one of the girls that he had spent the night with her.'

the Tipperary Brigade. Mrs Cohen's, which features in *Ulysses*, was 82 Montgomery Street.

The place of women in the nationalist movement and their relations, sexual and otherwise, with its fighting men are interesting. For instance, the Minister of Labour in the First Dail was the Countess Markievicz, who was perhaps the first woman to reach such a status in any government. She was the first woman elected to the British parliament and, ironically, refused to take her seat. Though sexual equality and complete adult suffrage was taken for granted by the Free State constitution, many women in the suffragist movement met with general resistance in Ireland from most nationalists, the Church and even the Unionists in Ulster. 'In Ireland,' Hanna Sheehy-Skeffington observed, 'there is always, as in agricultural communities generally, a strong prejudice against women working on independent lines.' She was herself the object of such prejudice. The role of some women, the War Widows, was of great influence later on: the Republicans during the Civil War were derisively referred to as the 'Women and Childers Party'.

Yet the old inhibitions of a rural society changed a little as British rule crumbled. These were, in Ireland as elsewhere, the roaring twenties, living lightly after the hardships of war. The cinema and jazz arrived, girls came out, skirts went up, lipstick became fashionable for more than prostitutes. Some women reached for a place in life they could never have had in the old Ireland. The young men of the IRA, who came and went by night, were romantics. Frank O'Connor remembers how hard so many of the girls worked for the Republican cause. 'When I look back at this period it is of them rather than their brothers that I think.' Some, like the girl in O'Faolain's 'Fugue' offered the boys something more comforting than a cup of tea. What a contrast there is between the group of women photographed on the Dublin street in 1902, and the girls young enough to be their daughters, posing as Women Scouts of the Republican Army in late 1922. For a while, in the eagerness of a new world, an easiness emerged between the sexes in Ireland, a newer younger sense of spirit. What became of this new feeling we shall shortly see.

Political and emotional freedom were obviously linked before our day raised sexual liberation to a philosophical level. One has only to think of Russia after the revolution, or Berlin during the hectic Weimar years. There was nothing so extreme in Ireland. Sean O'Faolain in writing about how he met his future wife, describes what must have been the more typical relationship of the period. He met her at a Gaelic summer school.

> From that we became intimate friends, from that intimate comrades, and on that chastely warm ground we pitched our separate tents for years. This may, for all I know, still be a normal relationship between young men and women in Ireland; it was the common pattern during those idealistic years, and the more so as they grew more and more troubled. Certainly in the really hot revolutionary years all animal passion was sublimated in the overriding passion for Ireland and liberty. I should speak only for myself, since I do not know how it may have been for others, though I imagine that in those hot years far older men than I, engaged in the most dangerous adventures, strained constantly to the highest tension, must have found a way of dissociating themselves completely from their own bodies, driving them before them like animals in a fierce anger, death-devoted to Saint Gun. We are not a people to record such things, but others have done so, as in those two terrible, confessional pages at the opening of Lawrence's *Seven Pillars of Wisdom*, proving that, on the other hand, idealists, though exalted from the body, are often amoral in their contempt for it.[2]

What a strange contrast they make : the ascetic gunmen fighting for their country, and the girl in the kips with her patriotic lingerie. Both Irish in their opposite passions, both irreconcilable, both people of their own time.

Then, in the middle of the summer of 1921, the war stopped. Ernie O'Malley was in the south-west. On 9 July, a Dublin boy arrived at the house where he was lodging with a message for his eyes only. A dispatch rider was sent to bring in O'Malley. The boy handed him a typed order :

> In view of the conversations being entered into by our Government with the Government of Great Britain, and in pursuance of mutual conversations, active operations by our troops will be suspended as from noon, Monday, 11th July.
>
> Risteard Ua Maolchatha
Chief of Staff[3]

So it ended for O'Malley in the south-west. He had orders typed to the five brigades under his command, and then sat down to wonder about this sudden news. The IRA were willing to keep up the pressure on the British, which had been increasing; in a month or so, operations would have extended into the towns, and the flying columns would have operated in sections. (Others have argued more recently that the IRA was hard pressed and would soon have collapsed.)

What did this short, bald message from his superiors portend? Was it all over? They sat down and had their tea and wondered.

Frank O'Connor, just turned eighteen, was a member of a brigade in another division. For him the truce was an extraordinary event deserving, he later came to think, a whole book to itself. The British tanks, armoured cars, and troops fell back on Cork Barracks in long processions. As the Angelus rang out from the city churches that Monday morning, the watching crowds saw the great gates of the barracks close behind those hated khaki uniforms.

> Did it really mean it was all over? That there would be no more five o'clock curfew and that one could walk at night as late as one pleased without being shot? That one could sleep in one's own bed? That it really represented the end of seven hundred years of military occupation, the triumph of imagination over material power, the impossible become law.[4]

This was a heady feeling for people who had been at war for three years; the emotional tension gushed over, as elsewhere everybody burst out singing.

> All that perfect summer young men who had been for years in hiding drove about the countryside in commandeered cars, drinking and dancing, brandishing their guns. In the evenings the local Volunteers, their numbers vastly increased by careful young men who were now beginning to think there might be something in this for them, drilled openly and learned how to use rifles and machine guns.[5]

These 'Truceleers', as they came to be called, swelled the ranks of the IRA. Some of them were to become the most intransigent of the Republicans.

The year between July 1921 and June 1922 was a year of

growing division and argument. The basic division was over the Treaty settlement : de Valera and his party requiring a Republic in form as well as substance; Collins and Griffith accepting a compromise, 'the freedom to become free'. The events of the Treaty debates and the subsequent arguments have all been well covered by historians. Here we are concerned with more subtle feelings and more minor events, which illustrate the contest between imagination and material power, between what the girl in the kips and the ascetic gunman meant as ways of life.

That year between the Truce and the Civil War was not only a year of widening political divisions, it was also the year when the Church and bourgeoisie, the Faithful Brothers and Tim Corbin to use Michael Farrell's examples, came to terms with the new Ireland, and when the writers who had helped to make the revolution fell out of favour. This realignment can be seen in one episode, not of any consequence in political terms, but indicative of a new social order, which was to be uninformed by tolerance and charity. That, at least, is how Austin Clarke remembered it.

We have seen in *Thy Tears Might Cease* how Martin is disgusted at the treatment of the Dublin street walkers by the Sinn Fein vigilantes, and how he is dismayed to find that a feature of his childhood, Josie the cook from the Glenkilly home, has fallen into the trade.

Clarke recalls that in July 1922 (only a few weeks after the start of the Civil War), some thirty-one girls were taken from the brothels of Monto to a house in Church Street, where a well-known Franciscan preacher and members of the Legion of Mary tried to persuade them to give up their sinful ways and go on an enclosed retreat. 'The frightened girls, who had been taken from the brothels, believed this was a government plot to lock them up for life.' It was arranged with the Sisters of Charity at Baldoyle for the girls to use their school, rather than a regular retreat house. To avoid scandal the girls were to pose as a Sacred Heart Sodality from the city centre.

On the morning of July 14th a private bus was to leave from Myra House (the Legion of Mary headquarters) for Baldoyle at 11.30. Some hours earlier, a Franciscan from Adam and Eve's agreed to conduct the retreat subject to the approval of his superiors. As the girls came out of Myra House, a huge crowd waiting in the street sang 'Faith of Our Fathers', while old women knelt down on the pavement reciting the Rosary ... Soon afterwards, more brothels were entered and the whores taken away. So, with the connivance of the new Provisional Government, Night-Town was closed.[6]

The Legion approached Mr Cosgrave, then still Minister of Local Government, for assistance in finding some residence for the girls so that they could be kept together until reformed. He passed their request on to the Cabinet, who agreed to lend the Legion the use of a large house in Harcourt Street and donated £25 to the good work. (It must be admitted they also gave £200 to aid the publication in German of Rudolf Thurneysen's work on the old Irish sagas.) And in the end

Of the twenty-three girls who attended the Retreat, three were married in a few months, one became engaged, two had to go into hospital, two returned to their homes, employment was found for five, eight remained at the new Hostel, two went back to a life of sin. Two, who were Protestants, were received into the Catholic Church, one in August, the other in September.[7]

Now it is only to be expected that certain literary types should have a sentimental regard for whores: it is traditional. The notion that 'the prostitute is the only truly liberated woman' can be true only if she works for herself. One wonders about the girls in the Monto stews: were they truly liberated women? In the context of their exploitation by landlords and madames this was impossible. But their life, with its sexual liberty, was certainly an affront to the basic attitudes of Irish society at that time. One could only expect opposition to brothels from the new government, but what rankles with Clarke is obviously the cruel, highhanded manner in which they were closed. It was one thing for the gunmen to be amorally contemptuous of their own bodies but surely not of others'. The brothels and their inmates had featured in the writings of Joyce and O'Flaherty; they had provided refuge for Republicans during the war. And no matter what one feels about prostitution, whether it is a necessary outlet for sexual feelings or an exploitation of women by society, it has to be agreed that this episode shows a crass and cruel disregard for decent tolerance and the rights of the women. The writers saw the whores as celebrating life—a girl dancing with tricolour underclothes—the puritans had only a contempt for the body and so rejected the celebration of life. The vigilantes of the Catholic faith had set the tone of the new state with remarkable swiftness, as did the disparagement of women in politics.

The attitude of the state to its artists had been set a little earlier than this. On 18 October 1921, General Mulcahy appeared on the stage of the Abbey theatre at the end of a charity performance for Republican Dependents. 'It seems to me we have been deserted, at the present time and all through the fight put up in the country, by our poets and by our literary people.' His speech was given emphatic publication in the *Irish Independent*, and unthinkingly many must have accepted what he said as true. But it was not. Lady Gregory was astonished at the man's bad manners, the theatre having been given free for the benefit. She noted in her journal: 'I wonder if he has seen Yeats's poem and AE on Brixton Prison, and his pamphlets (my *Nation* articles not being signed don't count).' She might well have added to this Oliver Gogarty's aid to Collins, Darrell Figgis's work on industrial resources and economics, Erskine Childers's work for propaganda. All these were public knowledge.

Obviously Mulcahy had not considered them. But the charge made that night is one often made and is worth examining. The general, reared in the traditions of his class, had in mind the poetic figure of the Minstrel Boy and his love of Ireland:

> Though all the world betray thee,
> One sword, at least, thy right shall guard,
> One faithful harp shall praise thee.

The general had wielded his sword, and expected the poets to play their harps in praise of the soldiers' sing songs around the fire at night. But the poets were more interested in the realities of life than in providing sentimental war songs.

As a matter of fact his charge is false. If one takes the original members of the Irish Academy of Letters as the literary establishment that the period produced one sees that falsity clearly. Though its members were said by a prominent Jesuit to be incapable of giving a truthful picture of Irish life, one finds they are in fact a very mixed group. There were twenty-one full members, that is writers whose main distinction was in creative work. Of these, five were former members of Sinn Fein, the IRA, or had fought in the Troubles: Gogarty, O'Connor, O'Donnell, O'Faolain, Francis Stuart, leaving aside Yeats's early membership of the IRB. Eight others had written in support of Irish nationalist ideas; Colum, Higgins, Moore, O'Flaherty, O'Sullivan, George Russell, Shaw and Yeats himself. Of the remaining nine members, some like Forrest Reid were apolitical while St John Ervine was the only Unionist; some of the rest, including George Moore and Austin Clarke, were of nationalist Catholic caste; others, like Lennox Robinson and Edith Somerville, Protestants definite in their Irishness. This constituted a very mixed and representative group of people ranging from the far left (Peadar O'Donnell) to the extreme right (Yeats).

Lady Gregory mentions the contribution of Yeats, AE and herself. One should not forget also the active contributions of Erskine Childers, Darrell Figgis, Alice Stopford-Green, Gogarty, Corkery, Hyde, O'Faolain, and Desmond Fitzgerald. If these betrayed or deserted the cause, what did General Mulcahy define as support? The vigour, vitality and variety of the ideas of these people were obviously essential to the creation of a public life of any character in Ireland. Here the representative of the new regime with deliberate thought attacked and rejected the literary elite.

Many of the fighting men were simple people, frightened of the complexity and subtlety of the writers and poets, fearing the protean shapes of the imagination. Others saw such people as little better than the prostitutes, selling Ireland's honour for English money. Not all of them of course: P.S. O'Hegarty, the nationalist historian, wrote after the death of Yeats a more sympathetic assessment.

> I think that Ireland in the coming times will understand that the great poet who worked for a national culture was during his life one of the most revolutionary influences in Ireland. He worked for a liberation of the spirit, and it is the spirit that moves the body.[8]

This is very true. Yeats was working for a liberation of the spirit, but the new government was prepared to accept limits to the march of its people's emotions. One can only conclude that by the time the Treaty was signed in December 1921, the revolution had ceased to be really a revolution. The new leaders were not concerned as Pearse and Connolly, Yeats and his friends all were, with a liberation of the spirit, the creation of a national culture, with new shapes of life. The failure of the revolution had begun back in 1918, when such unlikely and narrow men as Griffith and de Valera were ushered by the quirk of history and the enthusiasm of an excited people to the first positions of leadership.

Attitudes to whores and writers represent the extreme ranges of opinion, but are a part of contemporary attitudes to life in general, and how it should be lived. If the ideas of Pearse and Connolly had any meaning, it was that new ways of living were needed in Ireland. New ways : did people think about such things during 1921? Sean O'Faolain is a witness. He had a job that summer as a booksalesman. Though spruce and dapper and riding a motor cycle, his only other possession was a long nosed Webley pistol, which he had yet to use. He was twenty-one, still caught in the dream time of youth, unhammered by reality. He was reading Gogol's *Lost Souls* and dreamed of writing an Irish counterpart, based on the ways of life he was seeing in his travels : 'I do not know any better job than that of a commercial traveller to get to know the life-ways of a country, the general character of its people and its distinctive personalities through whom one may approach the profoundest problems of the land.'[9] When he came to write *A Nest of Simple Folk* ten years later, his novel owed more than its title to Turgenev. It was filled with well realised, though slightly romanticised reality. But at this time he was still 'too young, too ikon-minded and too inexperienced'.

All that year [1921] I crossed the lives of hundreds of men and women who must have talked often about the one subject that was, or should have been, biting into everybody, the shapes of life that would emerge in a free Ireland. If they were talking in this way—but were they? Or were they, too, still caught by the dream?— I did not hear those worried voices of inspectors of schools, teachers, priests, hotel-owners, little shopkeepers, grubby-tailed waiters or the slattern maids who daily dished out the plates of potatoes, cabbage and bacon like a deck of cards around the commercials' table. I was happy, I was not frank-eyed, I was about to pay for it, dearly.[10]

And so were all those people, so was the country.

The *shapes of life* : the phrase betrays a concern which was far from most minds that hectic summer of victory. They had won, what more was there to say? They might have wondered, for instance, what were the social intentions of Ireland's new leaders.

Arthur Griffith, aside from wanting a dual monarchy, had no really developed social policy, perhaps no real ideas at all, and had been thrust almost accidentally into the place of leadership. Dying before peace was reached, it is difficult to assess what he might have done then.

To some of their admirers Michael Collins and de Valera now appear as irreconcilable leaders divided by civil war. This was not really so. Both men had nearly the same vision of a free Ireland, a vision derived from their rural boyhoods at Sams Cross in Cork, and Bruree in Limerick. It had the security of the familiar, the very Ireland that O'Faolain describes above and which went into his novel about rural Limerick.

Collins, for all his tactical expertise, remained the clever country boy. Whenever we seek the source of action in him, Frank O'Connor, one of his most sympathetic biographers writes, 'it is always in the world of his childhood that we find it'. Like his hero Peter Pan, he was a boy who never grew up. In him this was a vitality that protected him from too ready a compromise with the middle-class urban attitudes of some of his colleagues. But it also meant that he tended to judge culture from a warm seat by a Cork fireside on a winter night. P.S. O'Hegarty records one of Collins's few utterances on his utopia, which was made with difficulty in finding the right words. Collins wanted to be exact.

> I stand for an Irish civilisation based on the people and em-bodying and maintaining the things—their habits, ways of thought, customs—that make them different—the sort of life I was brought up in. . . . Once, years ago, a crowd of us were going along the Shepherds Bush Road when out of a lane came a chap with a donkey—just the sort of donkey and just the sort of cart that they have at home. He came out quite sud-denly and abruptly and we all cheered him. Nobody who has not been an exile will understand me, but I stand for that.[11]

And so did de Valera. He also was an exile, in a far deeper and more intimate way. The fatherless child raised by his mother's people on the small farm at Bruree, found there the permanence and the stability which all his life remained his standard. His vision of Irish life he has expressed in almost the same way as Collins :

> The Ireland we have dreamed of would be the home of a people who valued material wealth only as a basis of right living, of a people who were satisfied with frugal comfort and devoted their leisure to the things of the spirit; a land whose countryside would be bright with cosy homesteads, whose villages would be joyous with the romping of sturdy children, the contests of athletic youths, the laughter of comely maidens; whose fireside would be the forums of the wisdom of old age.[12]

The disruptions of the Civil War have obscured the striking similarities between the two men. They were natural allies, conservative with an agrarian Catholic base, giving an expression in politics to the ideals which we looked at in a previous chapter, which Corkery had elaborated for his young protégés.

Theirs was the ideal of the Catholic nationalists; other elements had other ideas, desired other shapes of life for the new Ireland. Not necessarily opposing ideals, but merely different. There were various disjointed left-wing elements, such as the Countess Markievicz, passionately seeking for social justice. These should have had their rightful place, given the contribution of Connolly in the years before the Rising and his part in that event. But there was no strong social democratic tradition in Ireland. Connolly's nationalism was taken up, but not his socialism. The Labour Party, which he had founded, stood aside to let the people decide on the nationalist question. When they did come to act as the opposition in the Free State Dail, they were caught in an unnatural position, between Cosgrave and de Valera. The return of de Valera to the Dail in 1927 and his advent to power in 1932 put paid to any chance the Labour Party might have had of gathering up radical republicans, who at that date drifted into the I R A. Labour lost their chance at the beginning and never really recovered.

If the Labour Party abdicated on social change, others did not. In the breakdown of British rule, there were a few attempts at socialisation. In rural Ireland, even in de Valera's Bruree, some few men were seeking newer shapes. During May 1920, the workers in the Cleeve creamery factory at Knocklong in County Limerick settled a strike by taking over the running of the factory. Their example was followed a year later, when the coal miners at Arigna seized the works there. The Cleeve factory was turned into a soviet in August 1921. The same month at Bruree the 'Workers Soviet Mills' declared 'We Make Bread not Profits'. By September Cork Harbour was also being run as a workers' soviet, and in Clare herders at Toorahara and Kilfenora took over lands and ran them collectively rather than as small holdings.

One recent historian of the Civil War, Eoin Neeson, gives a conservative account of these 'communists' as being 'mostly irresponsible and disaffected individuals, as great a danger to themselves as to the community'. So of course, in the eyes of the British, had been the IRA. The soviets received little support from the farmers, which was natural enough where the large ranchers were concerned. They issued cheques 'which had no credit, at the same time stirring up the unemployed to violence'. Here was a crisis for the hour. Credit they had in their labour, and the unemployed had as much right to obtain social justice as freedom. What might have been the fine flowering of the cooperative and labour movements was blighted. At Knocklong the farmers appealed to the Republican forces then holding the district: 'shots were exchanged'. The Republicans, or some of them at least, were satisfied with partial order, and Neeson admits they 'did not worry much about civic affairs'. (If they didn't, what were they fighting for?) On 29 July 1922, the retreating Republicans burned the factory behind them, leaving 400 workers unemployed. The Tipperary soviets were reduced by an Irish Farmers Union boycott; and those in Clare by groups of armed farmers aided by the National Army.

Whatever the motives of the soviets (their history is obscure: were they ordinary radicals adopting the fashionable terms of the collective, or were communists actually active there?) they showed that there were other factions in the country seeking other, perhaps more important goals, than the question of External Association. In this debate the Labour Party led by Thomas Johnson stood aside to let the people decide for themselves. Such honourable actions were not reciprocated: 'The man', said Griffith, 'who injures Ireland whether he does it in the name of Imperialism or Socialism is Ireland's enemy'. The Collins/de Valera pact of May 1922 was made, Gogarty reported to Yeats, from 'a fear of social revolution'. The fear was a real one. The latent division between the radical and conservative elements of the nationalist movement were appearing. Liam Mellows, who seized the Four Courts with Rory O'Connor, wrote that 'the commercial interests and the merchants are on the side of Treaty. We [the Republicans] are back to Tone—and it is just as well—relying on the men of no property. The stake in the country people were never with the Republic; they will always be against it until it wins'. Of course, there were no longer men of no property in Ireland; the land acts had made most people on the land into small holders. And they were in no hurry to support wild ideas about soviets, or young men who might disrupt their little lot in life. Failing to find widespread support, the Republic was lost before the fighting began, which explains perhaps much of the bitterness of the war.

So it seems that during that long year of debate, most people were not concerned with the shape of life any longer, but were hammering out the shape of the sword.

In seizing the Four Courts, Liam Mellows and his comrades were attempting to recreate 1916, to bring into existence what was only an imaginary concept, almost a poet's creation, the Irish Republic. The pragmatic realists opposing them were, of course, being true to their own ideals also. Yet one cannot help but feel that there was something in those willing to compromise which would have failed, which did indeed fail, to bring about any real revolution. There is a passage in Oliver Gogarty's memoirs where he is entertaining George Russell and some American visitors one evening, when General Collins calls. This is during the Civil War months. Russell is orating at length in his high fantastic manner, whether about the National Being or rural cooperation we are not told. Collins takes out a note-book and, pencil ready, leans forward to ask, 'Your point, Mr Russell, your point?' Mr Russell had many points, but not all of them were such as the man of action could appreciate. There was no bridging this gap. Imagination and material power, the poet and the gunman, the culture-heroes of Ireland, stared at each other across the hearth. And were silent.

A vivid impression of this interregnum (as it turned out to be) can be found in the paintings of Sean Keating. The war had been won, and he was anxious to record something of this great passage in Irish history. In the summer of 1921 he went down to Cork and for several months sketched and drew the scenes and personalities of the war. The result was a series of paintings which he exhibited at the Royal Hibernian Academy in the summer of 1922. By then they had taken on an additional irony, as Stephen Gwynn, the Irish correspondent of the *Observer* noted.

Keating's paintings seem to be the only records by an artist of this period. One of the paintings, *Raids*, looks forward to his allegory of the Civil War, but the other paintings such as *The Republican Court* and *Men of the South* are realistic and were drawn on the spot or from sittings by real people. His painting of Cork Number One Brigade Flying Column was intended as a companion piece to an earlier picture *Men of the West*. The earlier picture had shown a group of posed Western peasants armed—'in ambush' it later seemed to Yeats; it was a part of that Arcadian vision of Ireland which Keating had shared with Jack Yeats, for despite the armed men, it is an innocent picture. The faces in *Men of the South* are the faces of members of a real flying column. There is nothing innocent in this picture or in the landscape of *Raids*. By the time *Men of the South* was exhibited, the men in it were fighting again—this time amongst themselves, through the same hills and glens in which they had defeated the British.

The Heart Grown Brutal

WRITERS THROUGH THE CIVIL WAR

To think of the Civil War as a failure of imagination would be wrong. It was quite otherwise. Too much imagination was involved. As Yeats put it, with his increasing insight into the violent nature of man :

> We had fed the heart on fantasies,
> The heart's grown brutal on the fare;
> More substance in our enmities
> Than in our love.[1]

What had begun so simply with gun shots at Soloheadbeg, now moved with more terrible events into some awful rehearsal of the twentieth century. Of all wars, a civil war is the worst, because it is fought by brothers who hate with the hatred only possible between brothers. From the Civil War, the hatred of brothers, Ireland emerged into a newer reality in public life and a revised romanticism in literature.

At the beginning it was still possible to indulge oneself. Oliver Gogarty describes an evening, early in January 1922, on the eve of the Dail ratification of the Treaty, which seems to epitomise so much of the period. He and his guests sought to satisfy their anxiety for their future by invoking omens. Happily men with knowledge of the classics and their tradition were present, among them Father Dwyer and Professor Alton : 'We decided to put the *Sortes Virgilianae* to the proof. Virgil through the Dark Ages was regarded as a necromancer. . . . And his book was used to foretell the future, for had he not foretold the Golden Age that Christianity was about to bring in his Fourth Eclogue?'[2] So that they might discover whether some new saturnal was due, or another dark age, with ceremonial seriousness Professor Alton

called for a Virgil and a large key, both of which Gogarty brought
out. The question set was 'What will become of Arthur Griffith?'
Father Dwyer, the chaste person required by tradition, inserted
the key among the leaves of the volume and passed it back to
Professor Alton. Alton paused with shock before reading out:

> . . . spretae Ciconum quo munere matres
> Inter sacra deum nocturnique orgia Bacchi,
> Discerptum latos juvenem sparsere per agros.

The meaning seemed clear: 'What will become of Arthur
Griffith?' *Spretae quo munera*—spurned by which gifts—repudiated by the Treaty; *matres Ciconum*—the Maenads—the mad
women in the celebration of the god's ritual amid orgies of night-
wandering will tear the young men in pieces and scatter them
over the plains.

A remarkable prophecy indeed. Alton laid the folio down
solemnly in silence. 'I felt', Gogarty confesses, 'all the terror of
the fabulous darkness when such prophecies were fulfilled with
import for those whose minds were credulous and necromantic.'

A second trial was made: 'What will de Valera do?'

> Quaere age et armari pubem portisque moveri
> Laetus in arma jube et Phrygio, qui flumine pulchro
> Consedere, duces pictosque exure carinas,
> Coelestum vis magna jubet.

The standard translation of Virgil rendered that passage as
follows: 'Rouse thee now, and with joyful heart bid the young
men arm themselves and move to the fray and destroy the foreign
oppressors who have settled on our beautiful river, and burn their
painted ships. The might of heaven orders this to be done.' At
these words there came into Gogarty's mind the story of that
weak and egotistical young man, Turnus the Rutilian—'another
de Valera if ever there was one'—'how Juno, ever harassing the
Trojans, even as some malign fate seems to sow perpetual discord
among the Irish peoples, sent Alecto disguised as Madame
Markievicz, or rather as Calybe the priestess, to urge Turnus to
attack the Trojans'. The classical parallel came easily to mind,
but Gogarty did not choose to recall the final fate of the Trojans.

At that moment Turnus—or rather de Valera—was about to
make his famous speech that as a labourer's child he knew his

people so well he had merely to look into his own heart to know what they wanted. It was a new sentiment suitable for a democratic age : le Peuple, c'est moi. He had also issued in the Republican paper *An Phoblact*, a warning to his followers not to be tempted into accepting the Treaty. They must refuse it. 'If you quail at the consequences, what will they not ask you to surrender next to this ignoble fear?'

However, if de Valera like other prophets urged on his people —on 16 March he was talking of wading (Anath-like) in the blood of his opponents—he was not to be found among the garrisons at either Limerick where strife had then just been avoided, or later at the Four Courts in Dublin.

Who in fact led whom? By the final vote on 4 January 1922, the Dail accepted the Treaty by sixty-four votes to fifty-seven. The Dail under the presidency of Arthur Griffith proceeded to constitute a provisional government to implement the Treaty. De Valera as leader of the Republicans withdrew from the Dail. But he was not the leader of the IRA, and it was the IRA and not the deputies who were dedicated to defending the Republic.

The situation was serious. The government began to build up a Free State Army in which there were to be only a few veterans of the Tan war, and a new police force. The IRA began to reorganise itself, and a GHQ was established in Barry's Hotel in O'Connell Street. Inevitably the armies clashed : by 6 May eight men had been killed and nearly fifty wounded in incidents.

De Valera came to make a pact with Collins at the election in May to preserve the status quo. At this time a pogrom of Catholics was under way in Belfast. Ulster and the question of partition might have provided enough common ground to unite the divided south; Collins went so far as to provide the IRA in Ulster with arms to defend the northern Catholics, then being harried and burned out of their homes. However, on 7 June, British troops drove the IRA out of the border towns they held, and on 14 June the IRA leaders in the Four Courts rejected a comprehensive unity plan, but held their hand. The election on 16 June returned only thirty-six Republicans as against fifty-eight for the government; Labour and others got thirty-four. The vast majority of Irish people were for the Treaty. The Labour Deputies took their seats; the Republicans refused to.

The British government, given the appalling events in Ulster, feared any moves towards unity in the South, which would have meant almost certainly action on Ulster. Pressure was brought to bear on Collins and Griffith and on 14 June, two days before the election, Collins repudiated the pact with de Valera. The election showed that though the country was largely in favour of the Treaty, there was still a sizeable minority for the Republic. But the Republicans themselves were split on the question of further fighting.

On 22 June, General Wilson, the military adviser of the Northern Ireland government, was shot dead in a London street by two IRA men acting it would seem on previous orders from Michael Collins. The next day Lloyd George sent Collins an ultimatum to clear the Four Courts. Collins hesitated. On the 24th General Macready, commanding British forces in Ireland, was ordered to act, though the order was wisely withdrawn the next day. On the 26th a new ultimatum was sent to the Irish leaders who now gave way.

At dawn on 28 June, Free State troops demanded the evacuation of the Four Courts by 4.00 a.m. They wheeled field guns (borrowed for the occasion from the British) into positions along the south bank of the Liffey. When the garrison refused to surrender, the bombardment was ordered at 4.30. The old hammer of reality had shaped the inevitable sword: the Civil War had begun.

One of the garrison in the Four Courts was Liam O'Flaherty. Just before the very end, he and some others were dismissed and so escaped the final bombardment in which the Four Courts were burned, O'Connell street ruined again and Cathal Brugha died fighting madly. All this O'Flaherty watched with the crowds held back by the police.

When he had returned from wandering around the world for two years, early in 1922, Liam O'Flaherty felt ready for direct political activity. On a previous short visit home he had found the Tan war uninteresting: it held no openings for a communist. But now with Civil War looming, he became involved in efforts to foment communist activity. As self-styled 'Chairman of the Council of the Unemployed', in January 1922 he led a party of workers which seized the Rotunda Theatre at the head of O'Connell Street. They declared an Irish Soviet Republic, and for one brief moment the Red Flag fluttered bravely in a Dublin breeze.

They held out for some days, but were finally persuaded to capitulate by a Free State officer. O'Flaherty then joined the Republican garrison in the Four Courts, from which he was dismissed as well. Watching the last fighting in O'Connell Street he overheard a rumour of his own death in Capel Street. A friend tried to persuade him to go down the country and join a Republican group in Cork, to continue the fight. But he realised that the rumour was right : one Liam O'Flaherty was dead, another was yet to live.

To escape arrest he fled to England. He had been doing some writing already, mainly articles for small Republican papers like *The Plain People*, but no fiction. In London, in September 1922, he began to write in earnest at last, finishing a novel of 150 thousand words in a few weeks. 'At least two million people were slaughtered during the course of the story' : it was rejected. Three days after it came back he began *Thy Neighbour's Wife*, of which his socialist brother remarked that a novel should be 'something more than a bar room story'.

Among the stories of the West and of animals which he published as *Spring Sowing* in 1924 was one about the Civil War called 'The Sniper'. Mrs Hamilton, who had first published the story in the *New Leader* and had been amused by the author's threat to blow up the office if he was not paid, advised him to send it to Jonathan Cape. There he came under the protective wing of Edward Garnett, who was to do so much to encourage other Irish writers, among them Sean O'Faolain. Garnett's strenuous resistance to faulty work encouraged O'Flaherty in writing *The Black Soul*. The revolutionary was dead; the writer come alive.

'The Sniper' is a simple story, told directly. The fighting is going on in the streets around the Four Courts. Across the width of O'Connell Street two snipers face each other. The Republican has the face of a student; thin and ascetic, his eyes have the gleam of the fanatic. They were deep and thoughtful, 'the eyes of a man who is used to look at death'. By a ruse the wounded Republican kills the Free State soldier. He feels a sudden curiosity to see who the man is and whether he knows him from the old days.

He decided to risk going over to look at him. . . . The sniper darted across the street. A machine gun tore up the ground around him with a hail of bullets, but he escaped. He threw himself downwards beside the corpse. The machine gun stopped.

Then the sniper turned over the dead body and looked into his brother's face.[3]

And there, in a sentence, was the Civil War.

The Civil War was, far more than the fight against the British, the experience that made the difference. And not only for Liam O'Flaherty. In the introduction to his collected stories, Sean O'Faolain dates his first successful story 'Fugue' from 1927; he wrote it in America where he was then studying at Harvard.

> I had come out of an experience which had left me dazed—the revolutionary period in Ireland. Not that it was really an experience as I now understand that word. It was too filled with dreams and ideals and a sense of dedication to be an experience in the meaning of things perceived, understood and remembered. I perceived alright, I remembered alright, but it had all been far too much to understand; especially the disillusion at the end of it all, for, as few people who are not Irish now remember, that revolutionary period ended in a civil war, and civil war is of all wars the most difficult for its participants to understand. Besides, as I found myself yesterday making a character in a novel I am writing say, 'It's a terrible and a lovely thing to look on the face of Death when you are young, but it unfits a man for the long humiliation of life'.[4]

For his generation, a younger one than O'Flaherty's, it was difficult to understand what was happening when the dreams of revolution dissolved into the nightmare of civil war, leaving in so many only bitterness in place of dedication. Being poor the Irish had only their dreams, and their dreams were trodden in the mire. For the country this was a difficult transition; for Irish writers there was another difficulty.

They had to describe what was happening, despite the unmanning face of death. This was their only material. They had to face the long humiliation of life disillusioned with the strange new country, which seemed to them so mediocre and stifling, then emerging from the long struggle. In such a state it was a thankless task to be honest; as Yeats wrote

> The rhetorician would deceive his neighbours,
> The sentimentalist himself; while art
> Is but a vision of reality.
> What portion in the world can the artist have
> Who has awakened from the common dream
> But dissipation and despair?[5]

The common dream, which the poets had shared with the patriots, had been of the new Ireland they would create. But the revolutionary visions of Pearse and Connolly were strangely transformed into the abstractions of de Valera, the vacuous violence of the gunmen.

In 1916 Yeats had wondered whether too long a sacrifice would make a stone of the heart; now writing in 1922, he realised that for hearts filled with the dreams of nationalism, the consequences were bitter.

> We had fed the heart on fantasies,
> The heart's grown brutal from the fare;
> More substance in our enmities
> Than in our love;[6]

Hatred's peculiar love provides the theme of the civil war writing. After so many years of fighting, the gun had become an answer-all. It was easier to shoot than argue, to fight rather than talk. Rory O'Connor seized the Four Courts to force the new government as the British had been forced. But the same war could not be fought again. The country would not support, as it had in the years before, the continued fighting. As the Civil War went on into the autumn of 1922 with murder, reprisal and counter-reprisal, Rory O'Connor and some seventy-six others were executed by the government. By the time the fighting ceased after the winter of 1923, Michael Collins and Arthur Griffith, Erskine Childers and Liam Mellows were dead. It was, if anyone cared to see it that way, but a small part of the turmoil of post-war Europe trying to find new ways, the beginning of what Yeats had glimpsed in 'The Second Coming'.

Early in 1922, Yeats returned to live in Ireland permanently;

he had spent the years of the Tan war in England, hearing of its horrors second-hand. He bought a house at 82 Merrion Square, in the calm heart of old Georgian Dublin, a mere two doors from the house where George Russell was then planning *The Irish Statesman*. The tower at Ballylee was now habitable, and the Yeats family spent the summer there, near Lady Gregory at Coole. In a letter written while he was working on 'Meditations in Time of Civil War' (9 August), Yeats explained to a friend that he lived 'in a medieval tower in the West of Ireland, beside a bridge that may be blown up any night'. He was not exaggerating the danger.

Yeats had already described Thoor Ballylee and its associations in *The Celtic Twilight*, and he had taken George Moore to see it on his return to Ireland and told him all about it. Blind Raftery, the famous Gaelic poet, had written of the beautiful Mary Hynes who lived there, as if she were Helen and he Homer. Yeats always sensed that poetry had the power to eternalise the smallest of places; perhaps Troy and its topless towers were no more than this, even though 'a ballad singer had sung it all'. He was attached to the tower 'for our feet would linger where beauty has lived its life of sorrow to make us understand that it is not of this world'. So he would liken his room to the chamber described by Milton in *Il Penseroso*, which Samuel Palmer had drawn, where the Platonist toiled on

> . . . shadowing forth
> How the daemonic rage
> Imagined everything.[7]

There could not have been a better place for a poet to work in.

He had begun the set of poems on the Civil War, which were to be the major work of the year, in June. The reference to 'some fourteen days of civil war' would make the date 11 July 1922. In his own notes to the poem he explains that 'These poems were written at Thoor Ballylee in 1922, during the civil war. Before they were finished the Republicans blew up our "ancient bridge" one midnight. They forbade us to leave the house, but were otherwise polite, even saying at last "Good night, thank you" as if we had given them the bridge.'[8]

As well as such personal dangers—as a Senator, Yeats had a bullet put through a window of his Dublin home, and was followed everywhere by armed detectives for fear he would be kidnapped or murdered—there was a philosophical danger in civil war. It was the complete disruption of the public order which he held to be essential for complete liberty. Perhaps, as he wrote in a letter, 'there is nothing so dangerous to a modern state, where politics take the place of theology, as a bunch of martyrs. A bunch of martyrs were the bomb in 1916, and we are living in the explosion.'

'A bunch of martyrs' is an odd phrase to describe the men he had hailed in the poems written after the event in 1916. Did he praise them then only because they had failed, and the immediate danger of revolution was past, leaving only another glorious memory for the poets and ballad singers? The years had altered the poet's views, as they had matured his poetry. Though he was proud to become a Senator in December 1922—'We shall have much government in our hands', he wrote confidently—Yeats had abandoned the nationalism of his early associates. He was now angered at the radical views of those once beautiful young women Maud MacBride, Constance Markievicz and her sister Eva, the poet.

What had caught his imagination was not the politics of independence, but the Cuchulain-inspired act itself. At the end of his life he claimed that he 'was not a nationalist, except in Ireland for passing reasons; State and Nation are the works of intellect, when you consider what comes before and after them they are, as Victor Hugo said of something or other, not worth the blade of grass God gives for the linnet's nest'. That is the poet speaking, for the politician had more exact views on the Nation and the State. His are not, certainly, nationalist views, and the Irish habit of seeing politics only in relation to nationalism has obscured the fact that Yeats had a remarkably coherent political ideal.

Earlier I quoted at length an early political statement of Yeats's which betrays the influence of Morris and the vogue for socialist ideas that he shared with Wilde and Synge and Shaw. Yeats was naturally conservative, and what he took from Morris was the ideal of individual excellence which socialism might liberate. With his increasing regard, however, for Anglo-Ireland, his political ideals became those of Burke, whom he now saw with Berkeley and Swift as a trinity of Anglo-Irish intellects.

It was from Burke that he derived his image of the organic state as 'that great rooted blossomer'. Such a state, from its deep roots in the soil to its airy blossoms, gave places to beggars and nobles, though he does not seem to have considered the bourgeoisie as the sturdy bole. This emphasis on excellence, on originality, on pride in what was individual, was worthwhile. Ireland lacked the distinction he longed for her to have, and he hoped to help her gain it. Other elements in his ideas, such as his sternly expressed will and his hatred for democracy led him to admire Kevin O'Higgins and later to flirt with fascism. This last episode was not, as he tried later to make out when covering his tracks, an aberration. He was consistent enough. It was O'Duffy, the leader of the Irish Blueshirt movement, who failed to come up to scratch as a Mussolini to his D'Annunzio.

As his poetry grew richer in the 1920s, Yeats flew above the limits of his past, the passions of his present, and found the universal, images out of the *spiritus mundi*, riding by his door in humble Irish forms :

> An affable Irregular,
> A heavily-built Falstaffian man,
> Comes cracking jokes of civil war
> As though to die by gunshot were
> The finest play under the sun.
>
> A brown Lieutenant and his men,
> Half dressed in national uniform,
> Stand at my door, and I complain
> Of the foul weather, hail and rain,
> A pear-tree broken by the storm.[9]

Here before him, in very real terms, was the contrast between the poet and the gunmen. All he could share with them in passing was a coarse joke, and the shattered pear-tree. Yeats perhaps fancied himself as a man of action, certainly as an influential public figure. He liked men of action.* But between the poet and these soldiers there was nothing :

*The poet Thomas McGreevy, later director of the National Gallery, remembers that :
   W.B., turned man of action, said : 'McGreevy,
   It is very hard to like men of action.'
McGreevy had called and found Yeats with the, to him, uncongenial company of Free State Army officers.

I count those feathered balls of soot
The moor-hen guides upon the stream,
To silence the envy in my thought;
And turn towards my chamber, caught
In the cold snows of a dream.[10]

The image of the moor-hen on the stream had appeared also in
'Easter 1916', where the natural life was contrasted with the
stream-troubling stone, which he feared the insurrection might
be. Here again, in the Civil War, he tried to relate these images
of life and destruction.

The series of poems in the sequence is built up around images
of fullness, hatred and the coming emptiness already envisioned in
'The Second Coming'. These soldiers at his door are images of
the hatred loose in the country. In the seething coldness of his
dream, the poet contrasts them with that prime Yeatsian image
of civilised fullness, the Anglo-Irish country house :

Surely among a rich man's flowering lawns,
Amid the rustle of his planted hills,
Life overflows without ambitious pains;
And rains down life until the basin spills . . .[11]

This connection between greatness of spirit and violence, and the
paradox of art's dependence on violence and bitterness for its
creation, was illustrated by the history of Thoor Ballylee itself.
His home with its meditative chamber, was in fact an old castle
where a Man-at-Arms had settled with his followers 'in that
tumultuous spot' where the poet now desired only peace.

Also he had another symbol of this peculiar relationship. In
New York in March 1920, a Japanese admirer named Sato had
presented him with a Samurai sword, wrapped in flower-embroi-
dered silk. It had been made 650 years before and had been a
family heirloom for 500. Sato pointed out along the sharp edge
of the sword the name of the Master, Montashigi,* who had
made it. This remarkable gift deeply moved Yeats's imagination,
reminding him of the sword which he had once thought his
favourite Irish poets should keep upstairs. The sword was now
before him on his work desk, with pen and paper by it,

---

* Actually Bishu Isajuné Motoshigé; an account of the sword is given by
Shotomaro Oshima.

that it may moralise
My days out of their aimlessness.[12]

This Samurai weapon, the weapon of the great aristocratic Japanese warrior class, was also an image of war and of artistry by generations of craftsmen, another object of art fashioned by the needs of violence. For Yeats it was symbolic of life rather than death, as he used it in 'Dialogue of Soul and Self', where he resigned himself to rebirth rather than escape from life. Yet when he was later asked by a retiring Indian visitor if he had any message about life to send to that resurgent country, he flourished the sword about his head and cried out, 'Violence and more violence'. This was a creed fashioned from his experience of war in Ireland.

His castle was now once again tumultuous with the alarms and excursions of war; sudden night visitors, soldiers, stopping at dawn, the dead trundled by on country carts. Leaving these, he climbed the tower to find bees building their nest in the cracked walls of the castle, sweetness out of strength as the old riddle had it, as if the tower were already falling into unredeemable ruin, his seed running out in the natural declension of soul.

Rumours of civil war were plentiful even in that remote spot, yet 'no clear fact to be discerned'. Pacing the height of the tower, he looked out over the long familiar country, yet even here

Frenzies bewilder, reveries perturb the mind;
Monstrous familiar images swim into the mind's eye.[13]

An image of hatred : a crowd crying for vengeance into which the poet feels himself caught up, as inevitably he is in such excitement. This, he tells us in a note, is intended as a 'fit symbol for those who labour from hatred and so from sterility of various kinds'. Against this he sets an image of fullness : those magical unicorns with beautiful women on their backs, symbolic to him of the soul's self-sufficiency.

These images are displaced by brazen hawks, a peculiarly telling image of 'the straight road of logic, and thus of mechanism', an image of the coming emptiness of the imagination :

Nor self-delighting reverie,
Nor hate of what's to come, nor pity for what's gone,

Nothing but grip of claw, and the eye's complacency
The innumerable clanging wings that have put out the moon.[14]

Considering his own vocation as an artist, his first loyalty to
his own imagination, he would have to subdue his envy of the
men of violence, the active gunmen. Their cause he sees as one of
sterility in the end; it cannot be his. In this raging bloody Civil
War there is no place for him. He must leave the soldiers of both
sides by the road, survey them from his tower, from the lonely
eminence of the artist. Violence disturbed him, because he wondered if it was not the only way in which to create that supremacy
of feeling which he admired.

> I turn away and shut the door, and on the stair
> Wonder how many times I could have proved my worth
> In something that all others understand or share;
> But O! ambitious heart, had such a proof drawn forth
> A company of friends, a conscience set at ease,
> It had but made us pine the more. The abstract joy,
> The half-read wisdom of daemonic images,
> Suffice the ageing man as once the growing boy.[15]

From this position, there was to be no turning back.

It may have been from an image in Yeats's poem on the Civil
War that Sean O'Casey picked up the title of his play on the
period, his most considerable work *Juno and the Paycock* (first
produced on 8 February 1926, though published in 1925). I am
not certain of this, but the poet's lines on the great houses:

> O what if gardens where the peacock strays
> With delicate feet upon old terraces,
> Or else all Juno from an urn displays
> Before the indifferent garden deities;[16]

make an ironic contrast between all this, what Yeats calls the
'inherited glory of the rich', and the tragic comedy enacted in a
Dublin tenement, between Juno Boyle and Captain Jack, the
strutting peacock husband.

If 'Meditations in Time of Civil War' is Yeats's masterpiece of
the period, *Juno* is O'Casey's. It is sometimes argued that *The
Plough and the Stars*, written later, is a greater play because it

more closely related to O'Casey's own experience. But *Juno* has a greater feeling for both the comedy and tragedy of the period; and it gains a great deal by omitting such blazing drama as the Rising easily provided.

The play is set late in 1922, during September and November. In the country the Civil War is being fought with great bitterness, but the Republicans have been defeated in Dublin and reduced to murders in the back streets. The newspapers were full of stories similar to the one which opens the play—'Out on a little by-road out beyond Finglas, he was'—announcing the death of Mrs Tancred's son. But the tragedy and the comedy arise not out of the influence of public events but out of the characters themselves. Johnny for instance, wounded in 1916, has now lost an arm in the O'Connell Street fighting of June. He is almost completely in the background for the First Act; but it slowly emerges that he is the informer who betrayed Mrs Tancred's son. Like most cowards, Johnny indulges in boasts about his fighting in Easter Week and losing his arm.

> *Johnny*: I'd do it agen, Ma, I'd do it agen; for a principle's a principle.
> *Mrs Boyle* : Ah, you lost your best principles, me boy, when you lost your arm; for them's the only sort of principles that's any good to a workin' man.[17]

The play revolves around the effect of an inheritance on the family, and—to adapt Yeats's phrase—the inherited glory of the poor, which amounts to little enough. Poverty is a state of mind, like respectability, an infection which has nothing to do with not having any money. Juno has had her good looks destroyed by her long struggle to support the family. Mary, the daughter who has inherited those looks, moves on the edges of socialist circles, attempting to read her way out of the slums. Jerry, her working-class boy friend, cannot offer her what the more superior Bentham seems to have, but the latter's theosophy (a dig at the higher nonsense of George Russell and his esoteric friends) seems to have little effect on his morals. But then in the end, the other's socialism is just as empty, for Jerry is seen to be trapped in the conventional morality of the bourgeoisie he despises. Johnny having turned Judas on the leader of his own political faith, has only the more superstitious forms of Irish Catholicism to fall back on when the crisis comes. Indeed all the creeds of the characters are false. Joxer, a former National Forester (like Uncle Peadar in the *Plough*) has also been betrayed by his faith; he spots his chat with fine quotations but his imagination has nothing to sustain it now but *Willie Reilly and His Colleen Bawn*. And the Paycock himself, with his philosophising on the mysteries of life—'What is the stars I'd ask meself, what is the stars'—his fine memories of Easter Week, tumbles to the play's end. 'The blinds are down Joxer . . . the whole world's in a state of chassis'.

The two key themes of the play, the inheritance and Johnny's fate, suggest how life must have been in troubled Dublin, where it was possible for the very banalities of life to be thus shattered by public violence. Ideals whether of nationalism, socialism, theosophy or whatever, where they were not bankrupt were turning in on themselves. Money, often seen by the poor as a universal panacea of all social ailments, was also an illusion. Nothing in the end remains but the drunken rhetoric of the Paycock, the splendid courage of Juno. The comedy of the spending spree is a common enough comic device: common, comic, and true. Mary's seduction is also of the common stuff of melodrama. But by setting these off against Mrs Tancred's impassioned grief and Juno's stalwart resignation, O'Casey raises the level of the drama to a higher plane. It is all trivial enough, but triviality altered by death: children playing in a square as the bombs fall. People desire only to live their lives, however trivial, but history thrusts itself into their lives with tragic results.

The tragedy of many lives is that those who live them out do not realise they are living history. History somehow seems something with dignity, with triumph and failure clear-cut; but often in war lives lack dignity, and failure and triumph become matters of squalid murders in back streets and country lanes. Such was the Civil War.

After the fall of the Four Courts, the fighting was mainly concentrated in the south, where Nationalist feeling had always been strong. The so-called 'Munster Republic', centred on Cork, was attempting to hold out. The Free State Army advancing by land was driving the Republicans from the small towns, and Cork itself was captured by a sudden landing from the sea. The

H

Republicans began retreating from village to village across the mountains of West Cork and Muskerry, till by the end of 1922 only Kerry itself was still holding out. Most other parts of the country experienced only what Yeats and O'Casey write about: the passing soldiers, the casual murder. Yet the circumstances of the war in Ireland were peculiar, in that each event of significance has its literary witness. We have

> Character isolated by a deed
> To engross the present and dominate the memory.[18]

Yeats and O'Casey provided material to engross the present and dominate the memory; so did the great public figures.

Many of the great scenes of the Civil War have been described for us, not by the politicians, but by writers sometimes involved, sometimes distant. No member of the government of the Free State having chosen to write his memoirs, we have to depend on writers like Oliver St John Gogarty to turn the events of the day into literature. And very often it is moving literature.

On 12 August Gogarty was called to St Vincent's hospital, where he was told Arthur Griffith, whom he had been treating, had collapsed. When he arrived he found that two doctors had opened an artery in the president's arm in an effort to revive him.

> President Griffith, the man who had believed in the Irish people, lay on his back. His left arm was outstretched and bloody. 'Take up that corpse at once,' I said, letting something of the bitterness of my spirit escape into the harsh word. A moment later, I regretted it. 'Take the President's body into the bedroom.' *I perish by this people that I made.*[19]

The words are Tennyson's on the parting of Griffith's namesake for the Isle of Avalon. Nothing sums up the whole paradox of the Free State more aptly than that an Irish poet should quote an English one on a British hero in memoriam of a Dubliner of planter stock whom he sees as creating the Irish people.

A nation haunted by its leaders' deaths finds always fitting words of parting. Griffith had his tributes at the graveside from Michael Collins and from Richard Mulcahy. And from Gogarty who, writing in *The Free State*, claimed 'it remains for Ireland to become worthy of Arthur Griffith'.

He shook from off him with a grand impatience,
The flesh uncomforted,
And passed among the captains in whom Nations
Live when these men are dead.[20]

Ten days later Michael Collins was in Cork, apparently in an attempt to contact old comrades in the IRA in an effort to make peace, or to talk to de Valera, who was in the district at the time. Skibbereen had been occupied by the Republicans in July, but they had left on 13 August, before the Free State troops arrived, leaving burning buildings behind them.

A few miles away, in remoter Castle Townshend, Edith Somerville was much relieved. 'We have been making history in West Cork,' she wrote in a letter, 'and have not finished yet'. On 22 August she and her brother Cameron drove into Skibbereen where they talked to Collins about the situation and restoring order. They found him sympathetic to their position, isolated in the country without police protection, but he had no troops to spare.

He drove on. Collins was a Clonakilty man. Before leaving Dublin he had said, 'I'll hardly be shot in my own country.' But later that day, between 8.30 and 9.00 at a place called Beal-nablath—the Gap of Flowers—his small column was ambushed by a Republican force. Encouraging his men, Collins climbed out of the armoured car he was driving in, and as the Republicans withdrew, a bullet caught him in the head. As Frank O'Connor wrote, years later, 'The tradition he had made had risen in the falling dark and shot him dead.'

Once again Dublin followed a leader to his grave. Sir John Lavery, the painter, was much moved by the scene at the lying in state. Collins, he thought, 'might have been Napoleon in marble as he lay in his uniform, covered by the Free State flag with a crucifix on his breast'. Of all the leaders of that time, perhaps only Collins survives with generosity in the memory of his country. The legend of the Troubles emerged into public life for a few short months, and died heroically.

Regret was the tone of some even then. The *Irish Independent* reported the arrest of Ernie O'Malley and the death of Harry Boland with a regret for the divisions in the national cause it had itself only so lately swung round to. But generosity was not for everyone, and not certainly for Oliver Gogarty. He wrote after Collins's death :

> Down the memorial ages, he shall have
> The fame of Judas who McMurrough clad,
> What alien schemer or deluded lout,
> What Cain has caught his country by the throat?[21]

The alien schemer may have been de Valera, but more probably Gogarty had in mind Erskine Childers. It is typical of the period that the gallant Childers, an Anglo-Irish liberal who had cast his lot with the Republic, should have been made the scapegoat by the Free State for any great crime committed, and been execrated in the crudest terms by Griffith and others as a foreign devil, a renegade, and 'an Englishman'. (This last, coupled with the accusation of being a spy, was the particular accusation of Griffith.) Childers however was a writer, and his one novel *The Riddle of the Sands*, a record of secret service, casts its own light on his complex career. The novel is quite well written, superior to Buchan by a long way, with a quiet and observant humour of its own; it is worth reading, not only for its story, but for its descriptions of small boat sailing in the Baltic and North Sea. Two young Englishmen stumble on the makings of a plot to invade England from the Frisian islands. Behind this scheme they find not only the Kaiser, but a former officer of the British navy who has gone over to the Germans. There are some curious passages here where Childers talks about the unmistakable nature of the Englishman, an ironic comment on his own end. The novel was intended as propaganda to warn the British public of the possibility of such an invasion. Childers was then a British patriot, and it was as a patriot that he first offered his services to Sinn Fein. But the book puts the lie to the calm, composed, yet nervous features Childers displayed to the camera. We can see he was a romantic, who believed that great events of state could be influenced by the courageous action of dedicated men working on their own. He was capable of the most rigorous analysis of political and economic problems, but when it came to action he became the romantic adventurer, out in the North Sea in his small boat, or in the west Cork hills with his small printing press. In 1914 he provided his boat the *Asgard* to bring into Howth the guns Darrell Figgis had bought in Germany. When the Civil War came there was only one place for him to be, however unsuited he was for the role; on the front line.

It was a great compliment to him that the Free State took him seriously. He was alleged to have blown up Mallow viaduct and destroyed the Valencia trans-Atlantic cable, and to have conducted other raids, all of which he never did. He was not a gunman, but a publicist, a writer at war with his words. He stamped on the Republican papers he edited a high-pitched, high-minded and cutting style that persists in some of them to this day. What irked his former colleagues was that he, almost alone, had considered in detail the relations possible in the Commonwealth. He insisted that Ireland hold out for what she wanted, that a change of status was not the only thing required, that social justice and democracy must be held in view. If the Republic had succeeded he would have emerged as one of its leading figures. If the Free State was to succeed it was necessary that the radical Childers be murdered. Like Dollman in his novel, he had changed his allegiance, but found he was mistrusted by those he wanted to help. In the end, this was the death of him.

Oliver Gogarty's biographer, among others, repeats the allegations against Childers, having failed to consult Frank O'Connor's account of Childers's activities given in *An Only Child*: thus are the lies of yesterday perpetuated. Yet we have O'Connor's word that when the news of Collins's death was received with joy by himself, Childers was moved to write an article in his praise. Certainly the obituaries on Collins and on Griffith which Childers wrote for *An Phoblacht* are just and fair and kind. After the defeat of the Republicans in the south Childers, anxious for a peace settlement, made his way back to the Wicklow home of his cousin Robert Barton. It was ironical that in that house where the little English boy had begun to grow into the Irish man, he was arrested by Free State soldiers. He had a gun on him, which he was unable to use, a miniature one with an ivory handle worn pinned to his braces, which had been a present from Michael Collins. He was swiftly brought to his final end in a gaol yard at dawn before an Irish firing squad.

This confrontation of former friends in the horrors of civil war was not a struggle between opposing views of external association or dominion status. These were merely the fronts for two opposing views of life. Liam Mellows spoke of the Republicans being back with 'the men of no property' and the Free State made no secret of its desire to preserve a status quo agreeable to large economic interests. It was in a small way a class war, the clash of different philosophies.

We shall come shortly to the symbolic figures of the Republic, but first we shall look at the Free State through the eyes of its literary supporters Yeats and Gogarty.

One day, later in December 1922, Yeats and his wife returned to Number 82 Merrion Square to find chalked on the door: *Senator W.B. Yeats*. Gogarty had called to report that his efforts with the President, W.T. Cosgrave, had been successful and both he and Yeats had been nominated by the new government to the Senate. Finding Yeats out, he had chalked his message for all to see.

Such a gesture was typical of Gogarty. Some Dubliners saw in him only a scurrilous snob, as James Joyce certainly did, in making him Malachi Mulligan, Ireland's gay betrayer. Yeats saw him indulgently as the man of action he was not. His admiration for this second-self who dared to carry a gun and use it, was taken to the extreme of including seventeen poems by Gogarty in *The Oxford Book of Modern Verse*. In Yeats's introduction to that anthology there is a remarkable passage.

> Twelve years ago [in January 1923] Oliver Gogarty was captured by his enemies, imprisoned in a deserted house on the edge of the Liffey with every prospect of death. Pleading a natural necessity he got into the garden, plunged under a shower of revolver bullets and as he swam the ice-cold December stream promised it, should it land him in safety, two swans. I was present when he fulfilled that vow. His poetry fits the incident, a gay, stoical—no, I will not withhold the word— heroic song. Irish by tradition and many ancestors, I love, though I have nothing to offer but the philosophy they deride, swashbucklers, horsemen, swift indifferent men; yet I do not think that is the sole reason, good though it is, why I gave him considerable space, and think him one of the great lyric poets of his age.[22]

Yeats was always kind to his friends, and may have taken Gogarty over seriously as a poet. Nowadays we are more interested in the writer as a man of action than as a poet.

As a poet, he has a spontaneous and witty felicity which can be quite charming—as in his little poem 'After reading Tolstoi' on going to live with a red-headed whore in Ringsend :

> Where the little lamp blooms.
> Like a rose in the stew;
> And up the back garden
> The sound comes to me
> Of the lapsing, unsoilable sea.[23]

His novels have a rumbustious recklessness which is outweighed by a mannered style, at once over-grand and facetious. He made a parade of his classicism from his student days at Trinity under the legendary Mahaffy. Joyce's mockery of this in Malachi Mulligan—'The snotgreen sea. The scrotum-tightening sea. *Epi oinopa ponton*. Ah, Dedalus, the Greeks.'—stung him deeply : 'That Joyce, whom I kept in my youth, has written a book you can read on all the toilet walls of Dublin.' Gogarty even saw St Patrick as bringing Roman culture to Ireland—a dubious historical notion indeed—blending the qualities of classical culture with the spirit of the Celts. Such a blend he thought he saw in Collins, and admired.

He called his autobiography, which deals mainly with these years, with more honesty than other writers, 'a phantasy in fact'. It is an illuminating document of what a Republican would doubtless call 'the Free State mentality'. His fawning admiration for Griffith and Collins we have already seen; here we look at his treatment of the Yeatsian theme of the Big House.

Gogarty owned a country house at Renvyle in Galway, a beautiful house on one of Europe's finest coasts. During the guerrilla war in the final stages of the Civil War, it was one of the many houses which the Republicans burned down. (Moore Hall, owned by George Moore, and the home of Maurice Moore his more patriotic brother, was another, as was the home of Sir Horace Plunkett.) The wantonness of this campaign, for it served little real political purpose, was to be deplored, though the Free State balanced the atrocity account in the end. Gogarty devotes a very characteristic chapter to a paen to all that these houses stood for, one very different in tone from John Synge's lament quoted earlier.

Leisure, and all the accroutrements of leisure, lakes preserved, pictures, silver, and motor-cars, these are as red rags to the congenital 'Reds'—the underdogs of all time. We shall be 'taught a lesson'. In other words, all we possess that is the outcome of the creative imagination of artists who had the leisure to dream and to give their dream a local habitation, all that took time and loving care to accomplish, be it the cover of the Book of Kells or a silver inkstand, by all that appertains to a household of continuance, aye, even the house itself must be destroyed. And not that anything may live but hate.[24]

Yeats wondered if he himself had not contributed to 'that whereby a house lay wrecked', whether he had not helped let slip the forces of anarchy he feared so much. Gogarty might have wondered the same thing, but he did not. 'Books, pictures, all consumed : for what? Nothing left but the charred oak beam quenched in the well beneath the house. And ten tall square towers, chimneys, stand here on Europe's extreme verge.' The question is not answered. Gogarty was unable to realise within himself, as Yeats was, the dichotomies dividing the country. Yet Gogarty was far more active as a politician in Sinn Fein, and later in the Senate, than Yeats ever was. Yeats realised how fragile a thing this inherited glory of the rich was; and that the classicism of which Gogarty made so much was no defence against the Asiatic hordes of chaos. He answers Gogarty's classicism with lines of complete finality :

> Odour of blood when Christ was slain
> Made all Platonic tolerance vain,
> And vain all Doric discipline.[25]

Ireland, where the odour of blood when Cuchulain was killed had made tolerance and discipline vain for Ireland. So Yeats thought, and this belief lay behind the sombre themes of his later poetry.

But these views do not, perhaps, fully represent the reality. In Cork during the year of the Civil War, Edith Somerville was turning over the same theme of the destruction of the Big House for her last major novel, *The Big House at Inver*, which was to be published in 1925. Meanwhile at Bowen's Court, Elizabeth Bowen's family suffered the visitation of Republican raiders. That summer of 1922 the old house was occupied by a force of seventy retreating Republicans, who mined the walls and the driveway in case they were suddenly attacked by National troops.

Having done this [she writes in *Bowen's Court*], and seen that it was good, they rested. If the house had never had more numerous, it had never had quieter visitors. Even prejudice allows they behaved like lambs. The young men—they were mostly very young men—were very tired. The bedding was gone from the few beds; the leaders lay on the springs, the others lay on the floor—there was much floor, for the house had now many empty rooms. Outside the rows of windows, the summer of 1922 droned on—and evidently the summer glare was too strong, for soon many windows were shuttered up. When the men woke up, they read. They were great readers, and especially they were attracted by the works of Kipling: a complete set of these, in flexible scarlet leather, with gilt elephants' heads, had been given to Mary, and were available. Once a day the men rose from their floors and beds and went through the country on reconnaissance.[26]

So much for the rapacious louts of Gogarty's imagination: the odour of blood had not, it seems, quite made *all* tolerance vain. When they went, this band of Republicans left Bowen's Court still standing, as others left Coole and Castle Townshend. The friendly houses stood; elsewhere the arrogance and pride of the gentry were their own downfall.

This band at Bowen's Court, so pathetic in their youth, were typical of the small groups scattered in retreat across Munster at the end of 1922. The Free State made much out of the Republican outrages, so it is as well to remember that in the final days of the drive through Munster, the National Forces were themselves responsible for fearful atrocities in Kerry. Prisoners were tied together and blown up with landmines, or shot down in groups. But these were the final bitter moments of the Civil War which had begun with such high devotion and idealism on the part of those young men quietly reading Kipling.

The Civil War had begun with the shelling of the Four Courts by the Free State army. Of this event, another of those young men, who lived through the war, Frank O'Connor, writes in his memoirs:

Rory O'Connor and Liam Mellows in seizing the Four Courts were merely echoing Patrick Pearse and the seizure of the Post Office, and Michael Collins, who could so easily have starved them out with a few pickets, imitated the English pattern by blasting the Four Courts with borrowed artillery. And what neither group saw was that every word we said, every act we committed, was a destruction of the improvisation and we were bringing about a new Establishment of the Church and the State in which imagination would play no part, and young men and women would emigrate to the ends of the earth, not because the country was poor, but because it was mediocre.[27]

The land's imagination, in Yeats's phrase, was not to be satisfied. The Civil War resulted in a devitalising sterility of spirit which encouraged neither prosperity nor writers. All this came about through the circumstances of the Republican defeat.

Both Frank O'Connor and Sean O'Faolain were involved in the embattled last days of the Munster Republic. For both of them this was the only fighting they ever saw, and it played an important part in moulding them as writers.

O'Connor, in hindsight, admits seeing everything through a veil of literature. Retreating with Erskine Childers, he strutted around preposterously armed to impress the country girl he had fallen in love with on the farm where they were based. 'Unfortunately I had no notion of how to make love to her, because she appeared to me through a veil of characters from books I had read. Most of the time she was Maryanka from *The Cossacks*!' But, as he admits, Tolstoy was not then in Childers's line. At a dance the night before a big ambush, the boys of the flying column stacked their rifles in the corner and danced *The Walls of Limerick*. An American correspondent remarked to Childers how like the eve of Waterloo it was—'There was a sound of revelry by night'—to which the writer anxiously replied, fearing the man's mind was wandering to other things, that he 'would be sure not to forget an article about "Women in the War".'

O'Connor was still caught in the ties of literature when Erskine Childers was executed.

I was in a house on the Wellington Road the morning I read of his execution, and I wrote the date over Whitman's lines on the death of Lincoln in a copy of *Leaves of Grass* that I always carried with me at the time—'Hushed Be the Camps Today'. Like everything else I did at the time, it reeked of literature, and yet when I recite the lines to myself today, all the emotion comes back and I know it was not all literature.[28]

The situation was too serious merely to be that.

O'Connor began to come to his senses when, later in the year, a 'job' was suggested, shooting unarmed National Army soldiers out courting in the streets of Cork. He refused.

It was clear to me that we were all going mad, and yet I could see no way out. The imagination seems to paralyse not only the critical faculties but the ability to act upon the most ordinary instinct of self-preservation. I could be obstinate enough when it came to killing unarmed soldiers and girls because this was a basic violation of the imaginative concept of life, whether of boys' weeklies or the Irish sagas, but I could not detach myself from the political attitudes that gave rise to it. I was too completely identified with them, and to have abandoned them would have meant abandoning faith in myself.[29]

O'Faolain also recalls in his own memoirs some of the incidents which O'Connor describes : the arrival of the Republicans, tired and defeated, at Macroom Castle; Erskine Childers at work on publicity; Dave Robinson, Childers's cousin, leading the raid on Inchageela, that nearly ended in tragic farce. After that episode, O'Faolain began to realise how pointless these activities and his own bomb-making all were. But it was only after months on the run in the wilds of west Cork, and after taking part in his one and only battle at Ballymakerra—a skirmish only—that he finally took the advice of a friendly priest and went home to Cork.

Later in his short stories 'The Bombshop' and 'Fugue', O'Faolain was to re-create these events of Civil War, just as Frank O'Connor was also to do in his own work. But there is a point worth emphasising. The material of 'Fugue'—which we have already looked at in an earlier chapter—derives from those days of flight in the autumn of 1922, yet in the story the author has his two young men in flight from the Black and

Tans. The same transposition of time is also true of 'Mid-summer Night Madness'. O'Connor in his stories does the same. One cannot help wondering whether these writers thought it was easier for their foreign readers to grasp what was happening in the Tan war than in the Civil War. Perhaps they felt the facts of war were the same, though on their own evidence the emotional flavour of the Civil War was gall in the mouth after the war with the British. The facts were altered and some of the truth may be jeopardised by such blurrings of historical reality. And it was this failure to face the facts of historical reality that made the aftermath of the Civil War such a difficult period. Writers did not help by blurring the events.

Undoubtedly it was a very grim historical reality they faced. 'The romantic improvisation was breaking down,' O'Connor writes, 'and the real killers were emerging'. Most of those involved in the fighting were amateur soldiers, rather than amateurs of war. Most but not all. Grim reality in the form of 'unfortunate incidents' was frequent. But the feeling of the period is not in the fiction of O'Connor or O'Faolain, but in the novels of Liam O'Flaherty. Reading the latter's fiction in the context of its creation, Yeats's lines come first to mind :

> The best lack all conviction, and the worst
> Are full of passionate intensity.[30]

That is the best phrase for some of O'Flaherty's writing : passionate intensity among the awful dregs of warfare.

His are the facts of the Civil War, rather than its elevated theories. His short stories, especially, are lean and spare, the picked bones of the subject, concentrating on action, incident, moments of death, love, or despair, rendered with an almost primal innocence. Not that O'Flaherty himself is an innocent. As Frank O'Connor observes, 'his is a divided character, and his secondary personality blows up into outrageous, uproarious and sometimes absurd novels'. That is very just, but there is another side to the novels. Yeats, writing to his English friend Mrs Shakespeare (13 March 1927), urges her to read *The Informer* and *Mr Gilhooly* : 'I think they are great novels and too full of abounding natural life to be terrible despite their subjects. They are full of that tragic farce we have invented. I imagine that part of the desire for a censorship here is the desire to keep him out. He joyously *imagines* where Moore *constructs* and yet is more real than Moore.'[31] Though the remark about Moore is slightly snide (Yeats continuing his campaign against the novelist), this comparison is illuminating. Moore, of course, had set himself up as the great realist in the nineteenth-century sense; his solid sense of construction was the means towards the higher aims of his art. But Yeats the poet instinctively finds the imagination more congenial than any reality. Yeats's taste in novels was limited. He began *Ulysses* with admiration but went back to Trollope before he had finished it. He liked novels with an edge of wildness, like O'Flaherty's and Francis Stuart's, for theirs was 'an Ireland the poets have imagined, terrible and gay'. It was also a narrow one. In the novels of Dublin life O'Flaherty limits himself to the soi-disant revolutionaries in shabby trench-coats and other social drop-outs caught up in their activities. For with the end of the Civil War, Donagh MacDonagh points out in a perceptive introduction to an American edition of *The Informer*, 'all that was left was the smudged fifth or sixth carbon copy of revolution, a body moving by instinct towards chaos, divided against itself, the mind groping towards release in action'.

Thus the ideals and aspirations of Pearse and Connolly were brought down to squalid little murders in back streets and the fantastic nightmares riding through O'Flaherty's fiction. Yeats, writing again to Mrs Shakespeare (April 1933), says of the situation in Ireland, that no sooner does a politician come to power than he begins to seek unpopularity (at this time de Valera was clamping down on the IRA who had helped him into power the year before).

It is the cult of sacrifice planted in the nation by the executions of 1916. Read O'Flaherty's novel *The Martyr*, a book forbidden by our censor, and very mad in the end, but powerful and curious as an attack upon the cult. I asked a high government official once if he could describe the head of the IRA. He began 'That is so-and-so who has [a] cult of suffering and is always putting himself in the position where he will be persecuted'.[32]

Yeats was right in seeing this cult as going back to Pearse. Writing in 'The Coming Revolution', a tract well known in IRA circles, Pearse claimed that 'bloodshed is a cleansing and sanctifying thing, and the nation which regards it as the final horror has lost its manhood'. A high sentiment indeed, but it follows the extraordinary statement that Pearse would like 'to see any and every body of Irish citizens armed. We must accustom ourselves to the thought of arms, to the sight of arms, to the use of arms. We may make mistakes at the beginning and shoot the wrong people. . . .' The time had now come when the Irish people were more than accustomed to the sight of arms and when the wrong people were being shot as a matter of policy.

In Pearse's imagination this cleansing sacrifice, by which he plunged the country into the revolution, was modelled on a curious amalgam of Cuchulain and Christ. At the end of his play *The Singer* this idea becomes explicit, when MacDara goes out to fight the foreigner and dies against great odds : 'One man can free a people as one Man redeemed the world. I will take no pike, I will go into battle with my bare hands. I will stand up before the Gall as Christ hung naked before men on a tree.'[33] The unavoidable end of all this occurs at the 'very mad' conclusion of *The Martyr*. The Republican Crosbie, a religious maniac, is crucified and burned on the cross by Tyson the National Army officer. Tyson is a proto-fascist, who wishes someone to die for Ireland to purge the nation and make it strong. The novel ends with the fiery cross plunging into a lake : not perhaps the most sanctifying of events. O'Flaherty has attempted to suggest some of the underlying characteristics of the Civil War and their perverted nature, but the madness of his own creation overwhelms the competence of his writing which descends to a lower level than the tragic farce intended.

These flaws are not so apparent in *The Informer* (1925). Because of the film version this is the best known of his novels, which makes the author disdain it.

In Dublin [during 1924] I worked out the plan of *The Informer*, determined it should be a sort of high-brow detective story and its style based on the technique of the cinema. It should have all the appearances of a realistic novel and yet the material should have hardly any connection with real life. I would treat my readers as a mob orator treats his audience and toy with their emotions, making them finally pity a character whom they began by considering a monster.[34]

The novel was completed the next year in England, and turned out just as planned. When it was published it had just the intended effect.

> The literary critics, almost to a man, hailed it as a brilliant piece of work and talked pompously about having at last been given the inside knowledge of the Irish revolution and the secret organisations that has brought it about. This amused me intensely, as whatever 'facts' were used in the book were taken from happenings in a Saxon town, during the sporadic Communist insurrection of about nineteen twenty-two or three. My trick had succeeded and those who had paid little attention to my previous work, much of it vastly superior from the point of view of literature to *The Informer*, now hailed me as a writer of considerable importance.[35]

Now O'Flaherty is being perhaps a little too off-hand here. One Irish critic, mainly because the 'Revolutionary Organisation' in the book is a communist one, says the book 'reminds one of a bad German or Polish novel'. However, O'Flaherty's own political experience in the first days of the Civil War was with just such a group led by Roddie Connolly, and through the novel there runs a personal experience of terror and its effects.

The treatment of ex-soldiers of the Great War by Dubliners is clearly based on what happened to the author on his first return in 1920. The shooting of the secretary of the Farmers' Union for which McPhillip is wanted, sounds as if it were based on some actual incident during the suppression of the soviets, but this is not certain. There is, however, no doubt that the atmosphere of the underworld is authentic.

Those familiar with John Ford's film version of *The Informer* will be surprised to find that the novel is set later than the Tan war, and that Gypo betrays his friend for the price of a night's lodging, not a passage to America as in the film. By altering the period and the motivation, much of the point of the Civil War, on which the novel depends, is lost on the screen. When he is called before the council of the Revolutionary Organisation, Gypo is able to invent a story and manages to escape. He is now loose with his Judas money, in flight from the gunmen. He goes to ground in the Monto, but is captured again in a brothel. Escaping once more, he takes refuge with Katie Fox, the kindhearted whore. But again he is traced. Shot down outside a church, he staggers down the aisle to fall by McPhillip's mother at her prayers. With his last breath he asks for her forgiveness, which she gives.

All very sensational and melodramatic. But when one American reviewer described the novel as 'a libel on the people of Ireland' he was being sentimental. 'The men and women Mr O'Flaherty describes to us', he went on, 'are not martyrs in a noble cause. They are merely a collection of brutes.' Just so. By 1924 O'Flaherty's cynicism about martyrs in a noble cause was justified. The noble cause had killed more people than was ever justified, and had produced a sentimental chauvinism. His brutes are the other side of a true story which many would rather have forgotten.

But not all his characters are brutes or ghouls or cowards. In the brothel Gypo hides with Connemara Maggie. Here is the rural character whom O'Flaherty loves completely—indeed the character around whom so much of the Irish literary revival had grown —'big-boned, red-faced, strong, handsome', a woman 'with her great soft eyes swollen and gentle like the eyes of a heifer'. She is another version of the now familiar Irish figure, another ox-eyed Juno. 'She busied herself tending to her man, just as if she had never left the purity of her Connemara hills and she were tending her husband after a hard day's work in the fields; instead of tending a casual lover in the sordid environment of a brothel'. A fresh wind from the Western world of *Spring Sowing* blows for a moment through the Dublin slums, mixing the stark realism with a touch of the romantic ideal.

Granted that O'Flaherty is at his best in that rural life, he does give a true account of the gratuitous violence of this period. McPhillip is wanted for a murder connected with the agrarian upheavals of rural Ireland. Gypo Nolan betrays his friend in an act so thoughtless that it would be hard to call it even greed. But in the rebel cause of Ireland, betrayal is the sin mortal and unforgivable against the people : unable to fight society any longer, the revolution fights itself. The avenging angel of the novel is Commandant Dan Gallagher, the gunman gone wrong. 'His brand of communism', the International is informed, 'is that type that appeals most to the Irish nature. It is a mixture of Roman Catholicism, Nationalism, Republicanism and Bolshevism'. He is a ruthless man, interested only in the satisfaction of a lust to kill, at war with the rest of his species. He *thinks*. He is the type that intrudes into the wholly personal tragedy of *Mr Gilhooly*, another novel Yeats admired. O'Flaherty describes the rise of those who make up this type in a passage in that book, seeing them as a reaction to the Black and Tans, but once their use was past, the government found it necessary to destroy them or they would have destroyed the state.

But the destruction of the state can only be achieved by killing individuals, and Gypo Nolan blundering through the Dublin slums, the implacable Gallagher searching him out, are such individuals. Gypo's death represents the final end of revolutionary politics when the revolution fails. Literature such as this, rather than politics, shows how history works itself out through individuals.

The course of political action was at an end; it now remained to see not only what kind of society had emerged from the revolution (if such it was) but also what sort of literature it would produce.

It would not certainly be of the old kind. Among the poems which he gathered into *The Wind Among the Reeds* in 1899, Yeats included a very strange and prophetic one called 'The Valley of the Black Pig'. In later editions he had to explain in a note what the poem was about.

All over Ireland there are prophecies of the coming rout of the enemies of Ireland, in a certain Valley of the Black Pig, and these prophecies are, no doubt, now, as they were in Fenian days, a political force. I have heard of one man who would not give any money to the Land League, because the Battle could not be until the close of the century; but, as a rule, periods of trouble bring prophecies of its near coming. A few years before my time, an old man who lived at Lissadell, in Sligo, used to fall down in a fit and rave out descriptions of the Battle; and a man in Sligo told me that it will be so great a battle that the horses shall go up to their fetlocks in blood and that their girths, when it is over, will rot from their bellies for lack of a hand to unbuckle them. If one reads Rhys' *Celtic Heathendom* by the light of Frazer's *Golden Bough*, and puts together what one finds there about the boar that killed Diarmuid, and the other old Celtic boars and sows, one sees that the battle is mythological, and that the Pig it is named from must be a type of cold and winter doing battle with summer or of death battling with life.[36]

> The dews drop slowly and dreams gather : unknown spears
> Suddenly hurtle before my dream-awakened eyes,
> And then the clash of fallen horsemen and the cries
> Of unknown perishing armies beat about my ears.[37]

Nothing could be more typical of the Yeatsian method and accomplishment than this poem and its explanatory note. From the strangest melange of mythological scraps, Yeats hammers out a strangely compelling vision of mystical warfare. This was the sort of intervention by the gods of which he often spoke in the 1890s, taking his own words more lightly than others took their ideas.

It was while hunting the slopes of Ben Bulben that Diarmuid was killed by the boar. And on those same slopes a less mythological battle took place during the Civil War. The Republican crew of an armoured car, who had tried to dismantle the local railway line, were surrounded by National forces and retreated to the mountains. The National forces closed in. When the six Republicans, armed with the Lewis gun from the armoured car, appeared on the crest of a hill they were shot down. One of the six was Bryan MacNeill, son of Eoin MacNeill, the founder of the Irish Volunteers. The bodies were brought down to Sligo, where a jury returned an open verdict. Three days later they were buried. There were no more soldiers' funerals in Sligo after that. The war was at an end.

The Winter of 'Twenty-Three

WRITERS AND THE END OF REVOLUTION

'You are all abstract fanatics', Sean O'Faolain was told by Eileen Gould, when they met again on her release from Cork Women's Prison. 'You are suffering, if you are suffering, not out of love of your fellow men but out of love of your own ruthless selves. Some morning you will wake up to find yourself standing in the Grand Parade behind green iron railings holding up the torch of liberty, not a man at all but a statue made of stone or lead.'[1] She was right, as the women often were, and in the end helped him escape such petrification of heart and body.

By this time O'Faolain had come to see himself as the last guardian of the Republic, 'a last redoubt of the minority's resistance to the majority'. In succession to Erskine Childers, he was still churning out publicity for the cause. But slowly the light came through: it was no use. In May 1923 it ended. Still on the run in rural Cork, he was out painting a tree when a boy brought him the news, as another had to Ernie O'Malley two years before.

'So it's all over?' the boy said. O'Faolain looked up at him coldly and said: 'As long as that tree stands the Republic stands.'

The boy turned away. 'So does my arse,' he said.

O'Faolain stayed till January 1924, working in Dublin for what was becoming a dream Republic. Then he got a letter from the Acting President of the Irish Republic thanking him for his services. He tore it in pieces and went home to Cork, a bitter and disillusioned young man.

It was to the same prison from which Eileen Gould was released that Frank O'Connor was taken after his arrest. His detention for him was a relief from responsibility, and as the danger of actually being executed passed, became in a strange way a sort of blessing. Yet while he was in that prison he saw a youth tortured: the Free State soldiers drove bayonets through his buttocks. A few days later the enfeebled boy was taken out and shot.* So this was what romanticism came down to: burnings, tortures, hopeless prayers, free whiskey for the firing squads.

After defeat, prison was the next bitter experience of many Republicans. Peadar O'Donnell was taken prisoner early on, after the fall of the Four Courts. He began writing to escape the bare walls of his cell. He found it stimulating, for human nature was great stuff. It had just two enemies in his experience: fear and poverty. Poverty, so familiar to him from his life in Donegal, was an enemy that he would fight in the years to come, during the Land Annuities Campaign, and in the councils of the IRA. Now, however, fear was the great enemy against which human nature was pitched. In gaol the opening scenes of *Storm* were written, the episodes for *The Knife* remembered, just to escape from the paralysis of fear.

O'Donnell also began to rethink his political situation. Early in *The Gates Flew Open*, his account of his prison experiences, there is a notable passage on Michael Collins. His death at Bealnablath had been greeted with joy by most of the imprisoned Republicans, but Dick Barrett, who had known Collins well, told O'Donnell that Collins merely intended the settlement as an aid towards his own assumption of power. He intended to operate 'a dark hand' and assassinate rivals as they appeared.

> From Barrett I got a picture of Collins that always made him a tragedy to me. Without any guidance except his own turbulent nationalism, with the weakness for intrigue and conspiracy that secret societies breed, he confused the conquest with the mere occupation of the country with British soldiers and the personal influence of the 'undesirables'. He failed to recognise that the military occupation was merely to make the imperial exploitation possible and so he guaranteed to safeguard the exploiting interests if the soldiers were withdrawn, without recognising that he was thus making himself a bailiff of the Conquest. He confused the bellowing of the group who were losing office with imperial resentment and he mistook the

*His name was William Healy: shot 13 March 1923.

cheering of the new throng of office-seekers with the tramp of the national masses returning into their inheritance.[2]

Whether this is a just appraisal of Collins—though from what we have seen, it comes close to being one, I think—it is quoted here because it gives some impression of Republican feelings about the intentions of the new state. If Collins—'with the outlook of a Fenian home ruler and the code of a tinker swapping donkeys'—was wrong-headed, were Republicans any cleverer? What were their intentions? Time had shown that for the most part they were little better. For many Republicans the goal of an undivided Republic of Ireland was enough, and social aims were of no interest.

To O'Donnell's credit, he shows us not the terrors of prison, but the experiences that made him a writer. For him 'this was not the end of a book, this defeat, but the end of a chapter'. The stubbornness that had maintained the idea of the Republic through the Civil War, 'must be collected and stated in new terms'. For him, as a novelist, this meant writing.

I know that I know the insides of the minds of the mass of the folk in rural Ireland : my thoughts are distilled out of their lives. Therefore, it is not my task to say anything new but to put words on what is in confused ferment in their minds. How would I say it? Write? I could try and I did : I wrote the scene where Charlie Doogan leans on a spade in *Islanders* and sees the gannet circle over the little dark patch where no cloud could be reflected. . . . If I could say their lives out loud to these remnants of the Irish of history until they would nod their heads and say 'this is us'. A powerful, vital folk they are but too blasted patient; muling along carrying manure on their backs, draining bogs, blasting stones, while out beyond was their inheritance.[3]

This new determination towards realism, to speak of life as it was, is yet tempered with a sense of idealism. This, I hope to show, is the dominating tone of the new Irish literature. The dreadful experiences of prison—the executions on 8 December 1922, of Liam Mellows, Dick Barrett, Rory O'Connor and Joe MacKelvey without trial as a reprisal for the death of two T.D.s; the judicial murder of Erskine Childers while in the jurisdiction of the courts; the long slow lingering deaths of the hunger strike begun late in 1923—these were incidents merely. They were not comparable to the new determination that grew in a handful of men to do something new, to try and grasp that heritage beyond the fields.

This was especially true of the young men who were to emerge as writers in the thirties. One of these was Francis Stuart. Though born in Australia in 1902, his childhood was spent in Ireland. He had joined the Republicans, and was captured in the Dublin streets after the fall of the Four Courts. He had 'lost' his Parabellum, but his captors provided him with a loaded gun to ensure his conviction. He was sent to Maryborough Prison, where the conditions were so bad that the prisoners set their hut on fire and were shot at by the guards.

In prison his friend Paddy Hunt described to him the execution he had witnessed in Dublin, when Joe Spooner and two others were shot in November 1922. This is the real end of all war :

They came out without hats and I noticed that Joe hadn't bothered to lace his boots all the way up. It must be funny putting on your boots and knowing you'll never take them off again. There was an officer with a gun in his hand walking beside them. It was very muddy in the yard. The other two boys had rosary beads hanging from their hands, but Joe had his hands in his pockets. When they came to the wall they turned round and the two boys put their beads over their heads so that they hung round their necks. Then they stood to attention but Joe kept his hands in his pockets and his shoulders hunched up. The sergeant said something to him and he shook his head. Then the sergeant stepped back and took the gun out of his holster. The firing squad was standing about fifteen paces away. When the officer gave the word they brought their rifles up to their shoulders. The two boys had their eyes shut and Joe was looking at the mud just in front of his boots. There were tears streaming down the face of one of the boys from under his shut eyelids. There was the rain on their faces too but I saw the tears. When the soldiers fired he put up his hands to his chest and tore at his coat as though he wanted to open it. He swayed forward without falling. His coat came open with the buttons ripped off and the blood ran down his hands. Then he fell on his knees with his head bowed over the other boy who had fallen sideways, his face in a pool. Joe had fallen back against the wall but his feet were still firm on the ground and he was choking with blood and spittle coming out of his mouth and his face turning dark. The other boy fell from his knees and the two boys lay across one another. The sergeant put his gun to the side of Joe's head and fired four or five shots into it. The side of his head was torn open, then he fell sideways with his shoulders slipping down along the wall.[4]

This clear and horrible account is the realism of the young, doing away with the rhetoric and the ideals, facing what it means to die at dawn for one's country. Though it was published in 1934, there are things that one cannot easily forget. By then Stuart claimed he was used to living on the side of lost causes; at twenty he was bitter and felt defeatist. 'Now [in 1934] I understand that the romantic, the inspiring, the lyrical will always be a lost cause in this dark age which is organised for businessmen and commerce.' It was a lesson he was lucky not to have to learn at dawn in another muddy yard.

Others were not so lucky in the Troubles, but with the exception of Thomas MacDonagh, there is no one whose death seems a tragic loss to literature. And even in his case, perhaps his fine talents as a poet and his sympathies as a critic would not have survived the Troubles without fading or turning bitter.

For those who did survive the fighting, the prison camps of the Free State were the first stage in coming to terms with the new reality. In a small, almost imagist poem by Thomas McGreevy called 'Autumn 1922', we are told:

> The sun burns out,
> The world withers
>
> And time grows afraid of the triumph of time.[5]

These few lines are explicitly about the failure of the revolution. In those terrible dark last days of the autumn and winter, it seemed that everything of value to the idealist was vanishing, burnt up and withered. But such a victory is costly to win, and even those who win must come to wonder if their triumph was worth it in the end.

Art's intention is always to rescue man's time, his life as lived, from the triumph of time. For this, words alone are certain good, to speak in such darkness is to be human. For many writers the serious practice of their art began in those prison camps. In contrast to the lines above, here are some written by Francis Stuart, dated Tintown Camp, May 1923:

> The rain in all its little peacefulness
> Falls into the bright sepulchre of earth
> At this full flow of spring-tide . . .
> . . . .
> Stars shed their light, Olympian, seasonless
> Upon earth's latest May, and bright no less
> Upon my heart's unearthly Italy.[6]

The sense of renewal here came, not through romantic poetry, but through the names Stuart sets over another poem in his small first volume of verse, most appropriately called *We Have Kept the Faith*, the names of the great Russian realists Gogol, Tolstoy, Dostoievsky, Turgenev and Chekhov. These were the writers the young men were reading, and their views of life became the touchstones of the new literature. Frank O'Connor wrote an essay on Turgenev in Irish for a national competition. Though he was to be heavily influenced in his early stories by the exotic romanticism of violence in the *Red Cavalry* stories of Isaac Babel, what finally emerges in his writing is much closer to these realists, more like a synthesis of the two streams which had flowed into the war, a union of Moore's realism and the romantic attitudes of Yeats. But it was a long time before the romantic edge was blunted, and a more satiric sharpness came to the stories of O'Connor and O'Faolain. O'Faolain, as we have seen, was reading Gogol and seeing Irish life in Turgenev's terms. O'Flaherty, uninfluenced by anyone, except his own vital sense of existence, beginning with *Spring Sowing*, in the untilled field, described life as he saw it.

The war had been a hard school. For some the camps were almost a university, the only one they would know. In cell blocks and camp huts classes were organised. Like the medieval monks

of Ireland in their remote monasteries, these civil prisoners cultivated learning. There were many remarkable people in those
cells and camps, among them the best minds in Ireland perhaps,
creative and intelligent. 'It was a joy to sit and talk with them',
O'Connor recalls of Gormanstown Camp, 'and feel I was back
with the sort of people who had really started the Revolution—
men who read books and discussed general ideas.'

O'Connor himself, in trying to teach Irish, discovered the
miracle of grammar. Some order was brought to his mind by
this, the idea of an object and an accusative case steadying the
emotional young man. Once grammar had brought order in, he
began 'to have doubts about many of the political ideas I had
held as gospel'. Coming to his senses, coming back to reality, was
a painful experience. It meant doing something he had never
done before, taking an unpopular stand without allies. He noticed
that Shelley and Meredith on death were quoted too frequently
in the camp papers. He took to inserting near them, whenever he
could, a line remembered from Goethe : 'You must be either the
hammer or the anvil'. Frank Gallagher, a great admirer of
Shelley and so an adherent of de Valera, gave the camp a lecture
on Erskine Childers which completely changed the quiet intellectual man that O'Connor had travelled with. He began to ponder
seriously, in the light of this romantic remaking of a complex
man, about the connections between Irish Nationalism and the
Romantic movement. Once that began, his political days were over.

His scrappy education completed itself with what he learnt
from the other prisoners. Sean T. O'Kelly lent him Anatole
France in French, and Sean MacEntee gave him Heine, and he
found that Corkery had been right when he told him that Heine
was the only poet for a man in prison. Then his essay in Irish
won the competition : literature was replacing politics. When the
hunger strike began he took no part in it. An article in the *Irish
Statesman* (which had begun to be published late in 1923) by
George Russell persuaded others to give it up, and another prime
piece of Shelleyan fantasy came to an end. The strike was called
off, and the relieved prisoners gorged themselves like pigs. The
romantic improvisation was over, yet years later O'Connor was
still to meet men whose lives had been bewildered by what had
overwhelmed them. He himself was to be haunted by the memory
of that young man he had seen tortured in Cork prison; on quiet

nights when he was reading after work in Pembroke Public Library, that ghost would enter, and his spirit would be shaken again by all the old fears and horrors.

In the mornings, Francis Stuart remembers from the last days in the camp on the Curragh, they would look out through the wire at the race horses he so paganly admired for their grace, out for the morning gallops.

> And far away climbing a small hill I saw a woman in a red dress and I watched her in astonishment, not having seen any-one but men for a long time. She seemed like an incredible invention of God that had just appeared on earth. If I had been close enough to see her face I should probably have turned away in disappointment.[7]

Even his romantic spirit was facing up to things as they were.

Now no one thought about anything but release. All illusions had dropped away. At Gormanstown, where O'Connor was, they had a foretaste of what this meant.

> Two audacious girls, realising that the fighting was over and that no one was likely to kill them in cold blood, walked coolly across the fields one evening from the main road and stood outside the wire by the Limerick hut, asking for some relative. In their high tower the sentries fumed, waiting for the military policeman to take the girls away. In no time a crowd gathered, and two or three men who knew the girls stood on the grass bank overlooking the wire and talked to them. The rest of us stood or sat around in complete silence. It was years since some of the group had heard a woman's voice. Nobody cracked a dirty joke; if anyone had, I think he might have been torn asunder. This was sex in its purest form, sex as God may perhaps have intended it to be—a completion of human experience, unearthly in its beauty and staggering in its triviality. 'Mother said to ask did you get the cake. Jerry Deignan's sister asked to be remembered to you.'[8]

To speak in darkness is human : and out of the darkness came a woman's voice. Men had had enough, it seemed, of the inventions of the intellect, of the Nation and the State, and wished to return to the inventions of God. The Civil War resulted for some in a devitalising sterility of spirit, which was not encouraging. Yet in the transition from war to peace there was a passing from abstractions back to humane concerns. This passage of feeling is caught in the vignette above and in a story of the period by O'Faolain called, suitably, 'The Patriot'.

Norah and Bernard return to Youghal for their honeymoon. They had first seen each other there three years before when Bernard had been taken there by his teacher Edward Bradley. It was in Youghal also, during the troubles, that Norah had spoken first to Bradley. Bradley is the patriot, modelled suitably on Daniel Corkery, the great teacher hoping to be a lasting influence on his pupils.

During the Civil War Bernard sides with the Irregulars. The last days of the Revolution have been reached at last. The Republican Army is broken, undisciplined, the men given to drinking and stealing. Bernard's capture when it comes is almost a relief. After his release he and Norah marry. And on their first day in Youghal they see a notice :

SINN FEIN ABU
A Public Meeting Will Be Addressed
by Edward Bradley

They go to it. His eloquence is as rich as ever, despite his whitening hair. They do not introduce themselves.

Later, in their hotel bedroom, Bernard standing by the window in the dark hears the sound of a fast approaching car :

Over his shoulder he could see her pale body in the dim light, but where he stood by the window with one hand raised to draw down the blind his eyes fell on the passing car. He saw the white hair of their orator friend, the old bachelor, the patriot, driving out of the town into the country and the dark night. The hedges would race past him; the rabbits skip before his headlights on the road; the moths in the cool wind would fly around his flushed face and trembling hands. But the wind would not for many miles cool the passion in him to which he had given his life.

'Bernard,' she whispered again, and her voice trembled a little. He drew the blind down slowly. The lamp shadowed the framework of the window on it. Slowly he turned to where she gleamed even in the dark.[9]

PART THREE: REACTION

Above him there was now only the sky—the lofty sky, not clear yet still immeasurably lofty, with grey clouds creeping softly across it. 'How quiet, peaceful and solemn! Quite different from when I was running,' thought Prince Andrei. 'Quite different from us running and shouting and fighting. Not at all like the gunner and the Frenchman dragging the mop from one another with frightened, frantic faces. How differently do those clouds float across that lofty, limitless sky! How was it I did not see that sky before? And how happy I am to have found it at last!'

Tolstoy : *War and Peace*

After Aughrim's Great Disaster
LIFE AND LITERATURE IN THE
FREE STATE

By the spring of 1923 the Civil War was over. The government
of the Free State was in control everywhere; the Republican
forces were dead, in prison or on the run. So on 23 May 1923
de Valera addressed himself to the IRA:

> Soldiers of Liberty! Legion of the Rearguard! The Republic
> can no longer be defended successfully by your arms. Further
> sacrifices on your part would now be in vain, and the con-
> tinuance of the struggle in arms unwise in the national interest.
> Military victory must be allowed to rest for the moment with
> those who have destroyed the Republic.[1]

To his followers these were noble, patriotic words, the last words
of a great cause, a last gesture of rhetoric to the old ideal of the
Irish Republic. And many who heard them were content, like
Bernard in O'Faolain's story, turning in the darkness to his wife,
to go home to more humane affairs.

The aftermath of the Civil War, the first decade or so of the
new state, was a period of political and social adjustment. With
the restoration of public order 'after the rebels were scattered and
bate' as the old ballad about Aughrim's great disaster put it, a
way back to political and social stability had to be found. When
de Valera came to power in the election of 1932 in an orderly
transfer of authority, democracy could clearly be seen to have
triumphed over conspiracy. The stability of the country was no
small achievement for the rulers of the Free State.

Yet for many of the writers whose lives we have been following through the events of the revolution, the atmosphere of the
new state was inimical to literature. In the next three chapters
we will explore the feelings of the older generation associated
with Yeats and the work of the younger writers who emerged

after the Civil War. In this chapter we will survey rapidly the politics and society of the new state, with its puritan outlook and increasingly clerical nature. This survey is of necessity perfunctory, for it is difficult to catch the full flavour of the period in a few pages. Then in the writings of Daniel Corkery, whom we have already met as the mentor of Sean O'Faolain and Frank O'Connor, we will examine an apologist for the way of life which the new state, especially after the advent of de Valera, claimed to cherish and which many Irish writers rejected.

The governments of both William Cosgrave and de Valera were conservative on economic matters. The Free State government had a free trade policy which was successful for the first few years of the state, but the coming of the world-wide economic depression in 1929 made the isolationist and protectionist ideas of de Valera attractive to the small farmers who at that time bulked large in the population. Self-government brought few real solutions, and Ireland remained beset with social problems. Emigration which had been a great drain on the resources of the country continued at a high rate during this time, and increased under de Valera. Families were still large, though the marriage age remained later than in other European countries. Irish life became increasingly bleak up to the beginning of the Second World War, and many people would have admitted that the country's problems could no longer be blamed on the British.

Not everything was bleak however. The Shannon hydroelectric scheme (begun in 1925) which led to the gradual electrification of rural Ireland by the Electricity Supply Board (set up in 1927), brought about the transformation of Irish life by electric light, mechanisation and radio (the state station began broadcasting in 1926). This was one bright feature. Electricity brought the promise of a better life for everyone and of new industries which would keep the people at home.*

Yet agriculture remained the major industry. Irish farms were small, Irish farmers inefficient. Agrarian difficulties had caused political unrest and it was this which brought de Valera to power in 1932. By then he had broken with the Republicans in Sinn Fein and had formed his own conservative party. He was a man with a vision of Ireland who would not be defeated. In 1927 he

*A promise largely unfulfilled until after de Valera retired from politics, and there was a reversal of government policy under Sean Lemass.

and his new party Fianna Fail were forced by a new law to take
their seats in the Dail. They refused the Oath of Allegiance to the
King of Ireland. De Valera said it was an 'empty formula'. There
were critics who wondered why he had not been able to see it that
way in 1922, and so prevented the blood-bath of the Civil War.

Others feared his radical rhetoric, but once in power de Valera
proved to be quite conservative. His main interest was in dis-
mantling the last remnants of British authority over the Free
State. In 1937 a majority of the people were persuaded to accept
his new Constitution which included corporatist ideas with
Catholic overtones. The secular Free State was transformed into
the confessional state of Ireland. His critics thought with sour
irony that Ireland was no longer a free state in more ways than
one, what with censorship and divorce prohibited and the Catholic Church acknowledged to have a special constitutional place.

De Valera had achieved a democratic solution for his ideals.
There remained a very small minority of Republicans who wished
to continue the fight in the 'orthodox way' even after 1932.
They felt betrayed by de Valera. For them the secret Army
Council of the IRA was the only legitimate authority in Ireland :
the fantasy Republic lingered on.

And it was from among these still dissident Republicans that
the last blow of the Revolution had been struck. On a Sunday
morning ten years before, 10 July 1927, while walking to mass
in Booterstown, a quiet seaside suburb of Dublin, Kevin
O'Higgins was assassinated by a party of gunmen in a parked
car.

O'Higgins as Minister of Justice and Home Affairs in the
Cosgrave government, was the man popularly held responsible
for the executions of the seventy-seven Republicans during the
Civil War. Many saw him as the strongest personality in the
government, a potential leader of the state. After his murder
the government acted quickly. Arrests were made, but though
rumours were rife, no one was ever charged with his murder. The
government was, however, determined that this would be the last
incident of the kind. Proper parliamentary activity would have to
return, and the farce of the major opposition party abstaining
from the Dail would have to end. The next month new legislation forced de Valera and his party to take their seats.

An Ireland even more disillusioned and embittered than in

I

1891, had returned to parliamentary politics. The Dail was now a real assembly. But there was no one there now to equal de Valera in stature. The architects of the Free State, Griffith, Collins and O'Higgins, were all dead, two of them murdered by Republicans.

Constitutional rule was no longer a farce. Democracy was fully restored. Ireland had been saved from the gunmen at long last. O'Higgins's death was the last death of the Irish revolution.

The revolution had completely altered the political scene in Ireland. The social factors of pre-revolutionary Ireland had also been largely changed, except for the unique position of the Irish Catholic Church.

The social circle which had revolved around the Viceroy collapsed. With the coming of the Free State there was an exodus of Anglo-Irish people to England and the Colonies. Since then the Protestant community has slowly withered away: in 1900 one Dublin parish had 3,000 Anglicans, last year it had less than 300. The estates belonging to many of these people were bought up by the Land Commission and redistributed among small farmers. The country lost not only capital in this flight abroad, but also educated skills and managerial experience.

Those who remained had, at first, some difficulty in adjusting to the new conditions, their prejudices being replaced by another set. The pages of the society journal *Irish Life* reflected a desire to continue the old ways while accommodating the new: the wedding photographs now featured Free State officers. But *Irish Life* ceased publication in 1926, its readers and their way of life a thing of the past.

For the small farmers, many of whom came into possession of parts of the old estates, there was little improvement in life. Their small farms had ceased to be economic propositions at the turn of the century. What was wanted was a radical reorganisation of Irish rural life, the opportunity for which existed in reallocating the old estates entire. What was wanted was more large-scale cooperative ventures rather than more small farms. But the farmer, the family, and private property were sacred tenets of Irish life. There was no revolution on the Irish land.

The temper and tone of the new state did not really alter when de Valera came to power. The basic bourgeois assumptions about what was good for the country did not change. And very often what was good for the country was what the politicians thought might be acceptable to the Catholic hierarchy. There was no need for pressure by the Church on the Dail. Between de Valera and the Primate of Ireland there was an agreeable convergence of social ideas.

From a literary point of view, it is remarkable that though the peasants, workers and gentry all produced writers—one thinks of O'Donnell, O'Casey, Behan, Lord Dunsany—there seems to have been no one writing about the middle classes, the new masters of Ireland. Foxrock rather than Kerry was now the real Hidden Ireland.

A sombre greyness seemed to descend on Irish life. Yeats could have repeated his lines written in dejection in 1913 with equal bitterness in 1931 :

> Was it for this the wild geese spread
> The grey wing upon every tide;

and earlier in the same poem :

> What need you, being come to sense,
> But fumble in a greasy till
> And add the halfpence to the pence
> And prayer to shivering prayer, until
> You have dried the marrow from the bone?
> For men were born to pray and save.[2]

This last line might almost have been the motto of the new Ireland—from the writer's point of view of course. Like most members of the Revival who were of Protestant background, Yeats had an instinctive respect for the Catholic religion when it was a part of the life of the peasantry of the west of Ireland. But they did not care for the Church as an institution. And it was the Catholic Church, as guardian of the faith and morals of the vast majority of the people, that set the tone of the new Ireland and not, as they had once hoped, the poets. In Ireland the bishops were very much 'the unacknowledged legislators of mankind'.

The Church made no overt interference in public affairs. The ministers of all governments were of the same mind, and were prepared to introduce the required legislation without pressure. The laws relating to censorship, divorce and contraception were matters that particularly roused the opposition of Irish intellectuals.

These were major issues which concerned Irish writers, and writers remained a small but persistent liberal-minded minority. The larger issue, the creation of a Catholic confessional state by de Valera also concerned them. But their position in a closed society was difficult.

The interior life of Irish Catholicism was hermetical and this was reflected by Irish writers. The popular religion was a closed world of the heart and soul, in which the privations of Matt Talbot, the apparitions at Knock and the miracles at Templemore and Kerrytown were a few examples. For many Irish Catholics, 1932 was one of the great occasions of their lives, when the Eucharistic Congress was held in Dublin. Half a million people attended the final mass held in the Phoenix Park. Nothing was more appropriate than that this great religious pageant should be attended by all the rituals of the state.

This enthusiastic atmosphere was not congenial to many artists. For the first few years of the Free State many of these, such as Russell, Yeats and Gogarty, were active in public life. But gradually there was a withdrawal from public life by Irish writers and a growing feeling of isolation.

The Ireland which de Valera cherished was given memorable expression in the speech quoted earlier. He was speaking from the heart, a heart that had found its greatest happiness in the warming love of childhood among the small farmers of Bruree in Limerick. This was not a vision of Irish life that was totally rejected by Irish writers, for Peadar O'Donnell, Liam O'Flaherty and Sean O'Faolain all draw upon it in their early novels. But the whole-hearted apologist for that vision, and for the cultural attitudes of de Valera's Ireland, was Daniel Corkery. By now, however, he was writing not as a creative artist, but as a literary critic.

In the election of 1932 de Valera represented to the people an ideal which had lain behind the ideas of the other leaders of his generation. When Daniel Corkery wrote the book which appeared in 1931 as *Synge and Anglo-Irish Literature*, he was writing a cultural polemic on behalf of that ideal. He was defending what his young protégés were by then abandoning, disillusioned as they were by the Civil War.

At that time Corkery was known not only for his activities as a language revivalist and a Republican, but also as the author of *The Hidden Ireland,* published in 1925. The earlier book had made a great impression and the title came to stand for the whole submerged world of the Gael under British domination in the eighteenth century. The Ireland of that date was only too easily seen, by Yeats for instance, as Georgian Ireland, the Ireland of Burke, Berkeley and Swift. Corkery in what he subtitled 'a Study of Gaelic Munster in the Eighteenth Century' pointed out that there was a genuine Gaelic culture which found expression in the poetry of that province.

Corkery, largely conditioned by the Irish revival, drew many of his historical ideas from Father Dineen, whose editions of the Munster poets were then the standard ones. Corkery saw the themes of nationality, religion and rebellion which had dominated his own life as the chief features of the poets of the earlier period. For him these men were oppressed peasants speaking out against the tyranny of British rule.

Yet this was not the case, as L.M. Cullen points out in a re-assessment of the whole concept of 'the hidden Ireland'. The poets Corkery discusses, far from being peasants, were professionals, writing mainly for a group of prosperous Catholic landowners and cattle ranchers. Their verse reflects the life of 'hard riding country gentlemen' as much as anything later written by Anglo-Irish writers about their class. These poets looked backward to a royalist restoration, rather than forward to a republican revolution. The concept of a hidden Ireland rests on 'a misreading of certain significant features of the period, and on certain assumptions flowing from his reading of the poetry, in part from the character of the national revival'. Cullen's conclusion might stand as a judgment on others in the Revival besides Corkery:

His Hidden Ireland simplifies Irish history, putting it in a simple context of land resettlement, oppression and resentment with predictable and stereotyped relationships and situations flowing from it. It also impoverished Irish nationality and the sense of identity, seeing it in the context of settlement and oppression, and not in the rich, complex and varied stream of identity and racial consciousness heightened in the course of centuries of Anglo-Irish relations.[3]

Corkery wished perhaps to rewrite Irish history, to remake the Irish character as revealed by Merriman and Synge, for instance, into something closer to his own. But in doing this, he denied all that was vital, creative, vigorous and joyous in Irish literature. He is important not for the truth of what he says, but because he is seemingly so popular and influential. (Both of the books referred to here have been through many recent printings in paperback editions.)

Continually Corkery does what some politicians do. He reduces the complexities of life to a simple pattern. This appeals to those who share his viewpoint, but does little to reveal the truth. The simple pattern, merely because it is simple, cannot resemble 'the complexities of blood and mire' which life and history really are.

The Hidden Ireland seems to have been written as a direct reaction to the Free State, so very different from the new nation that the Republicans had dreamed of. His thesis was a deliberate rejection of the idea of Irish culture which Yeats was trying to build up, that the virtues of the Gaelic had passed over into English and were the marrow in the bone of modern Irish literature.

Corkery, as a cultural isolationist, did not believe this. His new book continued the attack begun on modern Irish writing in *The Hidden Ireland* by examining the particular example of John Synge. As Synge's main subject had been the Irish peasant, it was particularly important for Corkery to undermine his position as a writer. Indeed Corkery denied that anything written in English by Irish writers could in fact be called 'Irish literature': that term should properly be applied only to what was written in Gaelic; anything else was merely Anglo-Irish.

What concerns us here is not so much what Corkery thought about Synge, but his description of the position in Ireland of the Anglo-Irish writer. He gives a long list of authors, some thirty-six in all, who were not then resident in Ireland. (Yeats, incidentally, was not among them, as he spent most of the year in Ireland.) They were therefore expatriates writing for a foreign market, and could not claim to speak for the people of Ireland. The only writer who could 'speak for Ireland' was, it would seem, a Gaelic writer who lived in one of the remoter parishes of Connaught where he devoted himself to celebrating the hardships of life and the beauties of nature.

As an ideal of literature this was naïve, sentimental and dangerous. Naïve because it was a rejection of the modern world; sentimental because it imposed on Irish rural society values which were not really its own, but those of an unsettled urban man; dangerous because the exclusiveness and disdain for the work of the Revival encouraged others in their narrow-minded attitudes, thus making Ireland introverted and backward-looking in the twenties and thirties.

Corkery was a racist. His theories of Irish history and literature depend on the notion that there is an identifiable and purely Irish stock, 'the Irish of history', and that there was also an Anglo-Irish stock. He mistakes what were really class divisions for race divisions. No competent anthropologist looking at the make-up of the Irish people today would agree with such an idea. Even the Aran Islands and the Blaskets, often thought of sentimentally as the last bastions of the Irish of history, have mixed populations; one of the most celebrated writers on the Blaskets, Peig Sayers, had an East-Anglian name, and many of the Aran Islanders are the descendants of a Cromwellian garrison that 'went native'.

Purity in a racial sense does not then exist in Ireland. But for Corkery racial purity was synonymous with spiritual purity. The Irish in the views expressed in these two critical books became a pure-minded, gentle-hearted folk, bent upon religion and love of their neighbour. The experiences of Corkery's own life hardly supported this. Yet this dangerous racism about the Irish as a people had far-reaching consequences. It excludes, for instance, anyone of Protestant or Planter stock from being 'really Irish'. It creates and maintains divisions which might long ago have vanished from a modern society. Corkery's ideas as expressed in these books lie behind the political ideas of many concerning the place of Protestants in Irish society and politics.

Corkery's rejection, in favour of a nearly mythical Irish culture, of all writers in English as being 'un-Irish', confirmed the prejudices already widely held by many nationalists. This Irish culture needed to be protected, hence the introduction of censorship of books and films. Yet one has only to look at some of the books published around the same time as Corkery's by other Irish writers, banned as some of them were, to see how unjustified his claim was; this we will do in chapter fifteen.

Those writers whom Corkery called 'expatriates' might have preferred to call themselves 'exiles', for among them were George Moore, James Joyce and Gerald O'Donovan. There is a psychological difference between the two states of mind : an expatriate is someone who sloughs off his country like an old skin; an exile, on the other hand, however far he may go, has his country always on his mind. Stephen MacKenna, another of those listed by Corkery, said of Yeats (who was not), that if the poet were in the Gobi Desert and 'someone mentioned Ireland, he would be all aquiver'.

Exile has always been an honourable fate in Ireland. From Columcille to James Joyce, those who left for other countries, might have echoed the saint's words : 'my mind is upon Erin, upon all the little places where my people are'. This old sense of exile dominates the mood of Irish writing after the revolution, in both the young and the old.

14

Going into Exile (1)

DRAMA AND POETRY:
REALISTIC ROMANTICISM

A LANDMARK of this period was the publication in Paris in February 1922 of James Joyce's *Ulysses*. For Irish idealists this novel was a stunning refutation of what they believed. George Russell had optimistically expected a great idealistic flowering to follow on the victory of those heroic young men in dirty trench-coats. He was dismayed at this manifestation of complete realism. He had not wanted it from Joyce in 1904; and he did not want it now. Though Joyce had little direct influence on the Irish literary scene—young writers would visit him in Paris, talk to him in cafés, but fail to understand him, fail to follow up on the lead his books had given—the uncompromising sense of the real world in *Ulysses* was to be the dominant mode of the new Irish writing, which was reflecting the harsher realities of life in the new Ireland.

For the older generation, for O'Casey and Yeats himself, the case was different. All they could manage to do was to take up political stances, to try and influence opinion, and temper their romantic outlooks with some sense of the new realism.

Beginning with *The Shadow of a Gunman* in 1923, we have already looked at much of what began to appear, in the context of the events described. Other books and plays we will come to below, but the actual impact of this new writing ought to be looked at in the context of the new state.

In October 1923 Yeats was awarded the Nobel Prize for literature. The prize was rightly regarded as recognition not only of his own creative work, but also of the movement he had fostered. The terms of the Nobel Prize are that it shall reward the expression of idealism in literature. The first telegram that arrived during the celebrations that evening was from Joyce in

Paris; he was one writer who would never get the prize.

With the appearance of O'Casey, the prospects were pleasing that literature would flourish in the new state which it had helped into existence. Yeats realised that the general trend was away from his own ideal, and though he persisted in following his own creative instincts, he also did all that he could to encourage younger writers and to preserve an encouraging literary climate in Ireland. When the Tailtenn Games were revived in 1924, awards were made, in the ancient Irish fashion, to both athletes and poets. Stephen MacKenna refused a medal for his monumental translation of Plotinus on political grounds. The poetry medal went to Francis Stuart for *We Have Kept the Faith*, and he had the ineffable pleasure of being crowned by Yeats with a laurel wreath.

In 1924 Liam O'Flaherty's first volume of stories came out. *Spring Sowing* was a deceptively simple yet realistic set of observations of life in the west of Ireland. Work had begun again on the untilled field. It was as if the revival were starting off again.

With the cheek that young writers need to survive, O'Flaherty then published an attack on Yeats and all the revival had stood for. Yeats was most interested to meet him. O'Flaherty blushed on leaving when the poet remarked that 'It is nice of all you famous young men to call on an old man like me.'

Famous young men were indeed common enough. George Russell was then publishing the first stories and translations of Frank O'Connor and Sean O'Faolain in the *Irish Statesman* (as *The Irish Homestead* was now called, with a suggestive change of emphasis), a journal which attempted to impart a civilised standard to the public life of the Free State.

This alliance of the old poets and the young gunmen, as Yeats fondly imagined them to be, was a necessary one. Remembering the beauty of the young Con Markievicz, Yeats wrote:

> The innocent and the beautiful
> Have no enemy but time . . .[1]

A nice thought on his part, but this was not so in the Ireland of the 1920s. A narrow ideal of Catholic conscience was being brought to bear upon public morals, and this narrowing down of views would affect both the young and the old.

In May 1923, less than a month before the end of the Civil

War, a Censorship of Films Act was quickly passed 'to protect the youth of the country'. Speaking in the Senate on an amendment that school-children should be allowed into cinemas only in parties supervised by teachers (in most cases this would mean a religious), Yeats remarked scornfully that the Senate 'could leave the arts, superior and inferior, to the general conscience of mankind'. This the government had no intention of doing. The amendment was defeated, but the bill became law. It is perhaps significant that films, always in Ireland the most popular form of entertainment, should have been among the first objects of legislative attention. The coming of the cinema, as Liam O'Leary remarks, had opened up Irish society to foreign ideas; censorship was an attempt to close it off again.

This act was the beginning of a reactionary movement. Though much of their youthful idealism had vanished in the Civil War, enough remained for young writers to be optimistic about what might be done in the new state. How mistaken they were is shown by the *cause célèbre* of the small literary paper *Tomorrow*.

A group of young friends, Francis Stuart, Con Leventhal and Cecil Salkeld, decided to bring out a paper in which they and their contemporaries could publish their work and discuss the topics of the day. Yeats was enthusiastic about the scheme, and after suggesting that they should found their editorial policy on the doctrine of the immortality of the soul ('most bishops and bad writers being obviously atheists'), he wrote them an editorial which appeared in the first issue over their names. He had hopes of 'a most admirable row' and there was one. It was not over his paradoxical editorial, but over a mischievous story by Lennox Robinson about a simpleminded country girl raped by a tramp, who comes to think she is carrying the Son of God. Yeats contributed an early version of 'Leda and the Swan' in which a similar theme received a somewhat more elevated and distinguished treatment.

The paper may have been founded on the doctrine of the soul's immortality, but it foundered on the Immaculate Conception. The printer refused to print the material for the next issue and asked for changes. The paper was eventually printed in Manchester and published from Maud Gonne's house. The little paper was discussed and denounced, and there were more serious consequences. The admirable row that followed—what Lady

Gregory tartly called 'a storm in a chalice'—caused the resignation of Robinson from his position as secretary of the Carnegie
Trust. After the second issue the paper folded.

The scandal created by *Tomorrow* was a sharp indication of
which way the current of opinion was moving. It recalled the
'souls for gold' controversy over *The Countess Cathleen,* except
that now those who were offended were in a position to influence
relevant legislation. The new establishment had no intention to
leave the arts, superior or inferior, to the general conscience as
Yeats wished. Conscience was indeed considerably less valued by
them than obedience to authority.

A manifestation of this was the introduction in 1925 of a bill
to prohibit legislation for divorce in the Free State. In the Senate
Yeats made this the occasion for an impassioned defence, not of
the liberal ethic as some might have expected, but of the minority
rights of the Anglo-Irish Protestant community with which his
whole imagination was more and more involved.

> I am proud to consider myself a typical member of that
> minority. We against whom you have done this thing are no
> petty people. We are one of the great stocks of Europe. We
> are the people of Burke; we are the people of Grattan; we are
> the people of Swift, the people of Emmet, the people of Parnell.
> We have created the most of the modern literature of this
> country. We have created the best of its political intelligence.[2]

This was a fine reactionary stand, flying in the face of the
revolution.

But his speech was not all sectarian invective. He pointed out,
how rightly events have shown, that such legislation, inspired by
Catholic dogma, would eventually stand in the way of a united
Ireland, as the people of Ulster could not be expected to give up
what civil rights they had under British law. Then speaking over
the heads of the protesting senators to the younger generation
outside the house, he told them that the victory of narrow
opinion would not last, and was not worth their bothering about.
It was like an iceberg in warm water, and when the iceberg
melted Ireland would be a more tolerant country. He invoked
the examples of O'Connell and Parnell as men of irregular lives
of whom the country was still proud. He sat down amid further
cries of outrage from his fellow senators.

Having thus provided his young Catholic friends with a literary creed of a suitably reactionary kind; and having so splendidly defended what Burke himself would have called 'his little platoon', Yeats turned next to that prime source of Irish identity, the Gaelic language.

Gaelic had become in the minds of pious nationalists the language of a pure-minded and chaste Ireland. It had also become a compulsory subject in all Irish schools. This was the informing ideal of Daniel Corkery when writing *The Hidden Ireland*, in which the exuberant Brian Merriman, whom I have used as a touchstone of the genuine in Irish literature, is casually dismissed in favour of more settled imaginations. Yeats felt that this was not the true nature of the language at all, and in 1926 he wrote an introduction to a new translation of *The Midnight Court* made by his young friend Arland Ussher.

'This, vital, extravagant, immoral and preposterous poem', Yeats calls it and points out that though 'so characteristically Gaelic and medieval' it was actually inspired by Swift's *Cadenus and Vanessa*, 'read perhaps in some country gentleman's library'. For the classical allusions of Swift, Merriman had substituted the living fairy mythology of Clare. In the rhythm of classical verse he had contained the passions of the Feakle peasantry. Yeats concludes:

> Certainly it is not possible to read his verses without being shocked and horrified as city dwellers were perhaps shocked and horrified at the free speech and buffoonery of some traditional festival.[3]

Surely there is an echo here of the shock and horror with which Dublin greeted the free speech and buffoonery of Synge's plays, a memory of the Puck Fair at Kilorglin in Kerry which Synge had described in one of his essays, where licence once a year celebrated the crowning of a goat? Yet Yeats finds Standish O'Grady's opinion that *The Midnight Court* is the best poem written in Gaelic to be extravagant praise, though he feels that had the political circumstances been different Merriman 'might have founded a modern Gaelic literature'.

Yeats's intention here was clearly subversive, as had been his editorial in *Tomorrow* and his speech on divorce. He was attempting to acquire Merriman for his own Anglo-Irish tradition, to add him to Swift, Burke and Berkeley as a Protestant who just happened to write in Gaelic, an Irishman of the first rank.

The political situation which had isolated Merriman, that of an Ireland subservient to a foreign nation, had now been altered. Yeats seems to be suggesting to contemporary writers in Gaelic that Brian Merriman and *The Midnight Court* might be their best model, their source of a new subject, if they wished to establish a modern Gaelic literature. This was not to be. A later translation of *The Midnight Court* by Frank O'Connor was banned in 1945.

With such opinions and activities it is not surprising that Yeats and his associates should have come under attack from clerical sources; the *Catholic Bulletin* made a speciality of attacks on the 'pagan' Yeats and what it delicately called 'the sewage school'. Inevitably such attitudes were soon enshrined in the law of the state.

After film censorship, a move to introduce censorship of books had been resisted by Kevin O'Higgins while he was Minister of Justice. He and other members of the government were aware of the real merits of modern literature. Desmond FitzGerald, then Minister of Propaganda, who had been a friend of Ezra Pound in his Kensington days, had wanted to forward to the Nobel Prize Committee the name of James Joyce for *Ulysses*. Their sentiments were not common however; indeed the style of Desmond Fitz-Gerald was a particular bugbear of some Republicans.

After O'Higgins's murder, with almost indecent haste the government rushed through the Censorship of Publications Act in 1928. This enabled the banning by a board not only of publications considered obscene and indecent, but also of any work advocating or explaining birth control or abortion. This clause was scornfully attacked by Oliver Gogarty in the Senate : 'the men of Ireland must find another way of loving God than by hating women'. It was not until 1935 that the new government of de Valera got around to banning the importation and sale of contraceptives themselves under a section of the Criminal Law Amendment Act. On this occasion a veiled reference by Gogarty to the possible uses of the salad oil on the dining table was lost on his audience : cotton soaked in oil had been a common contraceptive in Victorian times.

In 1928, when the censorship bill came up in the Senate,

Yeats was no longer a Senator, so he published in *The Spectator* what would have been his speech against the bill. Censorship was, he thought, the one subject that might unite the otherwise politically divided writers. He remarked that a Christian Brother had denounced as obscene the medieval Cherry Tree carol which he had come across in a school book. This was the sort of mentality that was demanding censorship, from a fear of the present day. Yeats underlined this in his article :

> They do not understand that you cannot unscramble eggs, that every country passing out of automatism passes through demoralisation, and that it has no choice but to go on into intelligence. I know from plays rejected by the Abbey Theatre that the idealist political movement has after achieving its purpose, collapsed and left the popular mind to its own lawless vulgarity. Fortunately, the old movement created four or five permanent talents.[4]

The bill became law with results which are familiar. The censors worked with zeal, if not with lawless vulgarity, and ended by banning the books of every writer in Ireland of any distinction, and many of the most important writers of modern times, including Catholics. Not merely literary works, but also scientific and social books were banned. As well as cutting ordinary people off from the intellectual currents of the modern world, the censorship made the country a mockery in the eyes of the civilised world. But the Irish had turned inwards, and the people did not care what the world thought about them or anything else.

By the four or five talents which he referred to so casually, Yeats probably meant himself, Synge, Lady Gregory, George Russell, and Sean O'Casey. In coupling the collapse of the idealist movement with plays rejected by the Abbey, he brings to mind the case of *The Silver Tassie* in 1928. In this affair we can see something of the situation of drama after the revolution.

Just as Synge had been the great dramatist of the decade before the revolution, so O'Casey was the dramatist of the aftermath. As play followed play through the early twenties, each with a greater showing of his talent, it seemed again that the old days had returned. But they had not. And the difference between Synge and O'Casey may suggest why this was so.

O'Casey's first play *The Shadow of a Gunman*, produced in
1923, was well received, being only slightly critical of the nationalist ideal. *Juno and the Paycock* followed in 1925 and that too
was a success, for the pathetic tragedy and the rich comedy
covered his attack from the critics. O'Casey realised he had not
written about the Rising, and his third play was intended to be
a *drama à thèse* constructed around the happenings of Easter
Week and the impact on the people of the Dublin slums.

Controversy greeted the first production of *The Plough and
the Stars* in 1926. Hostile critics of the play have been laughed at
for their want of sense; but in truth, they were quite right. They
complained that O'Casey was mocking the nationalist ideal. And
so he was. But they were wrong in saying that he had no regard
for those who died in the fight. It is clear from the play that he
feels deeply the pity of their loss, even when he sees their ideals
as dangerous. Mrs Hanna Sheehy-Skeffington was particularly
outraged by the play; though she later modified her opinion of
the author when O'Casey's tribute to her murdered husband was
brought to her attention. This incident shows that very often the
extreme nationalists acted with little thought or consideration.
The swift rhetoric of denunciation came all too easily to them
now, and that perhaps is why they were becoming ineffective.

'The admirable row' generated by the play gave Yeats another
opportunity—the first since the *Playboy* riots in 1907—for a
histrionic display, again from the stage of the Abbey. 'You have
disgraced yourselves again,' he told the protesters, 'you have
rocked the cradle of another man of genius.' The dispute flowed
over in a more literary form into the columns of *The Irish Statesman*, where the play was attacked from another quarter by
younger writers such as F.R. Higgins, Liam O'Flaherty and
Austin Clarke. Higgins felt that O'Casey lacked the sincerity of a
true artist; that his play should have set people to destroying the
slums of Dublin and not the Abbey Theatre. Clarke, writing
from London, was also severe: 'Several writers of the new Irish
school believe that Mr O'Casey's work is a crude exploitation of
our poorer people in an Anglo-Irish tradition that is now mori-
bund'—clearly he had not seen the play and did not know what
he was writing about.

The wife of Kevin O'Higgins was less critical, but felt that
'O'Casey has missed the soul of the insurrection—a simple people's

sublime act of faith in themselves and their right to nationhood'. She also thought that the introduction of the Tricolour into the public house scene hurt aesthetically. Indeed this was unlikely to have happened in real life, she said, for the national flag was always given into the charge of some man of good character who would respect it and would not bring it into the presence of a whore.

Such comments as these are nice examples of the sentimental indulgence settling over the Rising and which were beginning to hide the real motives of Pearse and Connolly behind patriotic platitudes. One can understand the opinions of the writers, who were after all trying to remake Irish literature in the wake of the Civil War and shake off the dominance of Yeats. But the opinions of Mrs O'Higgins, and her description of a foolhardy indulgence in violence by oath-bound members of a secret society 'as a simple people's sublime act of faith' comes very near to nonsense. Such pompous cant and sentimental nonsense outraged O'Casey. He decided to move to England to escape from such people and such an atmosphere. And it was from England that he sent his next play *The Silver Tassie* to the Abbey. He was greatly surprised when the directors of the theatre rejected the play in the spring of 1928. Annoyed by what he regarded as high-handed treatment, O'Casey vowed to separate himself completely from the Abbey and from Ireland. He went to live in Devon, to become an exile. All writers are exiles of a kind, but a sense of exile does seem to permeate the slow dying fall of the Revival.

Curiously the reasons for the rejection of the play centred on the question of realism as against idealism. Yeats, who had begun the theatre with a desire for a high remote poetic theatre, now rejected the play because it was not realistic enough. One could not write about what one had not experienced, and O'Casey had not experienced the trenches of the Western Front, where part of the play was set. You must find a new theme, he said; but clearly he intended that new theme to be Irish; the Western Front would not do. Yeats rejected the play because, in its own way, it was dealing with a dreadful reality in a manner other than the merely realistic. Like many of his fellow countrymen, Yeats tended to forget how many Irishmen had served in the trenches, how for them that was the central experience of their lives. O'Casey had not forgotten. But Yeats's opinion carried the Abbey board, some of whom had felt that the play should be produced anyway. After all, O'Casey had written three successes in a row; he had earned the right to experiment, the right to fail. And the Abbey was there to serve artistic and not commercial standards. But the theatre lost O'Casey to exile, where he continued to experiment, while the Abbey retrenched itself and grew dowdy.

O'Casey's plays were as shocking to the sensibilities of the nationalists as Synge's had once been. The row over the *Playboy* had centred on the portrayal of Irish character; with O'Casey it was Irish nationalism itself. Where Synge had written an anarchic pastoral, O'Casey was writing proletarian drama. As a socialist he felt that economic justice could not be achieved while England ruled Ireland, but that the sufferings involved in the struggle to throw off that rule, which the patriots grandly overlooked, had been very terrible.

This anti-heroic view contrasts with Yeats's. Yet Yeats, writing of one of Liam O'Flaherty's novels, speaks of 'that tragic farce we have invented'. It was just such tragic farce—the noisy party interrupted by the mourning mother—that disturbed some critics. But like the parricide condoned and admired in Synge's play, such contrasts were part of the careless pattern of Irish life. Synge and O'Casey disdained patriotic rhetoric and sentiment, for their art was 'a vision of reality'.

The socialist sympathies in Synge's imagination became quite explicit in O'Casey's life. The poverty he had known and the ravages of the war made him what he liked to call a Communist. Both were trying to find some political stance that would cover a loving concern with their own people, a stance divorced however from the squalid tactics of party hacks. O'Casey was thus no more a convinced Communist than he was a complete realist. O'Casey was a romantic humanist with a soft heart. His hero was not Parnell or Pearse but Jim Larkin :

> Here was a man who could put a flower in a vase on a table as well as a loaf of bread on the plate. Here, Sean thought, is the beginning of a broad and busy day, the leisurely evening, the calmer night.[5]

But Larkin had failed to take advantage of the revolution in Ireland, and Irish independence was barely able to keep the loaf of bread on the plate let alone put flowers on the table.

Whatever it brought to Ireland, the new peace after the Civil War was unfortunate for O'Casey's art. It was the beginning of the leisurely evening. He had written his first plays out of his own unhappiness. Dissatisfied with the Abbey and Ireland, he found happiness with his wife and family in Devon. The plays he wrote there, however interesting as dramatic pieces, were not made of the same rich pulsating stuff of life as the first three had been. Made into a dramatist by years of hard labour, when he relaxed at last, the tension went. In slippered contemplation, his greatness declined with his violence, just as Yeats had imagined that luxury sapped the necessary violence of civilisation in his poem on ancestral houses.

Yeats himself did not seek a refuge outside Ireland, but for him there was also a sense of exile in the new Ireland. O'Casey settled down in Devon : Yeats departed in imagination for Byzantium. He had now, in his own words, woken from the common dream, the political idealism of the last decades. Was there to be nothing for him now but dissipation and despair?

By now it was clear to him that the Free State would not be the ideal polity of his dreams. There was in his own mind an essential link between his politics and his poetry. The old politics with which his earliest inspiration was bound up, were done with; the present ones were unwelcoming; was there perhaps hope of some new political movement, and so of a new poetry?

The last decades of his life were for Yeats not only years of extraordinary poetry, but also of extraordinary politics. Where O'Casey had moved towards Communism, Yeats moved towards Fascism. It is one of those mysteries of art that the brutal fantasies of Fascism were more productive for the poet, than the broad humanity of Communism were for the dramatist.

In a note to his poem 'Leda and the Swan', contributed to *The Dial* in June 1924, Yeats wrote :

I wrote Leda and the Swan because the editor of a political review asked me for a poem. I thought, 'After the individualist demagogic movement, founded by Hobbes and popularised by the Encyclopaedists and the French Revolution, we have a soil so exhausted that it cannot grow that crop again for centuries'. Then I thought, 'Nothing is now possible but some movement from above preceded by some violent enunciation'.

My fancy began to play with Leda and the Swan for metaphor, and I began this poem; but as I wrote, bird and lady took possession of the scene that all the politics went out of it, and my friend tells me that his 'conservative readers would have misunderstood the poem'.

The rather staid readers of Russell's *Irish Statesman* would certainly have been surprised. When Yeats's peculiar vision of that 'violent enunciation' had originally appeared in *Tomorrow* it had caused misunderstanding enough.

> A shudder in the loins engenders there
> The broken wall, the burning roof and towers
> And Agamemnon dead.
>   Being so caught up,
> So mastered by the brute blood of the air,
> Did she put on his knowledge with his power
> Before the indifferent beak could let her drop?[6]

Though it may seem perverse to some to regard such a passionate poem as political, Yeats did not think so. To the politically minded all things are political, and Yeats was politically minded. The intervention of Zeus harks back to the sudden appearance of Manannan in the moment of crisis of which Yeats had spoken in that speech of 1904. The Celtic gods had returned to Ireland at Pearse's invocation in 1916, and had brought with them 'The broken wall, the burning roof and towers/ And Agamemnon dead'. Now in this poem he explores a related image. But between the speech and the poem Yeats had become an admirer of Nietzsche. That sentimental socialism derived from William Morris had now completely gone. It was replaced by an admiration of fierceness, brutality, force; of men like O'Higgins and later de Valera, capable of imposing their will to power over the masses.

From such gods there was no salvation. The knowledge that Leda may have put on as a consequence of her violent rape leads on to the twins she bears, and eventually to the fall of Troy. In the system of historical cycles which Yeats had outlined in *A Vision* in 1925, the past is seen as eventually repeating itself. Troy was a potent symbol; for Yeats had in mind the burning of other roofs more recently and other broken Irish walls, and the possibility of yet another revolution.

'Among School Children' may also be seen as a political poem. We may picture the public figure of Senator Yeats passing down well-ordered ranks of desks, and all the while dreaming of a Ledean body, of Helen in her beauty, which suggests that image of life and imagination:

> O chestnut tree, great-rooted blossomer,
> Are you the leaf, the blossom or the bole?
> O body swayed to music, O brightening glance,
> How can we know the dancer from the dance?[7]

This ideal of the completed person, the child trained up to perfection of mind and body, is a political ideal. It implies, for Ireland at least, an attitude to life which was not encouraged in a Catholic state.

As a politician Yeats was a conservative, dedicated to the ideal of cultivated unity, of government by the educated, the intelligent, and the strong-willed. In his mind Kevin O'Higgins represented such authoritarian rule in Ireland. Then he was murdered. The night before, while Yeats was out walking with his wife, she had seen a phantom car, and when they had stepped inside their own door again, both heard bursts of music and of voices singing together. At the High Mass during the O'Higgins funeral which he had attended with the Senate, Yeats recognised what they had heard. 'Just before the elevation of the host, [the choir] sang in just such short bursts of song'. This was the *Dies Irae*. He wondered whether this clairvoyant warning was really a sort of participation in the 'race-process'.

> Had we seen more [he wrote to Mrs Shakespeare] he might have been saved, for recent evidence seems to show that these things are fate unless foreseen by clairvoyance and so brought within the range of free-will. A French man of science thinks that we all—including murderers and victims—will and create the future. I would bring in the dead.[8]

It was not everyone who had such an elevated theory of history, not everyone who could have found in O'Higgins's death a theme of redeeming sacrifice. With such extraordinary thoughts running in his imagination, Yeats began to work on a new series of poems 'partly driven to it by this murder', the last act of the Irish revolution.

Yeats, who had commemorated the deaths which had begun the revolution in 1916 with a series of important poems, now found that there was little left to say on this occasion. The poem he wrote immediately was called simply 'Death', and it might almost stand as a summary of the lessons of the revolution for Irish literature :

> Nor dread nor hope attend
> A dying animal;
> A man awaits his end
> Dreading and hoping all;
> Many times he died,
> Many times rose again.
> A great man in his pride
> Confronting murderous men
> Casts derision upon
> Supersession of breath;
> He knows death to the bone—
> Man has created death.[9]

Yeats was drawing to the close of his second term as a Senator, and decided against another term for reasons of health. The Public Man was one of his masks : who else could turn one of those shy chaste young girls at the Wexford Convent into a naked Ledean body? To the poet the daily events of the Senator's life were part of some great drama. He writes of the unclouded purity of the moon, contrasting it with the odour of blood on the ancestral stair of his castle at Ballylee.

> There, on blood-saturated ground, have stood
> Soldier, assassin, executioner,
> Whether for daily pittance or in blind fear
> Or out of abstract hatred, and shed blood,
> But could not cast a single jet thereon.[10]

There is in this contrast much of the tension of his later poetry, between the inspired products of the 'cold snows of a dream' and the real violence of life.

> And we that have shed none must gather there
> And clamour in drunken frenzy for the moon.[11]

This is a vision that carries us a very long way from O'Casey's view of life. Yeats was drifting off into his artificial paradise, to his sacred city of Byzantium.

O'Casey was more affected by another death in Dublin that month in 1927. On 15 July the Countess Markievicz died in the public ward of Sir Patrick Dunn's Hospital. There could have been no two deaths so different. As the senators in their silk hats, accompanied to the rear of the cortège by black-shirted Fascisti from Dublin's Italian community, followed O'Higgins's coffin, the other half of Dublin followed hers. Right and Left were burying the past. Eight lorry loads of flowers came after her, and also the divisions of the Free State, for the graveyard was crowded with soldiers under orders to prevent the traditional volley of respect from the IRA. De Valera made an oration, praising this departed friend of the poor who had put aside ease and station to serve the common people.

This was also a significant death for Yeats, though it did not call for peculiar apocalyptic meditations. If O'Higgins in his imagination had been a species of superman, Countess Markievicz brought back to him all the tangled emotions he felt for the landed gentry of his youth. He had written once of Constance's mind as 'a bitter abstract thing,/ Her thought some popular enmity'. Now in October 1927, in writing a poem in her memory he turns back in his own memory to their youth, recalling vividly

> The light of evening, Lissadell,
> Great windows, open to the south,
> Two girls in silk kimonos, both
> Beautiful, one a gazelle.[12]

What a different vision this from the blood-soaked dreams O'Higgins's death had conjured up.

Again he writes of Constance 'conspiring among the ignorant' to 'set the little streets upon the great'. Her sister Eva Gore-Booth, now grown old and gaunt, seemed also 'an image of such politics'. Yet in their youth together they had built their pleasure dome, that great gazebo of cultivated leisure, and now he wished them to bid him set time (the great devourer of all our passions) alight and burn it up. A beautiful and haunting image, yet how ironic it seems in retrospect for Yeats to claim

> The innocent and the beautiful
> Have no enemy but time;[13]

when the enemies of innocence and the haters of beauty were closing in like wolves around the pleasure gardens of Europe . . .

In the last chapter we will look at the poetry of Yeats's final years which deals with themes of the Irish revolution. Here something should be said about his politics in those years. Just as O'Casey in his exile moved towards Communism, becoming an uncritical admirer of Stalin, so Yeats in his spiritual exile at home in a country which was increasingly not for old men like him, moved towards Fascism.

He had been an early admirer of Mussolini and his brand of strong government. He was entranced by the rhetoric of will and power, as well as the anti-democratic aims of the movement. We even find him quoting Il Duce as early as 1924. By 1927 the Blackshirts themselves had appeared in Ireland. Yeats was not the only one to welcome the appearance of General O'Duffy's minions in 1932. This he saw as the new movement in politics he had been longing for since 1924.

O'Duffy was brought out one evening to visit Yeats by their mutual friend Captain Dermot MacManus. The general received a long lecture on the virtues of Italian Fascism, from which he came away little wiser. Yeats was right in feeling that the Blueshirts lacked the power of some informing philosophy. The old slogans of defending Christian civilisation and the need for strong government would not do when their opponent in power was de Valera, who believed in both. He had no difficulty in outmanoeuvring them. O'Duffy and the movement came apart, and the general took himself off to Spain with a small party of men to try and fight for Franco. After a brief inglorious hour, the coloured shirt went out of Irish politics. Such Continental movements did not have much appeal to a nation of individualists.

Yeats was disappointed. But not long after de Valera came to power and was seen not to be so dangerous as many had thought, Yeats came around to admiring him instead. Yet as the writers of the younger generation discovered, the new Ireland had but little interest in what concerned them.

It was fitting that the death of Kevin O'Higgins should have inspired both Yeats, the imaginative poet, and Liam O'Flaherty, one of the new realistic novelists, for it was between their two expressions of life that Irish literature hovered after the revolution —between, that is, Yeats's poem 'Death' :

A great man in his pride
Confronting murderous men
Casts derision upon
Supersession of breath;[14]

and O'Flaherty's novel *The Assassin*. Man had created death, could he now reinvent life?

Going into Exile (11)

THE NEW NOVEL: ROMANTIC REALISM

THE year 1932 was something of an *annus mirabilis* for Irish literature. Not only was this the year of the Eucharistic Congress, and the year that de Valera came to power, it was also a year remarkable for its new books.

Within nearly the same twelve months several important books by significant Irish authors appeared. First there was the new critical book by Daniel Corkery on Synge and the nature of Anglo-Irish literature. Then there were books by two older writers: *The Gates Flew Open* by Peadar O'Donnell; and *The Puritan* and *Skerret* by Liam O'Flaherty. And others by two newcomers: *Guests of the Nation* and *The Saint and Mary Kate* by Frank O'Connor, and *Midsummer Night Madness* by Sean O'Faolain. Francis Stuart published *Pigeon Irish,* and Michael Farrell began working on *Thy Tears Might Cease.* And finally there was the establishment of the Irish Academy of Letters, which was a last public effort on Yeats's part to protect what these writers were creating.

These books in their various ways illustrate very well the literary outcome of the Irish revolution. Those two streams of the Revival, Yeats's romanticism and Moore's realism, the thesis and antithesis of Irish literature, were transformed by the revolution. What emerged in the books of the younger writers was a peculiar synthesis of the two streams produced by the dialect of the revolution, a romantic realism, in which idealism was tinged with harsher overtones. This new literature was quite opposed to what Corkery seemed to be seeking in his critique. Before dealing with this synthesis and the writers who survived to develop it, I would first like to look at the career of one who failed, as failure is often as revealing as success, at the final years of Darrell Figgis.

Some details of his earlier life have already been outlined in chapter five. During the Troubles he was imprisoned twice, and was once nearly murdered in a ditch by a Tan officer. He was rescued at the last moment by the intervention of Colonel Maurice Moore, with whom he had worked on the Republican Land Commission. Figgis had also been a member of a committee looking into the potential industrial resources of the new state which the Dail had appointed, as well as having been Secretary of Sinn Fein in 1917.

After the Treaty he worked on drafting the constitution of the Free State, now regarded in the light of the 1937 constitution as a model of liberalism; and he published a small booklet explaining its origins and intentions. In the General Election of May 1922 he stood as an Independent for South Dublin, a middle-class constituency, after urging other Independents to oppose the Republicans wherever possible. His jaunty off-hand manner amused some : a news picture of the new deputies shows Figgis, hat at a rakish angle, cane in hand; the caption refers casually to his well-known nonchalance. Others disliked him, and it had been an eventful campaign : two Republicans had broken into his flat at gun-point one night and trimmed off half of his neat auburn beard.

He hoped for a ministry in the new government; but as Padraic Colum observed, he was not the sort of man to whom Free State ministries were given. He became involved in various dubious business ventures which came to nothing, including one to establish a casino in the Wicklow mountains. He now found himself isolated, a position not really new to him. 'A busy life had robbed from a wanderer whose time was mortgaged to necessity, the opportunity for other than the most casual of friendships even in his own city of Dublin,' he remarks in his memoirs.

His writing now became satirical. A new novel *The House of Success* was popular in 1922; it was about a peasant who comes into a fortune and the disasters that overtake him, and was seen as a satire on the new state. The next year he published, under a pseudonym, *The Return of the Hero*, a novel in which Ossian comes back to modern Ireland and holds the country up to ridicule and contempt. When it became known in Dublin that Figgis was in fact the author of the book everyone had been enjoying, Yeats remarked to a friend, 'Well, I suppose we'll have to admit Figgis as a literary man now.' Great hatred, little room . . .

This uneasy relationship with his country ended in tragedy. Figgis was an idealist of the type which the war had discredited. His new satirical mode was out of key with the attitudes both of the country and its writers. Neither his satires nor those of Eimar O'Duffy succeeded against the dominant realistic novels of the day, and are now quite forgotten.

Nor was his private life a success. In November 1924 his wife discovered he was having an affair with a dancing mistress named Rita North. She took a taxi out into the Dublin mountains and (after paying her fare) shot herself in the back seat. A few months later, when Padraic Colum during a visit to Dublin called on him, he found Figgis just as lonely as ever, working on a book about Blake's drawings. (This is still a valuable book incidentally, but also an indication of his bent of mind.) Figgis was hoping now for a seat in the Senate; and also, Colum later realised, hoping to marry again. However, he never got a Senate seat; and on 19 October 1925, his girl friend Rita died in a London hospital. The cause of death was peritonitis following an abortion. The couple in seeking the illegal operation had tried to hide their identity, and at the inquest Figgis made a poor showing as a witness. On 27 October he gassed himself in a Bloomsbury lodging house: too harsh a reality had finally destroyed the romantic idealist.[1]

This was a sordid, though tragic end for an Irish patriot. Like Gerald O'Donovan in an earlier generation, Figgis seems to have slipped completely through the sieve of his contemporaries' memories; Ernie O'Malley is about the only one to mention him. Figgis has never been forgiven his independence of mind, his atheism, or his suicide. It is worth while sketching out his career, partly because its features and its failures contrast so sharply with the success of others, and reveal the vindictive and petty side of Irish literary life. Figgis may well be a second- if not third-rate writer, but he does not deserve to be so completely forgotten. After all, it was he who bought the guns that started all the shooting. Perhaps he was lucky to die as he did, and not murdered at dawn by one of his own Mausers.

The romantic ideal of the Irish revival in the sense in which Figgis had tried to live it, would no longer do; nor was his satire an adequate response to the altered circumstances of the new Ireland.

A new approach was needed. What we find when we examine the books of the younger writers is that they all contain, not the complete realism of Joyce nor the more humane view of Moore, but a synthesis of what those realists had tried to do, along with something of the idealism which had gone into the making of the revolution. This new realism, for all that it drew from such familiar sources as rural life, war, or the difficulties of love, had a far harder edge to it now. The later work of Sean O'Casey and Yeats strives towards an art which was a mixture of a certain harsh realism with a heightened poeticism; *The Silver Tassie* and the Crazy Jane poems are examples. But with these older artists it is always their search for an ideal, either in Communism or Fascism, which dominates. With the younger writers the combination had different proportions: the idealism was there, but it was realism that dominated.

It was just this realism that many Irish people, and critics such as Corkery, found so distressing about the new writers. They seemed to dwell continually on the worst aspects of Irish life, and to have an inordinate interest in sex. Why could they not write about ordinary people the way Canon Sheehan or Lynn Doyle did? To us now it seems that this dislike of the new writers came from a fear of looking too closely into the patterns of Irish life, even into life itself. It was easier, especially after the Civil War, to let things be. And this was just what the young writers would not do. As well as writing fiction, they involved themselves in public life.

From them came a stream of critiques on what was wrong with Irish life. Peadar O'Donnell, for instance, as well as writing his moving novels of rural life, involved himself as actively in politics on the Left, as Yeats and Gogarty did on the Right. Liam O'Flaherty did not involve himself in politics beyond the escapade at the Rotunda, but found his own line. His *Life of Tim Healy* was a comic exercise in character assassination. Healy represented all that was most bitter and vindictive in the old post-Parnell politics that the revolution had been an escape from. Yet here he was installed as the first Governor-General of the Free State in the former Vice-Regal Lodge up in the Phoenix Park, which inevitably became known to Dublin wits as Uncle Tim's Cabin. He was personally a pleasant man, but he had a cruel and brutal public tongue. O'Flaherty took him apart with all the ready hatred of an Aran radical. In another small book, he did the same sort of hatchet job on the country itself. *A Tourist's Guide to Ireland* is a bitter little polemic, written with the savage anti-clericalism of the spoilt priest, which attacked the whole quality of Irish life as narrow and puritanical. Nor were the opinions of Sean O'Faolain and Frank O'Connor at a later date much different in content to these others.

Such polemics had ironical results. An O'Flaherty novel *The Puritan*, which satirised the state of mind that had introduced the censorship in Ireland, found itself banned. Neither did its story, closely based on an actual murder in Dublin of a whore called Honour Bright, help it much. Yeats attempted to have the ban lifted but failed; and it was his opinion that the censorship had been introduced from a desire to keep out writers like O'Flaherty.

Certainly Irish fiction suffered badly at the hands of the Censorship Board. Not that the books banned were always thought to be in any way outrageous or obscene outside Ireland. It was enough if even one short passage gave offence. A reference of a few words in Kate O'Brien's novel *The Land of Spices* to the sexual deviance of one character was enough to get an other-wise exemplary book banned. (A full account of the Board's activities during these years can be found in Michael Adam's book *Censorship, the Irish Experience*.)

What offended those who complained to the board was that such books discussed, as was only natural, aspects of life which no one in Ireland really cared to discuss. In those days, when censorship was still newsworthy, writers could suffer personally. Frank O'Connor was refused a hotel room because he was the in-famous author of a banned book. Sean O'Faolain felt hurt and insulted when *Midsummer Night Madness* was banned in 1932. Worse still, he was horrified by the public reaction in Ireland, where few could have known anything of the book's content. From the Cork command of the IRA he received a summons to appear before a court martial for insulting the Irish people. Not all his mail, or that of his wife or his mother in Cork was funny; one letter said : 'No detractor of Ireland's fair name must whine because we Irish want to clean our house after dirty little dogs like you have dropped your filth on our clean carpet, as a pup is whipped so shall you be.'[2] He felt the Irish people had now the quickness to take insult of the demoralised and insecure.

Irish laws and Irish attitudes effectively made the writer an outlaw in his own society : one did not have to leave the country to become an exile, there was also an internal state of exile. A writer's work was ever open to the irreversible decision of the law, which might prevent him speaking to his own people at all, though this was what Daniel Corkery felt he should do. When their own people were either unwilling or unable to hear them properly, writers could hardly be blamed for looking with an appraising eye to England and America, the great sin of Irish writers according to Corkery. To see why writers gave offence, and if there were real grounds for complaint, the books published in 1932 give some idea of their authors' attitudes.

They fall conveniently into pairs which can be related to the earlier phase of Irish realism. Liam O'Flaherty goes back to the George Moore of *The Untilled Field*, for *Spring Sowing* (and indeed O'Donnell's *Islanders*) takes up the exploration of Irish life where the earlier book left off. Except that now, as a measure of the revolution through which the country had passed, the authors were not landlords' sons but the sons of peasants.

Peadar O'Donnell's book that year was *The Gates Flew Open*, an account of his prison experiences after the fall of the Four Courts until he escaped from Kilmainham in 1924. Liam Mellows was a fellow prisoner and the book gives glimpses of him up to the day he was executed. This kind of book has a long tradition in Ireland, John Mitchel's *Jail Journal* being the most celebrated example. But though O'Donnell gives an absorbing account of prison life, of the alternations between fun and fear, it is still an account of men in an unnatural environment. To O'Donnell the community has always been as important as the role of the individual within it. This book was written to escape from the past. The Land Annuity campaign which was absorbing his political energies while the book was being written, was what he was concerned with at that time. Such political activity was the only way of saving the community he loved from total destruction. Though not in the same class as his novels, the book nevertheless speaks very directly out of the experience of many Irish people who had supported the lost cause.

O'Donnell's novels of Irish life are those of a natural communist; O'Flaherty's those of an intuitive anarchist. While *The*

Gates Flew Open, a completely political book, whose opinions were anathema to many, was (like the same author's novels) allowed to circulate freely, O'Flaherty's two novels were banned. *The Puritan*, being a morbid study of a murderous fanatic with an atheistic bent, naturally fell into disfavour. *Skerret*, a novel about the feud between a teacher and the local priest on Inismore (called Nara in the novel), is among the author's best books. Corkery would have approved of neither work. O'Flaherty deals nearly always with characters who depart quite widely from the normal. Yet there is no denying that O'Flaherty's view of life rises like a tree out of the soil from the western way of living. The gaiety, the easy violence, the tormented passions, while disturbing to the contemplative soul, are a part of our life which cannot be denied. There two writers were born and reared on Inismore and in northern Donegal; to claim they cannot speak for their people's experiences is almost to deny that right to anyone.

Corkery would have had difficulty denying either Frank O'Connor or Sean O'Faolain the right to their own visions of life. He had contributed himself a great deal to their early education, but the Civil War had been a more realistic and exacting master than the gentle old idealist had ever been. O'Connor's novel *The Saint and Mary Kate* was a study of obsessive religion and its relationship with sexuality: again a departure from the normal. It was banned. So too was *Midsummer Night Madness*, with the results mentioned above. Certainly these were both examples of realistic fiction, and it was their realism that got them banned. But they were both imbued with a romanticism which never existed in George Moore or Joyce, and which we also find in O'Donnell and O'Flaherty. All these writers have an exact eye and ear for their native material, yet behind the surface detail, there is a pervasive feeling of identification which can only be called romantic. This comes out especially in the descriptions of places, where the landscapes of Cork or Connaught become in a Wordsworthian way a reflection of the determination of their characters to survive.

The sense of a broken world (the title of one of O'Faolain's finest stories), the disillusioned sense of loss, which is found in O'Connor and O'Faolain, reminds one occasionally of Joyce though without the bitterness. Their concern with the Catholic

faith, loneliness and love, relates them more closely to O'Donovan, a writer both were aware of from their earliest days. There
is nothing immoral or indecent in the work of either writer. Their
consciences are profoundly Irish and Catholic, tempered with an
easy-going tolerance of humanity. Indeed the tendency of both
towards the preaching that is found in their non-fiction is an
indication of a great moral concern with their people. That their
books were banned is an indication of the moral failings of censorship. Early and late both felt that they were victimised.
O'Faolain failed to obtain the professorship of English at Cork
University, for which he was well qualified, being passed over
for the more acceptable figure of Daniel Corkery, whom he felt
had no qualifications for the position. That was in 1930. In 1952
Frank O'Connor wrote an article for the American magazine
Holiday about Ireland, which was mildly angry about aspects of
life here. Mothers killing their illegitimate babies loomed large in
his imagination at the time, for he had seen a dozen girls
sentenced one morning in Green Street Court. He made a mistake in writing too freely for a foreign magazine, and claimed
that for years afterwards the official Irish News Agency was trying to discredit him because of this. Early and late the puppies
were whipped.

The moral concerns of the earlier writers are more profoundly
studied in the novels of Francis Stuart and the single great work
of Michael Farrell. Here the romantic element becomes much
stronger, especially in Stuart, so much so that one wonders if he
may be called a realist at all. A brooding on the mysteries of life
and religion connects Stuart with the Moore of *The Brook Kerith*,
though his searchings into the instinctive sources of violence
which characterise so many of his books was derived in large part
from his experiences in the Civil War. The parallel with D.H.
Lawrence is often striking. Stuart's *Pigeon Irish*, which appeared
in 1932, is an extraordinary book with an enormous reputation
among those who read it when it was first published—like many
of his books it is long since out of print. It is pervaded with the
writer's instinct for the current of life, the real life of the individual perhaps, that lies beneath the surface of everyday events.
The plot of the novel about a future war in Ireland draws on his
personal experiences of the Civil War, but the theme of love
is treated in a manner far removed from the tradition of the

K

Irish novel. By setting the novel in the future Stuart is able to concentrate on his own peculiar interests : violence, sex and religion. In themselves these were enough to gain him the attention of the censor, yet one is struck continually by the religious note in his work. The social world is sloughed off as ephemeral, and we are introduced to an intensely private world of experience and vision.

Stuart's later career was also to lead him far from Ireland. He was lecturing in Berlin during the war and involved his wife Iseult with a German agent dropped on Ireland during the war. His alleged involvement with Fascism has damaged his reputation, but Stuart was not a politician and he alone of Irish novelists has followed in his fiction the fortunes of modern Europe. His interest in blood and instinct suggests that the very irrationality of Fascism must have made an intrinsic appeal to his nature. He lived through the fall of Berlin, was interned and saw the postwar desolation of Germany. His concern in his later novels with such events, central to the experience of our century, gives him a unique if hard-won place in Irish literature.

Here again we can also see that Corkery's standards are just not adequate to encompass some sorts of experience, that his definition of literature is too narrow to have any value in the modern world.

In contrast to the horrors of ravaged Europe, the haunted bourgeois world of O'Donovan is re-created with greater skill and insight by Michael Farrell. Behind O'Donovan's novels there is a liberal attitude which implies the possibility of reforming all that he sees wrong with the world around him. After the experiences of the war, which are described in detail in their effect on various kinds of people, Farrell could see no such possibility. Martin Reilly at the close of the novel has become a man at last, but in the process all that he loved has been torn away from him and destroyed. He has nothing left to live for except his own sense of existence. Though Farrell, who left Ireland to work in the Congo for several years, might also have been called an expatriate, his colonial experiences found no place in his imagination. His life had been formed, his character created, as had those of the other writers we have been discussing, by the experiences of war in Ireland. He lived only for the past and for his love of it. His great novel was fashioned slowly, as Joyce would have approved, in silence, exile, cunning, no one allowed to read it until he was close to death.

What Yeats called 'the images of thirty years' are provided by the literature we have been examining in the course of this book. Yet even here we can see how, after the Civil War, the writers themselves were reactionaries. None of those listed here were in any sense avant garde. They wrote outside of the modern movements of literature on the Continent. Their acceptance of conventional literary forms relates them to the reactionary outcome of the revolution itself. In neither society nor literature was there a seeking for new forms : the old would do. Like the country itself, they were ready to accept, as Joyce was not, as Beckett was not, the accepted forms of society and literature. They created something Irish which yet remained in the English literary tradition, as the state itself remains a democracy of English origin.

The mention of Joyce and Beckett should remind us that in the Dublin of the 1930s there were a few who were not a part of Yeats's Academy of Irish Letters. Outside this establishment were some like Hyde and Corkery who would move back towards a simpler way of life expressed in a Gaelic literature; and others who were self-consciously modern.

The Abbey seemed to dominate the theatre, yet there were small rival companies run by Lord Longford and his wife, and by Hilton Edwards and Mícheál Mac Liammoir. These were concerned, as Edward Martyn had once been, to bring to Dublin not only plays in Irish but also the best of the modern European drama. They tried to keep before Dublin audiences examples of what was happening abroad. And it was as an admirer of Ernst Toller, that Denis Johnston made his mark in the theatre with his avant-garde plays *The Old Lady Says 'No'!* and *The Moon in the Yellow River*. The first of these began a reappraisal of feelings about literature and revolution which was to continue, in the second, with an examination of the clash of the old with the modern in the shape of a German engineer and the local people near a hydroelectric scheme. These were dramatic examples which vigorously rejected everything to do with the Revival and the Revolution.

In poetry much the same was true. Thomas McGreevy, though he had fought in the troubles, wrote imagist poetry which related to nothing in the revival tradition. Denis Devlin and his friend

Brian Coffey were largely influenced, not by the Yeats they avoided, but by foreign poets such as St John Perse. They lived in European rather than Irish literature.

This rejection and renewal took the strangest shapes, the strangest of all appearing on the eve of the new war in Europe. At University College Dublin, Brian O'Nolan had been one of the well-known wits of the debating society, but he was also an accomplished scholar and linguist. The learning was lightly worn; his translations from the Irish which brilliantly reproduced the effects of the originals, never received the admiration they deserved. These distinctions all combined with a comic genius to produce *At-Swim-Two-Birds* which he wrote under the name Flann O'Brien. This 'novel' took the Gaelic tradition which Corkery had hallowed and stood it on its head. From a real and living knowledge of the language, Flann O'Brien invented a fiction which showed that such a source, which seemed to have run dry, could in the hands of a genius produce what was at once completely Irish, yet completely and outrageously modern. In Paris one old hand recognised in the book 'a real comic talent'. O'Brien was a collector of Irish clichés. *An Beal Bocht* (now translated as *The Poor Mouth*) demolished with loving hatred all those popular peasant biographies which the Blaskets produced between the wars: how else could one parody such books except in Irish? The cover by Sean O'Sullivan satirised the image of those same peasants as they had appeared in Irish art. What, one wonders, did Daniel Corkery make of Flann O'Brien?

These young members of the avant garde—a description which O'Brien would have sniffed at—were able to escape from the historical pressure of the Civil War. It did not really concern them; the gun was just another cliché. Denis Devlin put it all away from a generation in *The Tomb of Michael Collins*. Their slightly older contemporaries could not escape. 'Strayed revellers from the Yeatsian feast' was Frank O'Connor's description of their plight.

As young men, to recall a phrase of O'Faolain's, they had looked on the face of death, and it had unfitted them for the long humiliation of life. Their lives and their writing have ever since been at heart a continued protest against a reality which still betrays those ideals they fought for in their youth. In the heart of the country they love, they have become permanent exiles.

Two more events of the literary life are worth noting. In 1930, after a libel action which drained the meagre resources of the paper, *The Irish Statesman* was forced to close. (Horace Plunkett who had founded it and done so much for Irish agriculture had gone to England some time before.) It is no exaggeration to claim that nothing took its place, not even *The Bell* which Sean O'Faolain and Peadar O'Donnell edited from 1940 to 1954. George Russell's wife died the same year, and he decided to go and live in England. After a tour of the United States, his health gave way and, almost alone in the world, he died of cancer in a Bournemouth nursing home in 1932.

Exile, actual and spiritual, was claiming the Irish Revival. Russell dying in England, O'Casey in Devon, Moore in Ebury Street, Joyce in Paris, Yeats 'sailing to Byzantium'. These were the heart of the Revival and it could not long outlast them. The Irish Academy of Letters which Yeats and Shaw established in 1932 was intended to gather into it the best of the Irish writers young and old, so that they might have, along the lines of the French Academy, some public body which could speak for them with authority and protect their interests.

Yet even this effort at respectability was attacked : a great rally was organised by Father Gannon S.J. to oppose this new manifestation of Yeats's 'paganism'. The setting up of the Academy was the end of the Irish Revival : it did not really last till the deaths of Yeats and Joyce. For the few Irish people who gave any thought to the question, the pious enunciations about the Irish genius which Daniel Corkery set forth in his books, were the real voice of Ireland—the acceptable voice that is, because it raised no uneasy thoughts about the Ireland in the making. Peasants and the Irish language, all that they stood for was acceptable, so long as one was not required to do anything about them. So the peasants emigrated and the language died away. Was Yeats in his old age conscious of this failure to remake the country as he and his friends in the Revival, as Pearse and Connolly in the Revolution, had wanted so long ago? Failure?

> Fail, and that history turns into rubbish,
> All that great past to a trouble of fools.[3]

A hard verdict on a generation of Irish life and achievement. Yet all was not failure, certainly not in the life of Yeats himself and his brother Jack the painter. Their personal salvation of Irish history we will now turn to consider last of all.

16

The Images of Thirty Years

THE REVOLUTION
IN MEMORY AND IMAGINATION

THE imagination creates from memories of life and history those images which become either art or literature. Those prime images of Irish life which had been so important to the Revival, what Yeats called 'those images of thirty years', are provided by his own poetry and by the paintings of Jack B. Yeats, the greatest maker of Irish images. The finest achievements of the Irish Revival are to be found in the poetry and paintings of the Yeats brothers.

There is one painting by Jack Yeats, begun in 1925 but finished only in 1927, which can be associated with the final years of the Irish revolution and with the murder of Kevin O'Higgins. Jack Yeats would never have painted a direct depiction of such an event, but only a commentary on it or an interpretation of it. The picture is *Romeo and Juliet, the Last Act*, and it can be related to his brother's poem 'Death'.

A theatre audience along the lower edge and right-hand side sit watching the scene where Juliet, waking to find Romeo dead, kills herself and dies by his side. The dominant tone of the picture is a moonlit blue, a sombre colour which expresses the cathartic effect of the scene. For those who have seen it, the painting says a great deal about the last act of the Irish revolution. The state divided against itself, involves, implicates and finally destroys the love and life of two young people. Jack Yeats had an intensely literary mind. His pictures with their allusive titles often leave the viewer with the difficulty of working out in his own imagination the full implications of his paintings.

It is surprising that though they both shared in their old age a hard-won heroic style, W.B. Yeats seems to have thought little enough of his brother's work. Perhaps this may be because his myopia (so obvious in his own few paintings) prevented him from actually 'seeing' the pictures. He remarked once in a letter to Lady Gregory that Jack's new work is 'very strange and beautiful in a wild way' and that 'Joyce says he and Jack have the same method'. That piece of art criticism had been brought back to him from Paris by Thomas McGreevy, an early admirer of Jack's later style. Joyce owned one of Yeats's earlier paintings of the river Liffey, and McGreevy had been prattling about it one day : Joyce finally remarked acidly that 'there are great silences in that painting, McGreevy'. Then he made the remark about the painter and he having similar methods. This was perceptive of Joyce, whose taste in painting was limited. They both share a completely modern manner, difficult to penetrate, rich in allusions, yet basically made from the commonest of everyday events, epiphanies as Joyce called them, raised to the level of myths. Indeed both of them pass in their work from an exact, almost documentary observation of local life through a rich elaboration of that life to end at a level of dream-haunted imagination. Between *Dubliners* and *Quay Worker's Home*, *Ulysses* and *The Liffey Swim*, *Finnegans Wake* and *The Expected* there is the sharing of a common vision.

Joyce and some of the younger writers of the thirties understood what Jack Yeats was trying to do. But for many others the paintings remained merely 'very strange and beautiful in a wild way' and nothing more. What divided the brothers comes out in their politics. As we have seen, Sean O'Casey was a Communist; W.B. Yeats an elitist : these were basic attitudes of their day. Jack Yeats was a Republican in sentiment, an anarchist by temperament. Hilary Pyle, his biographer, says of him :

Jack Yeats's patriotism was intense and of a deeply idealistic nature. To him the Free Staters were middle-class, while the Republicans represented all that was noble and free. His patriotism had nothing to do with war or with the practicalities of the situation, but was rather a dedication to perfect life, without blemish, where no man was subject to another.[1]

Life could not provide such perfection, so he created the world of his pictures. He is reported by John Berger as hating morality, that last dubious defence behind which the bourgeoisie retreat. He loved life, and desired its full perfection, and people with their different possibilities for reaching that glory always interested him. This is the man that Louis MacNeice remembers as having a story about every flower seller in the city of Dublin.

The revolution, latent with many possibilities of perfection—for is not 'perfect happiness the only end of revolution'—stirred such a man deeply. 'Yeats hated war and evil,' Miss Pyle continues. 'His pictures of political subjects do not depict the conflict or moments of sacrifice, but the tragic or removed emotions of those who live on.'² Yeats was shocked when he called to pay his condolences to Mrs Childers after her husband's execution, to hear her small son Erskine exclaim 'the Republic fights on'.* He left the house, never to come again. Such a remark, he thought, betrayed in the family an unnatural obsession with political abstraction rather than with human reality. Such patriotism was putting the state before the people: he would never have that.

During the troubles Jack Yeats did little painting, partly because he was still recovering from a serious illness, partly because the events were too disturbing. However he was not without ideas on what art could contribute to the new Ireland, as his little pamphlet *Modern Aspects of Irish Art*, which hoped that a larger audience for art might develop, shows clearly.

Only in the 1920s did he begin to paint the events that had moved him personally. These seem, as was only natural, to be all events from the Civil War. One of them, *Communicating with the Prisoners* (1924) shows a group of girls calling up to Republicans at the barred windows of Kilmainham Gaol, and might almost illustrate the scene described by Frank O'Connor—'this was sex in its purest form, as God might have intended it to be'. This and another picture, *The Funeral of Harry Boland* (1922)—an event of August 1922, Boland having been shot by Free State soldiers in a Skerries hotel—are both elaborations of his earlier illustrative style. (The Boland picture is in fact the only record of the event, as soldiers prevented anyone bringing cameras into Glasnevin that day.) Both suggest his Republican sympathies. But he was not a man to involve himself directly in politics or polemics. His passions he saved for his work, and increasingly it was passion and energy that broke through in his paintings.

Joyce accurately observed the silence of Yeats's paintings.

*As President of Ireland, however, Erskine Childers was to be a great force for reconciliation and understanding in Ireland.

About to Write a Letter, His Thoughts to Himself : such paintings are all silence. But there is also the isolated eminence of an exiled imagination, the cunning of a master's execution. The limits of line and pattern are dissolved into explosions of colour literally daubed onto the canvas with a palette knife, even at times the nozzle of the paint tube, which resolve themselves miraculously, as in one painting, into a thrush singing on a bush top.

For Jack Yeats the revolution had involved a revolution in style, a liberation of artistic energy. That liberation of consciousness that Pearse and Connolly had wished for their people as a whole, never came to the nation. Afterwards writers and artists considered themselves the only really free people. They reached out for perfection in life when their countrymen seemed resigned to find that perfection only in the hereafter. As John Berger observes of Jack Yeats :

> He has continued to embrace mortality in the face of every moral warning. But he has been able to do this because his vision has its roots in his country; visually in the Irish landscape; poetically in Irish folklore; and ideologically in the fact that Ireland has only up to now been able to fight English imperialism with the image of the independent rebel.[3]

But the rebel is an ambiguous figure, rebellion often bringing a negation of what the rebels earnestly struggle for. That is the difference between rebellion and revolution. All too often the Irish rebel, a Dan Breen or a Tom Barry, settled for rebellion when a revolution was needed. Thus the revolutionary, a Maud Gonne or a Constance Markievicz, was isolated into impotency. In Yeats's paintings there are no impotent men, only heroic figures such as his man from Aran, sure of themselves even in their isolation.

It is important not to confine the immensity of Yeats's vision to the mere results of a national resurgence. The paintings of his later and better period are not in any way nationalistic; he provides no set pieces suitable for patriotic posters. Yet looking at a painting such as *Grief*, painted in 1950 as *Let There Be No More War* : a savage, awful violence is revealed, where the tall façades of the Georgian houses rise over the tormented turmoil of revolution and suffering, where the figures of the horseman and the striving soldiers contrast with the mother anxious only for the safety of her children. One realises that here is a painting impossible to separate from the artist's experience of history.

Yeats was not given to discussing his pictures, and only a few of his opinions have been recorded. 'No one creates, the artist merely assembles memories.' And 'each painting is an event . . . a creative work happens'. He believed that all fine paintings 'to be fine must have some of the living ginger of life in them'. His own are fine in that they are full of that very sense of life he admired in others—in the novels of George Moore for instance. It is not surprising then that his best critics have been, like Ernie O'Malley, in sympathy with his memories or, like John Berger, acutely aware of the movements of history that produced them.

It seems eminently suitable that Ernie O'Malley, having helped to create the IRA, should have later become in his capacity as an art collector a close friend of Jack Yeats. He was there the morning that MacNeice called and all three went out to talk to the flower seller. In an essay written in 1945, O'Malley contrasts the early and later stages of the painter, though without relating the change in style to the revolution. His early drawings had been transcriptions of reality, such as his pictures of life in the West of Ireland. But following the upheavals of Irish history

> His work no longer dealt with a perception of countrymen in relaxation or at ease in a folklore tradition. His figures now enter a subjective world in which they are related to the loneliness of the individual soul, the vague lack of pattern in living with its sense of inherent tragedy, brooding nostalgia, associated with time as well as variations on the freer moments of old.[4]

There is no better statement of the effect of the Irish revolution on the Irish imagination than this estimate of the great image maker from a leader of the revolution.

Thomas McGreevy, as one of the younger poets of the day, expressed in a poem in homage to Jack Yeats, not only something of what he felt about the painter's work, but also something of the same ambiguities of feeling about the consequences of the revolution. The poet who had emerged himself from the Civil War into the hard realities of peace, recalls the Limerick of Sarsfield's courage, Merriman's bawdry, the city's own distinctive Georgian style :

Grayer than the tide below, the tower;
The day is gray above;
About the walls
A curlew flies, calls;
Rain threatens, west;
This hour,
Driving,
I thought how this land, so desolate,
Long, long ago, was rich in living,
More reckless, consciously, in strife,
More conscious daring-delicate
In love.

And then the tower veered
Grayly to me,
Passed ...
I meditated,
Feared
The thought experience sent,
That the gold years
Of Limerick life
Might be but consecrated
Lie,
Heroic lives
So often meant
The brave stupidity of soldiers,
The proud stupidity of soldiers' wives.[5]

A great many of the myths about the revolution were indeed consecrated lies, the brave stupidity of soldiers, the proud stupidity of soldiers' wives. In his art Jack Yeats attempted always to escape from such lies, to create from the same materials something that was closer to the reality of what had happened, while yet raising it and the whole of life to a plane of perfected wholeness.

The aim of W.B. Yeats was very similar: 'something to perfection brought' was also his ideal of art. 'The artist merely assembles memories': with that too the poet Yeats would have agreed, as much of his own poetry was created out of memories and the living ginger of life. The images of the painter often find their echo in the poetry, and yet the visions of the two brothers are in the end very different. An anarchist cannot become an aristocrat. The painter found his images in the circus and the music hall, in the seemingly vulgar amusements of quite ordinary people. Even when he evokes, as he sometimes does, the images of an older Ireland, of Queen Maeve or the flight of Diarmuid and Grainne, he does it with a melancholy sense very different in its joy from the almost desolate reality of his brother's later poetry and plays.

To turn from the painter to the poet is a complete change : the poet's circus animals are very different beasts to the painter's. The minds of the two artists worked over the same events producing very different effects. This can be seen in one of the few poems that W.B. Yeats wrote which concerns paintings. In 1937, revisiting the Municipal Gallery, which had been founded by Hugh Lane, the poet found himself among his 'permanent or impermanent images' in some of the paintings hanging there, which recorded 'the images of thirty years'. For an old man living more and more into his memories, the experience was a revelation.[6]

The paintings he saw that morning are still in the gallery : none are by his brother, and none are, frankly, of overwhelming merit as pictures. Yet to Yeats they were impressive. There were portraits of political leaders : John Lavery's portraits of Arthur Griffith ('staring in hysterical pride') and Kevin O'Higgins ('a soul incapable of remorse or rest'), of Roger Casement on trial at the Court of Criminal Appeal. Then there were images of Irish life and of the Irish revolution : a bishop blessing a tricolour held by a kneeling soldier, a group of armed peasants from the West of Ireland (to Yeats's eye Keating's men of the West were waiting in ambush); a party of pilgrims making that most gruelling of pilgrimages to the medieval shrine at Lough Derg in Donegal. These are images directly from Irish history, or from that vision of Irish life which was central to the Irish Revival.

The complexity of the associations aroused by these images overcame Yeats and inspired the burning stanzas of one of his greatest poems. For here were also portraits of Lady Gregory, of her son Robert, the Irish airman killed in Italy, of those beautiful women he had known in his youth Lady Beresford and Hazel Lavery, of that solitary genius John Synge. Here were all his friends, while the other paintings epitomised all they had worked for, an Ireland grown strong and whole from an Antaeus-like contact with the soil.

> 'This is not,' I say,
> 'The dead Ireland of my youth, but an Ireland
> The poets have imagined, terrible and gay.'[7]

He had created such an Ireland in his imagination, finding the real Ireland growing, so he thought, grey and commonplace. This was no country for old men, he had decided years before, and he preferred the Byzantine holy city of his imagination. Compared with Parnell, that other hero of his youth, or Casement or The O'Rahilly, the politicians of the new Ireland were a disappointment. They were not god-like heroes, he thought recalling 'Parnell's Funeral' :

> Had de Valera eaten Parnell's heart
> No loose-lipped demagogue had won the day,
> No civil rancour torn the land apart.

> Had Cosgrave eaten Parnell's heart, the land's
> Imagination had been satisfied,
> Or lacking that, government in such hands,
> O'Higgins its sole statesman had not died.[8]

Only such a Dionysia, macabre to those aware of the fastidious and retiring characters of both de Valera and Cosgrave, would have satisfied the poet's imagination. But the politicians were not to be cast as sacred kings in some Druidic oak grove, and were in any case more concerned to satisfy the need for jobs and rural electrification than play their part in a sacred drama of Yeats's devising. The satisfaction of the land's imagination hardly concerned them at all.

As always Yeats stood at a remove, so necessary for him, from the course of his country's history, recasting it 'as though some ballad-singer had sung it all' : the death of Parnell, the Rising, the Troubles, the Civil War, even the paltry Blueshirts, into something new and closer to his heart's desire. He was closely concerned with all these events, as his letters and speeches as well as his poetry clearly show, for the public events of history often seemed to him to be the reflections of the moods of his own imagination. Now that great history seemed to have failed its promise.

> Fail, and that history turns into rubbish
> All that great history to a trouble of fools.[9]

Thus behind the excited passion of his politics and poetry, there was a panic need that history might not be rubbish, all those great men not merely fools.

Many people who lived through those days might find it hard to accept the critical influence of mere literature on political events. They cling to those hallowed myths of Irish nationalism in surprising ways. To suggest that Yeats might have greatly influenced the creation of the idea of modern Ireland that the rebels fought for, this strikes some people as almost blasphemous. They seem to actively resent the notion of a mere poet having any large part in their idea of their country, of perhaps insinuating his ideas so well into the current of thought that they themselves might unknowingly be his disciples. Joyce once remarked that Ireland might be important because it belonged to him; on a dull day one often thinks he was right. Ireland might also be important because it belongs to Yeats and all those other artists we have been discussing. Our politicians, our businessmen, our smart boys on the make, in the end it is not they who add to the dignity of Ireland. Ireland is great only in so far as she is an Ireland 'the poets have imagined, terrible and gay'. Otherwise she might merely be a speck of colour on the map a fly could walk over.

Yeats's little poem on politics—maintaining that they were unimportant compared with his passion for Maud Gonne—hardly reflects fully his feelings on the public questions of his country. He was, as must be clear by now, acutely aware of political trends. Anyone who was able to casually quote in Ireland in 1924 from both Mussolini and Lenin, was a man with a political mind. The trouble for Yeats was that after the revolution the actual politics of his country never rose to the level of the politics of his imagination. In the end he is forced to admit

> It was the dream itself enchanted me:
> Character isolated by a deed
> To engross the present and dominate the memory.[10]

Politics failed him; but in his imagination history and its great men could be saved. Among those masterful images, as he called them, was one which united the whole span of Irish culture from the Celts to the Republic: the heroic image of Cuchulain.

In 1938 the memorial to the Easter Rising was unveiled in the General Post Office. Created by Yeats's old school friend Oliver Sheppard, it showed the mortally wounded hero tied to a stone pillar in his last agony, the raven Goddess of Death perched on his shoulder.

This monument was the initial inspiration of 'The Statues', that magnificent avowal of Ireland's cultural destiny with the great civilisations of antiquity, the Egyptians and the Greeks. We Irish, Yeats says, echoing the famous phrase of Berkeley, 'climb to our proper dark, that we may trace /The lineaments of a plummet-measured face.' Ireland's is a destiny, however, which can only be accomplished by violence. What stalked through the Post Office, Yeats asks, when Pearse called on the name of Cuchulain during the Rising? Elsewhere he answers this question, with a serene conviction which ought to trouble his admirers when they themselves quaver at the thought of violence.

> You that Mitchel's prayer have heard,
> 'Send war in our time, O Lord!'
> Know that when all words are said
> And a man is fighting mad,
> Something drops from eyes long blind,
> He completes his partial mind,
> For an instant stands at ease,
> Laughs aloud, his heart at peace.
> Even the wisest man grows tense
> With some sort of violence
> Before he can accomplish fate,
> Know his work, or choose his mate.[11]

This also was a kind of perfection, but very different from anything his brother had imagined. If anything troubles us about Yeats's involvement with the Ireland of his time, it should be that he draws such a deep conviction from the experience.

In his hard-won work, created out of this fascination with violence in the imagination, Yeats 'something to perfection brought'. The image of Cuchulain, pre-eminently an image of violence which had dominated his imagination to the point of self-identification, the hero in his plays growing older with the poet, was itself brought in conclusion to a very different sort of perfection, a perfection more in tune with the world of his brother's paintings.

His last play and his last poems on Cuchulain were written on his own deathbed in the south of France. In *The Death of Cuchulain*, Eithne leads the hero into a hopeless battle by a false message, a prospect he faces bravely, forgiving her. When he is wounded, his wife Aoife seeks to revenge his killing of their only son. But ironically the hero is killed by the blind old beggar for a paltry reward. Cuchulain, the great hero of the national saga, meets his death at the hands of a coward. This is a dour comment on life, but an admission that the day of the heroes was over, cowards making up most of mankind. The play concludes :

> What stood in the Post Office
> With Pearse and Connolly?
> What comes out of the mountain
> Where men first shed their blood?
> Who thought Cuchulain till it seemed
> He stood where they stood?
>
> No body like his body
> Has modern woman borne,
> But an old man looking on life
> Imagines it in scorn.
> A statue's there to mark the place,
> By Oliver Sheppard done.[12]

But an old man's ironic scorn was not Yeats's final appreciation of the theme. Almost the last poem he wrote—it is dated 13 January 1939, a fortnight before he died—was 'Cuchulain Comforted'. And this poem may be seen also as the poet's consolation. The dead hero has been translated to the afterlife, 'a man violent and famous strode among the dead'. Cuchulain, meditating on wounds and blood, is told by one of the shrouded dead who gather round him that

> 'Your life will grow much sweeter if you will
> Obey our ancient rule and make a shroud.'[13]

This is work 'all must together do'. The hero takes up a sheet of linen and begins the work.

This is a curious poem for an aristocratic elitist to close his career with, but in the end it seems the poet moves away from direct political concerns to a purely human involvement. Cuchulain is told by the ghost :

> 'Now must we sing and sing the best we can,
> But first you must be told our character :
> Convicted cowards all, by kindred slain
> Or driven from home and left to die in fear.'
> They sang, but had nor human tunes or words,
> Though all was done in common as before;
> They had exchanged their throats and had the
> throats of birds.[14]

So in the end, for the brave and cowardly, the heroic and the merely human, there is reconciliation in the common labour of the dead. Human life is translated into the eternity of song. In the end art has a salvation for us all.

EPILOGUE: LIVE AMMUNITION

'The words of the dead are modified in the guts of the living: in Ireland this often means an expanding bullet in the large intestine.'

Epilogue: Live Ammunition

TRADITION AND IMAGINATION

FOR the next generation the troubles, as the events we have been describing came to be called later, became a legend. Was it possible to believe it had all happened here : those heroic actions, those famous patriots, those eminent writers? It seemed

> The great shocked art, the gross great enmity,
> That roamed here once, and swept indoors, embalmed
> Their lesson with themselves.[1]

For Thomas Kinsella, the author of those lines, and other writers of his generation, other matters, more personal affairs, became the proper subjects of poetry. But in Ireland all art is seen in relation to public life, and again and again, even Kinsella has returned to public themes in a mood of bitter disillusionment.

Yet the old slogans, the old gestures, lingered on. Schoolchildren sang ballads of revolution and defeat with hearty gusto. Passing down the quays they could examine the walls of the rebuilt Four Courts in search of bullet pocks, and turn over in the second-hand bookshops the yellowing sensations of yesterday's news.

The figures of the revolution left alive, growing old and frail, were becoming shrouded in the mists of their own pasts. The young James Plunkett, born in 1920, describes an encounter with one such ghost.

> Near the end of the evening, I turned the corner of a quiet road in Clonskeagh and found myself face to face with a ghost. It was a very tall, very thin old lady, dressed from head to foot in black drapes, with a wolfhound on a lead. Then she passed me, an apparition in October twilight. She was Maud Gonne MacBride, once the symbol of Romantic Ireland, now

so incredibly old to my young eyes that I thought of Oisin when his foot touched mortal ground and all his years in the blinking of an eye descended with the weight of an avalanche on top of him.[2]

This incredibly ancient woman was the same Maud Gonne, 'Pallas Athene in that straight back', whose startling beauty had irradiated the heart of the young Yeats and stirred the imagination of a nation a generation before with her appearance in *Cathleen ni Houlihan*. Had that small boy seen merely an old woman going down the road, or 'a young girl, and she with the walk of a queen'?

For most of my generation, a younger one than Kinsella's or Plunkett's, the image of that young girl existed only in the songs and ballads, and in some family stories of the period. The songs were all of great ideals, the agonies of loss; the stories of minor encounters, of burnt-out houses in the country or raids in a Dublin living under the heel of the Tans. But this was just the way in which Republican feelings were kept alive in nineteenth-century Ireland. We can now see what effect such songs and stories, and such schoolbooks as were used till recently in all the schools, emphasising the horrors of the past, yet so silent on the Civil War and later years, has had on the present generation. Once again history is repeating itself, and young people are throwing themselves into the madness of a discredited Republicanism, knowing only a history of poses and postures and lies. Instead of being content with the pleasures of youth and the beginning of life, they bomb and shoot and maim, and even if they live, they die at heart. One cannot kill at twenty-two and learn to live a normal life at forty-four.

For some then, the legends are potent things. For writers, for whom love is the central theme of literature, there was only the note of elegy. The Republicans, as Francis Stuart suggested, may have kept the faith, but his own poems of that time have a melancholy air of loss. Only the other day Peadar O'Donnell promised us, in the title of some memoirs, that *There Will Be Another Day....* But his most recent novel, where the proud island of his early writings comes to its final end in a blaze of protest, says otherwise.

Others were certain that a period was over, its like never to be seen again. This is the sense of Denis Devlin's magnificent poem 'The Tomb of Michael Collins'. Like Frank O'Connor at the death of Erskine Childers, it was to Walt Whitman that Devlin turned as a boy when he heard of Collins's death. 'When lilacs last in the dooryard bloomed', the lament for Lincoln, was the lesson of the day. By recollecting this coincidence, he absorbs the death of Collins into the tradition of lament :

> And sad, oh sad, that glen with one thin stream
> He met his death in; and a farmer told me
> There was but one small bird to shoot : it sang
> 'Better beast and know thy end, and die
> Than Man with murderous angels in his head.'[3]

Collins is, I suppose, the hero of those who would, perhaps rightly, forget the rancours of the Civil War. But those murderous angels of history, of peace and freedom, beat their heavy wings in too many minds for that. The Republicans had other heroes, more recent deaths : seventy-seven executed in the Civil War, forty-two others who died at the hands of the government or fighting for the cause, other deaths in Ulster. Of these Austin Clarke has written in 'The Last Republicans' :

> Because their fathers had been drilled,
> Formed fours among the Dublin hills,
> They marched together, countermarched
> Along the Liffey Valley, by larch-wood,
> Spruce, pine road. Now what living shout
> Can halt them? Nothing of their faces
> Is left, the breath blown out
> Of them into far lonely places.[4]

For many other writers, the sad and sorry story of the later IRA has provided an easy source of nostalgic pity and petty action. But on the whole Irish writers have ignored the topic in favour of rural sexual mores. Here Sean O'Faolain is an honourable exception, in this as in so many other things, though the novel *Come Back to Erin* is disappointing. His Republican character, so thoroughly unpleasant, suggests the moral desuetude that the seemingly romantic outlaw can descend to.

Other writers were not so concerned, the truth was easier to ignore. In the North this was not so. There the IRA were still a piece of the fabric of society, the gunmen ready to appear to protect the Catholic community.

Perhaps the most remarkable portrait of the 'Revolutionary Organisation' in fiction is in F.L. Green's *Odd Man Out*, based on events in Belfast during the forties. The film, directed by Carol Reed (in the same period as he made *The Third Man*), is now better known, but the original novel has its own remarkable qualities. Green claims he wrote it quite deliberately to escape from what he considered to be the largely superficial attempts to delineate the Irish character by other writers. He attempts in his own novel a subtle revelation of motive and character on a refined plane that often reminds one of his namesake, Graham Greene.

But the harsh reality of Ulster life did not often reach to such a metaphysical level. The reality was just too hard and too bewildering. Michael McLaverty, in a short story called 'Pigeons', describes the feelings of a small Belfast boy who looks after his brother's birds.

> Our Johnny kept pigeons, three white ones and a brown one that tumbles in the air like a leaf. They were nice pigeons, but they dirtied the slates and cooed too early in the morning that my father said that someday he would wring their bloody necks. That was a long time ago now, for we still have the pigeons, but Johnny is dead; he died for Ireland.
>
> 'What's wrong, Mamie?' I asked, looking up at her wet eyes. 'Nothing, darling; nothing, pet. He died for Ireland.' I turned my head and looked at the bed. Johnny was lying on the white sheet in a brown dress. His hands were pale and they were joined around his rosary beads, a big crucifix between them. There was a big lump of wadding at the side of his head and there were pieces up his nose. I cried more and more, and then my Mamie made me put on my clothes, and go downstairs for my breakfast.[5]

But it is not Green or McLaverty that we associate with the later IRA: the real laureate of the movement is Brendan Behan. Behan was born and bred a Republican, his family having been involved in the national struggle for decades: his uncle Peadar Kearney is the author of the National Anthem. At the age of sixteen Behan was arrested in Liverpool carrying a caseful of bombs for blowing-up letter boxes. Typically, the mission to England was his own idea, unauthorised by the IRA. His experiences at Hollesley Bay gave him the material for *Borstal Boy*. Released from there, he was arrested again in Dublin after trying to kill a policeman at Sean McCaughty's funeral. Jailed, he was released under an amnesty for political offences. He then turned to writing seriously, his first stories being published in *The Bell* by Sean O'Faolain.

We are still too close to Behan to measure his full worth, but *Borstal Boy* and *The Quare Fellow* are among the best things in modern Irish writing. His other books are, as they say, of interest. The celebrated *Hostage*, however, gets carried away in its Theatre Workshop version by the music-hall elements which swamp the delicate love story of the soldier and the girl.

The plot of *The Hostage* was derived directly from the kidnapping of a young British soldier in Northern Ireland who was brought down to Dublin and kept prisoner in a Nelson Street brothel. This incident from the same campaign in the fifties in which Sean South and Fergal O'Hanlon were killed, provided the immediate idea. But in Behan's imagination it fused with a story he had been told about from the Troubles. An old IRA man had once described to him how he had waited in ambush for a British troop train. The train came around a bend with the soldiers, some scarcely more than boys, singing happily. The next moment the shooting started. Behan could never forget that image of happy song obliterated by machine-gun fire.

His politics—the politics of machine-gun fire—clashed with his writing, his kind of happy song. He was intensely loyal to the family tradition of Republicanism—he often boasted how his father had snubbed de Valera at his uncle's funeral. But the artist had seen enough of life in jail and out to know that human beings were difficult characters, good enough in themselves, but often led by duty to awful deeds. If *The Quare Fellow* unleashes its jovial scorn on capital punishment, *The Hostage* is equally hard on the Organisation and its pietistic career rebels. Yet in the end it is the mad pride in the IRA—almost the pride of a St Cyr officer, Sean O'Faolain once observed—that comes through.

When Behan died, his old comrades in the IRA covered the coffin with the tricolour and fired over the Glasnevin grave a parting salute. Some of those in that crowd must have remembered a passage in his last book:

> The firing party for Sean McCaughty was held in Dublin and the Guard of Honour fired revolvers over his coffin.
> 'From your holster, withdraw.
> 'Fire. Fire. Fire.'
> Funnily enough, the Guard of Honour in the Free State Army only use rifles, *but in the I R A we never use anything but revolvers.* There are six men in our Guard of Honour and eight in the Free State Army who, strangely, give their shooting orders in Irish, whereas ours are given in English. *We also have the distinction of using live ammunition* (added emphasis).[6]

It is exactly this distinction of using live ammunition, of being an active force, that keeps the tradition of the IRA alive among young people. They have their traditions: for the rest of us the songs and the poetry are enough.

But it is through the songs and the poetry, for good or evil, that the Fenian tradition of this country, the memory of the dead, lingers on. Because of them that live ammunition modifies the guts of the living. In memory of those two boys, South and O'Hanlon, killed in raiding an Ulster barracks in 1956, Dominic Behan wrote a fierce song that should have been the last word:

> Come all you young fellows,
> Stay here while I sing,
> For the love of one's country
> Is a terrible thing.
> It banishes feeling
> At the spurt of a flame,
> And it makes you a part
> Of the Patriot Game.

True and terrible words, if only the gunmen would listen to them. But they do not. They have the distinction of using live ammunition. And here as in so many things, the poet makes his way into those minds and finds the final words, where tradition and imagination become one.

In the poems written while he was dying, Yeats calls again on the memory of the dead, in this case the men of 1916, remembering the actor Sean Connolly who died at the City Hall in

Easter Week. He was only one actor of many in the national drama, down to those boys left roughly buried in a country grave-yard at night, and the newer dead in this morning's news from Belfast.

> Some had no thought of victory
> But had gone out to die
> That Ireland's mind be greater,
> Her heart mount up on high;
> And yet who knows what's yet to come?
> For Patrick Pearse has said,
> That in every generation
> Must Irish blood be shed.
> *From mountain to mountain ride the fierce horsemen.*[7]

Yeats knows all about the distinction of using live ammunition, of 'violence and more violence', of why John Mitchel prayed that God might send 'war in our time', of how the gods of Ireland suffer an eternal return to trouble once again the mortal world, of how the cold stone of the heart stands always in the living stream.

If the political revolution in Ireland failed to be the social revolution its initiators had hoped it would be, it is saved from complete failure by the art it inspired. I have used as epigraphs in this book those two moments in the classic nineteenth-century novel where the solitary individual in battle realises in a moment the nature of history and personal experience. Waterloo is reduced to a series of confused encounters which leave Fabriozo del Dongo wondering if what he has seen was a real battle or not. He had thought of a battle as a clear historical event, but now he realises that historical events are actually total confusion for those who live through them. Prince Andrei on the field of Austerlitz, lying looking at the indifferent sky above the battle, realises that the stars in their courses are indifferent to the deaths of individuals. Later in Tolstoy's novel, Pierre emerges from the battle of Borodino as a man made whole by suffering through just such confusions, just such natural indifference.

From the literature of the Irish revolution, it is similar moments that we remember and which make it important, moments of confusion, loneliness, and suffering: Yeats in his personal confusion so clear about the forces of violence within each of us; Mrs Tancred lamenting her son, Juno's resolution, Joxer's world of chassis; the 'bloody stars' at the end of *Guests of the Nation*, Bernard turning back to Nora. In the end the politics fade, and the reality of history becomes these people living, dying, surviving.

I began this book with Yeats's doubtful questions to himself about his own role in history. The answers are now clear enough. Words of his—despite those who would wish it otherwise—did send out men to die, for he was one of the creators of the image of a new Ireland that they died for. This was the image that overwhelmed the imagination of his beloved Maud Gonne, and the imaginations of many others also, and led them on through many acts of reckless violence. Yet once uttered, no other words of his could have saved the great houses that he loved from the wreck of history. He had helped to conjure up the storm, and after the whirlwind no one heeded the still small voice of poetry.

There was another side of the story. And for some there still is, as we have seen in this chapter. In that forgotten film *The Dawn*, there is a single shot of a column of men moving across the distant skyline in the first light of the morning. It is an image redolent of all the hopes and expectations of the revolution. Something of that idealism which ended for so many in the cold light of morning with a bullet in the brain, is retrieved from the sordidness of history by the dignity of art. It is surely no disparagement to them or their ideals to claim that the art of the revolution now has more meaning for us than the revolution itself, for it is they who give meaning to that art. Men laid in forgotten graves live on in our imaginations, influence us with their hopes, their passions, warn us finally by the failure of their deaths. They are enchanted into stones to trouble still the living stream.

Reference notes

Epigraph : J. L. Borges : *Other Inquisitions*, New York : Washington Square Press, 1966, p. 176.

INTRODUCTION
1. W. B. Yeats, 'The Statues', *Collected Poems* (1956), p. 323.
2. Yeats, 'The Man and the Echo', *Collected Poems*, p. 337.
3. Birrell, evidence in *Royal Commission on the Rebellion in Ireland*. London : H.M. Stationary Office, Cmd. 8311 of 1916.

PART ONE
Epigraph : C. C. O'Brien : *States of Ireland*, London : Hutchinson, 1972, p. 23.

CHAPTER ONE (pp. 11–20)
1. Yeats, 'The Bounty of Sweden' in *Autobiography* (1965), p. 378.

CHAPTER TWO (pp. 21–41)
1. Yeats, 'A General Introduction to My Work', *Selected Criticism* (1964), p. 256.
2. Yeats, 'To the Rose Upon the Rood of Time', *Collected Poems* (1956), p. 31.
3. Yeats, *Collected Poems*, p. 36.
4. Yeats, 'The Dedication to a Book of Stories Selected from the Irish Novelists', *Collected Poems*, p. 45.
5. Yeats, 'To Ireland in the Coming Times', *Collected Poems*, p. 49.
6. Yeats, ibid.
7. Yeats, an unpublished speech quoted in Ellmann (1949), p. 116.
8. Yeats, *Essays* (1924), p. 370.
9. Synge, 'Autobiography' in *Collected Works: Prose* (1966), p. 7. A slightly different text is given in *Autobiography* (1965).
10. Synge, 'The Passing of the Shee' in *Collected Works: Poems* (1962), p. 38.

11. Maud Gonne in *The United Irishman* (Dublin), 24 October 1904.
12. Synge to MacKenna (13 July 1905), quoted in Greene and Stephens (1959), p. 187.
13. Synge to MacKenna, quoted in Greene and Stephens (1959), p. 264.
14. Quoted by Jack Yeats in 'With Synge in Connemara' (1911), p. 41.
15. Jack Yeats, ibid., p. 42.
16. W. B. Yeats, 'In Memory of Eva Gore-Booth and Con Markievicz', *Collected Poems*, p. 229.
17. Synge, 'A Landlord's Garden in County Wicklow' in *The Aran Islands and Other Writings* (1961), p. 202. Originally published in *The Manchester Guardian*, 9 May and 1 July 1907.
18. Moore (1887), pp. 57–8.
19. Yeats, *Collected Poems*, p. 93.
20. Yeats, 'A Woman Homer Sung', *Collected Poems*, p. 88.
21. Yeats, 'No Second Troy', *Collected Poems*, p. 89.
22. Yeats, 'At Galway Races', *Collected Poems*, p. 95.
23. Yeats, *Collected Poems*, p. 106.
24. Ibid.

CHAPTER THREE (pp. 42–64)
1. Moore, *Ave* (1911), p. 94.
2. Somerville and Ross, *The Silver Fox* (1897), ch. XII, p. 171.
3. See Moore, 'Literature and the Irish Language' in *Ideals in Ireland* (1901).
4. Moore, *A Drama in Muslin* (1884 edition), pp. 203–4.
5. Moore, *The Untilled Field* (1903 edition), p. 49.
6. G. B. Shaw, *Immaturity* (1931), preface.
7. Joyce, *Ulysses* (Bodley Head edition, 1960), p. 38.
8. Ibid.
9. Ibid., p. 432.
10. Ibid.
11. O'Donovan, *Conquest* (1920), p. 35.

CHAPTER FOUR (pp. 65–90)
1. Wright (1914), p. 3; p. 29.
2. Connolly in 1896, quoted in *Socialism and Nationalism* (1948), p. 11.
3. Connolly in *Irish Work* (Dublin), 19 December 1914, quoted in *Socialism and Nationalism* (1948), p. 180.
4. Yeats, 'The Death of Synge' in *Autobiography* (1965), p. 342.

5. Patrick Pearse, *Collected Works: Political Writings and Speeches* (1917), p. 38.
6. Pearse, ibid., pp. 98–9.
7. Pearse, *Collected Works: Plays, Stories, Poems* (1917), p. 44.
8. Thomas MacDonagh, *The Poetical Works* (1916), p. 91.
9. Pearse, 'I Am Ireland', *Collected Works: Plays, Stories, Poems* (1917), p. 323.
10. Pearse, *Collected Works: Political Writings and Speeches* (1917), p. 137.
11. Pearse, *Collected Works: Plays, Stories, Poems* (1917), p. 335.
12. Pearse, ibid., p. 324.
13. Pearse, ibid., p. 333.
14. Pearse, ibid., p. 341.
15. Yeats, 'The Municipal Gallery Revisited', *Collected Poems* (1956), p. 318.
16. Text in Whitely Stokes and John Strachan : *Theasarus Palaeohibernicus* (Cambridge, 1903), II p. 290.
17. Pearse, *Collected Works: Plays, Stories, Poems* (1917), p. 341.
18. Plunkett, *Poems* (1916), p. 50.
19. Ibid., p. 50.
20. Ibid., p. 62.
21. MacDonagh, *Literature in Ireland* (1916), p. 23.
22. Ibid., p. 28.
23. Pearse, *Collected Works: Plays, Stories, Poems* (1917), p. 337.
24. Clarke, *A Penny in the Clouds* (1968), p. 25.
25. The full text of the Proclamation is given in Macardle (1937).
26. Yeats, 'The Statues', *Collected Poems*, p. 323.

PART TWO
Epigraph : Stendhal : *The Charterhouse of Parma* (trans. M. R. B. Shaw). Harmondsworth : Penguin Books, 1958. Ch. 3, p. 60.

CHAPTER FIVE (pp. 93–101)
1. See evidence in *Royal Commission on the Rebellion in Ireland* (Cmd. 8311 of 1916).
2. Figgis (1915), p. 12.
3. Figgis (1927), p. 71.
4. Ibid., p. 144.

CHAPTER SIX (pp. 102–118)
1. Yeats, *Letters* (1954), p. 613.
2. Yeats, *Collected Poems* (1956), pp. 177–80.

3. Ibid., p. 178.
4. Pearse, 'Renunciation', *Collected Works: Plays, Stories, Poems* (1917), p. 324.
5. Yeats, 'Easter 1916', *Collected Poems*, p. 179.
6. Ibid.
7. Yeats, 'Sixteen Dead Men', *Collected Poems*, p. 180.
8. Yeats, 'The Rose Tree', *Collected Poems*, p. 181.
9. O'Casey, *The Plough and the Stars*, Act II.
10. Ibid., Act III.
11. O'Flaherty (1950), ch. II, p. 25.
12. Ibid., ch. VII, p. 63.
13. Townshend (1975), p. 16, quoting Breen (1924; new ed. 1964), p. 38.

CHAPTER SEVEN (pp. 119–140)
1. Farrell (1964), p. 330.
2. Ibid., p. 344.
3. Ibid., p. 351.
4. Ibid., p. 248.
5. O'Malley (1936), p. 8.
6. Ibid., p. 9.
7. Ibid., p. 104.
8. Ibid., p. 104.
9. Ibid., p. 77.
10. O'Connor (1965), p. 19.
11. O'Faolain (1964), p. 111.
12. Ibid., p. 112.
13. Corkery (1920), p. 36.
14. O'Faolain (1964), p. 132.
15. Ibid., p. 135.
16. Maire Mac Entee (1969), p. 60.
17. O'Connor (1961), p. 110.
18. Ibid., p. 111.
19. Ibid., p. 122.

CHAPTER EIGHT (pp. 141–158)
1. Yeats, *A Vision* (1937 edition), Introduction.
2. Yeats, *The Only Jealousy of Emer* in *Collected Plays* (1952), pp. 281–2.
3. Yeats, *Collected Poems* (1956), p. 132.
4. Yeats, dedicatory poem for *Responsibilities* (1914), *Collected Poems*, p. 99.
5. Yeats, 'A Prayer for My Daughter', *Collected Poems*, p. 185.

6. Ibid., p. 187.
7. Ibid., p. 187.
8. Yeats, 'The Second Coming', *Collected Poems*, p. 184.
9. Ibid., p. 185.
10. Ibid., p. 185.
11. Yeats, 'A Prayer for My Daughter', *Collected Poems*, p. 186.
12. Bowen, *The Last September* (1929), p. 29.
13. Ibid., pp. 43–4.
14. Bowen, *Bowen's Court* (1964 edition), p. 440.
15. Somerville and Ross, *Strayaways* (1919), p. 252.
16. Collis (1968), p. 203.
17. See *Irish Independent*, 3 Nov. 1920.
18. Yeats, *Collected Poems*, p. 205.
19. Yeats, *Letters* (1954), p. 680.
20. Allt and Alspach, *Variorum Edition of the Poems of W. B. Yeats*, p. 791. But see also T. R. Henn, 'Yeats and the Poetry of War' in *Last Essays* (1976), for other variations.
21. Yeats, *Collected Poems*, p. 204.
22. Ibid., p. 205.
23. Ibid., p. 207.
24. Ibid., p. 206.
25. Ibid., p. 205.
26. Ibid., p. 208.

CHAPTER NINE (pp. 159–177)
1. Fallon (1965), pp. 8–9.
2. Corkery (1920), dedication.
3. Yeats, 'September 1913', *Collected Poems* (1956), p. 106.
4. O'Donnell, in the afterword to *The Valley of the Squinting Windows* (1964 ed.).
5. O'Casey, *The Shadow of a Gunman*, Act I.
6. Ibid., Act I.
7. Yeats, *Collected Poems*, p. 207; p. 205; p. 202.
8. O'Connor (1931), p. 215.
9. Ibid., p. 19.
10. O'Faolain (1957), p. viii.
11. Ibid., p. 23.
12. Yeats, 'The Pity of Love', *Collected Poems*, p. 40.
13. Farrell (1964), p. 577.
14. Ibid., p. 486.
15. Yeats, 'Coole Park and Ballylee, 1931', *Collected Poems*, p. 239.
16. Farrell (1964), p. 532.
17. Yeats, 'Easter 1916', *Collected Poems*, p. 179.

L

18. Yeats, 'Nineteen Hundred and Nineteen', *Collected Poems*, p. 205.

CHAPTER TEN (pp. 178–192)
1. Clarke (1968), p. 99.
2. O'Faolain (1964), pp. 136–7.
3. O'Malley (1936), p. 326.
4. O'Connor (1961), p. 146.
5. Ibid.
6. Clarke (1968), p. 102.
7. Ibid., p. 103.
8. O'Hegarty (1939), p. 24.
9. O'Faolain (1964), p. 193.
10. Ibid.
11. Collins quoted in O'Connor (1965), p. 20.
12. De Valera in a radio broadcast.

CHAPTER ELEVEN (pp. 193–224)
1. Yeats, 'Meditations in Time of Civil War', *Collected Poems* (1956), p. 203.
2. Gogarty (1937), ch. 19, p. 259.
3. O'Flaherty (1924), p. 161.
4. O'Faolain (1957), p. viii.
5. Yeats, 'Ego Dominus Tuus', *Collected Poems*, p. 159.
6. Yeats, 'Meditations in Time of Civil War', *Collected Poems*, p. 202.
7. Yeats, *Collected Poems*, p. 199.
8. Yeats, notes to *Collected Poems*, p. 455.
9. Yeats, 'Meditations in Time of Civil War', *Collected Poems*, pp. 201–2.
10. Yeats, *Collected Poems*, p. 202.
11. Ibid., p. 198.
12. Ibid., p. 200.
13. Ibid., p. 203.
14. Ibid., p. 204.
15. Ibid., p. 204.
16. Ibid., p. 198.
17. O'Casey, *Juno and the Paycock*, Act I.
18. Yeats, 'The Circus Animals' Desertion', *Collected Poems* (1956), p. 336.
19. Gogarty (1937), ch. 9, p. 188.
20. Gogarty quoted by Ulick O'Connor (1964), p. 189.
21. Gogarty quoted by Ulick O'Connor (1964), p. 191

22. Yeats, 'Introduction' in *The Oxford Book of Modern Verse* (1936).
23. Gogarty, 'Ringsend', *Collected Poems* (1954), p. 102.
24. Gogarty (1937), ch. 9, p. 148.
25. Yeats, 'Two Songs from a Play', *Collected Poems,* p. 211.
26. Bowen (1964), p. 441.
27. O'Connor (1961), p. 147.
28. Ibid., p. 166.
29. Ibid., p. 168.
30. Yeats, 'The Second Coming', *Collected Poems,* p. 185.
31. Yeats, *Letters* (1954), p. 722.
32. Ibid., p. 809.
33. Pearse, *Collected Works: Plays, Stories, Poems* (1917), p. 44.
34. O'Flaherty, *Shame the Devil* (1934), pp. 189–90.
35. Ibid., p. 191.
36. Yeats's notes to *Collected Poems,* p. 449.
37. Yeats, 'The Valley of the Black Pig', *Collected Poems,* p. 63.

CHAPTER TWELVE (pp. 225–233)
1. O'Faolain (1964), p. 208.
2. O'Donnell (1932), ch. 5, p. 16.
3. Ibid., ch. 30, p. 75.
4. Stuart, *Things to Live For* (1934), pp. 219–21.
5. McGreevy, *Poems* (1934), p. 12.
6. Stuart (1923), p. 9.
7. Stuart (1934), p. 46.
8. O'Connor (1961), p. 189.
9. O'Faolain (1964), p. 69.

PART THREE
Epigraph. L. N. Tolstoy: *War and Peace* (trans. Rosemary Edmonds). Harmondsworth: Penguin Books, 1957. Part One, Book Three, ch. 16, p. 326.

CHAPTER THIRTEEN (pp. 237–246)
1. Text in Macardle (1937), p. 781.
2. Yeats, 'September 1913', *Collected Poems* (1956), p. 106.
3. Cullen (1969), p. 47.

CHAPTER FOURTEEN (pp. 247–263)
1. Yeats, 'In Memory of Eva Gore-Booth and Con Markievicz', *Collected Poems* (1956), p. 229.
2. Yeats, *Senate Speeches* (1961), p. 99

3. Yeats, introduction to Ussher's *Midnight Court* (1926), p. 8.
4. Yeats, 'The Irish Censorship', *The Spectator* (London), 29 September 1928.
5. O'Casey, *Drums Under the Window*, p. 221.
6. Yeats, 'Leda and the Swan', *Collected Poems*, p. 212.
7. Yeats, *Collected Poems*, p. 214.
8. Yeats, *Letters*, p. 727.
9. Yeats, *Collected Poems*, p. 230.
10. Yeats, 'Blood and the Moon', *Collected Poems*, p. 232.
11. Ibid.
12. Yeats, 'In Memory of Eva Gore-Booth and Con Markievicz', *Collected Poems*, p. 229.
13. Yeats, *Collected Poems*, p. 230.
14. Ibid.

CHAPTER FIFTEEN (pp. 264–276)
1. Obituary notice in *The Times* (London), 28 October 1925. For other details on Figgis, see also the Dail publication *Report of the Committee on Wireless Broadcasting* (Dublin, 1924).
2. O'Faolain (1964), p. 342.
3. Yeats, 'Three Songs to the Same Tune', *Collected Poems* (1956), p. 278.

CHAPTER SIXTEEN (pp. 277–288)
1. Pyle (1970), p. 119.
2. Ibid.
3. Berger (1971), p. 57; first published in *Permanent Red* (1960).
4. O'Malley (1945), reprinted in McHugh (1971), p. 68.
5. McGreevy (1934), p. 30.
6. See also the speech quoted in O'Faolain (1964), pp. 354–5, from the limited edition pamphlet *A Speech and Two Poems* by W. B. Yeats (Dublin, 1937).
7. Yeats, *Collected Poems*, p. 317.
8. Ibid., p. 276.
9. Yeats, 'Three Songs to the Same Tune', *Collected Poems*, p. 278.
10. Yeats, 'The Circus Animals' Desertion', *Collected Poems*, p. 336.
11. Yeats, 'Under Ben Bulben', *Collected Poems*, p. 342.
12. Yeats, *The Death of Cuchulain* in *Collected Plays*, p. 705.
13. Yeats, *Collected Poems*, p. 339.
14. Ibid.

EPILOGUE (pp. 291–298)
Epigraph : see p. 3 of the present work.
1. Kinsella (1962), p. 34.
2. Plunkett (1969), p. 193
3. Devlin (1963), p. 21.
4. Clarke (1974), p. 255.
5. McLaverty, 'Pigeons' in *The Game Cock* (1948).
6. Behan (1965), p. 101.
7. Yeats, 'Three Songs to One Burden', *Collected Poems*, p. 321.

Bibliography

The only primary sources consulted in writing this book were the papers of Ernest O'Malley in the Archives Department, University College Dublin (of which there is not direct use made in the text); and letters and other materials relating to Gerald O'Donovan in the National Library (Sarah Purser Collection MS 10201/17) and in the possession of his family. I would like to thank Professor R. Dudley Edwards and Mrs Jennifer O'Donovan for their kind help with these materials.

GENERAL
History
Beckett, J. C., *The Making of Modern Ireland 1602–1923*, London 1963.
Beckett, J. C., *The Anglo-Irish Tradition*, London 1976.
Curtis, Edmund, *A History of Ireland*, London 1936.
Lyons, F. S. L., *Ireland Since the Famine* (revised ed.). London 1973.
Meenan, James, *The Irish Economy Since 1922*, Liverpool 1970.
Murphy, John A., *Ireland in the Twentieth Century*, Dublin 1975.
Norman, Edward, *A History of Modern Ireland*, London 1971.

Politics
Beaslai, Piaras, *Michael Collins and the Making of a New Ireland*, Dublin 1926.
Kee, Robert, *The Green Flag*, London 1973.
Macardle, Dorothy, *The Irish Republic*, London 1937; Dublin 1951.
O'Brien, Conor Cruise, *States of Ireland*, London 1972.
O'Brien, Conor Cruise (with Maire Cruise O'Brien), *A Concise History of Ireland*, London 1971.
O'Connor, D. R. Lysaght, *The Republic of Ireland*, Cork 1969.
O'Sullivan, Donal, *The Irish Free State and its Senate*, London 1936.

Townshend, Charles, *The British Campaign in Ireland, 1919–1921*, Oxford 1975.

Literature
Boyd, Ernest, *Ireland's Literary Renaissance*, New York 1916; 1922.
Ellis-Fermor, Una, *The Irish Dramatic Movement*, London 1954.
Howarth, Herbert, *The Irish Writers 1880–1940*, London 1958.
O'Connor, Frank, *A Backward Look*, London 1967; title in U.S.: *A Short History of Irish Literature*, New York 1967.
Rogers, W. R., *Irish Literary Portraits*, London 1972.
Ryan, W. P., *The Irish Revival*, London 1894.
Ussher, Arland, *The Face and Mind of Ireland*, London 1949.

INTRODUCTION: THE DEATH OF CUCHULAIN
Cross, T. P. and Slover, C. H. (eds.), *Ancient Irish Tales*, London 1937.
O'Hegarty, R. S., 'W. B. Yeats and the Revolutionary Ireland of his time', *Dublin Magazine*, July–Sept. 1939, pp. 22–4.
Rolleston, T. W., *Myths and Legends of the Celtic Race*, London 1911.
Sjoestedt, Marie-Louise, *Gods and Heroes of the Celts*, London 1950.

CHAPTER ONE: THE MEMORY OF THE DEAD
Arnold, Bruce, *A Concise History of Irish Art*, London 1963.
Arnold, Matthew, *On the Study of Celtic Literature*, London 1863.
Arnsberg, Conrad, *The Irish Countryman, an Anthropological Study*, London 1937.
Connell, K. H., *The Population of Ireland, 1750–1845*, Oxford 1950.
Connell, K. H., 'Catholicism and Marriage in the Century after the Famine', in *Irish Peasant Society*, Oxford 1966.
Craig, Maurice, *Dublin 1660–1860*, London 1952.
Cullen, L. M., *Life in Ireland*, London 1972.
Donnelly, J. J., *The Land and the People of 19th Century Cork*, London 1975
Edgeworth, Maria, *Castle Rackrent* (edited by George Watson), London 1964.
Flanagan, Thomas, *The Irish Novelists 1800–1850*, London 1958.
Hyde, Douglas, *The Love Songs of Connacht*, Dublin 1893.
Kinsella, Thomas and Yeats, W.B., *Mangan, Davis Ferguson? Tradition and the Irish Writer*, Dublin 1970.
Merriman, Brian, *The Midnight Court* (translated by Frank O'Connor), Dublin 1946.

Miller, David W., *Church, State and Nation in Ireland 1898–1921*, Dublin 1973.
Norman, Edward, *The Catholic Church and Ireland in the Age of Rebellion*, London 1959.
O'Brien, R. Barry, *Life of Charles Stewart Parnell*, London 1899.
O'Connor, Frank, *A Backward Look*, London 1967.
O'Faolain, Sean, *The Irish*, London 1946; 1970.
O'Hegarty, P. S., *Ireland Under the Union*, Dublin 1926.
Whyte, J. M., *The Independent Irish Party*, London 1958.
Whyte, J. M., *Church and State in Modern Ireland*, Dublin 1971.

CHAPTER TWO: THE RETURN OF THE NATIVE (I)
Coxhead, Elizabeth, *Daughters of Erin*, London 1962.
Ellmann, Richard, *Yeats, the Man and the Masks*, London 1949.
Ellmann, Richard, *The Identity of Yeats*, London 1954.
Ellmann, Richard, *Golden Codgers*, New York 1973.
Greene, David H. and Stephens, Edward M., *J. M. Synge*, New York 1959.
Gregory, Isabella Augusta (ed.), *Ideals in Ireland*, London 1901.
Gregory, Isabella Augusta, *Cuchulain of Muirthemne*, London 1902.
Henn, T. R., *The Lonely Tower*, London 1962.
Jeffares, A. Norman, *W. B. Yeats, the Man and the Poet*, London 1949.
MacBride, Maud Gonne, *A Servant of the Queen*, London 1938.
Moore, George, *Parnell and His Island*, London 1887.
Price, Alan, *Synge and Anglo-Irish Drama*, London 1961.
Pyle, Hilary, *Jack B. Yeats*, London 1970.
Synge, J. M., *Collected Plays* (with an introduction by W. R. Rogers), London 1952.
Synge, J. M., *The Aran Islands* (with illustrations by Jack B. Yeats), Dublin 1906.
Synge, J. M., *The Aran Islands and Other Writings* (edited by Robert Tracy), New York 1961.
Synge, J. M., *Collected Works*, Oxford 1962–66. Poems (1962), Prose (1966).
Yeats, W. B., *The Celtic Twilight*, London 1894.
Yeats, W. B., *Synge and the Ireland of His Time* (with a note on a walk through Connemara with him by Jack B. Yeats), Dublin 1911.
Yeats, W. B., *Collected Poems*, London 1956.
Yeats, W. B., *Autobiographies*, London 1965.
Yeats, W. B., *Memoirs* (edited by Denis Donoghue), London 1974.

CHAPTER THREE: THE RETURN OF THE NATIVE (II)

Collis, Maurice, *Somerville and Ross*, London 1968.

Denson, Alan, *John Hughes Sculptor*, published by the author, Kendal 1970.

Ellmann, Richard, *James Joyce*, New York 1959.

Gwynn, Dennis, *Edward Martyn and the Irish Revival*, London 1932.

Hone, Joseph, *The Life of George Moore*, London 1932.

Joyce, James, *Dubliners*, London 1914.

Joyce, James, *A Portrait of the Artist as a Young Man*, New York 1916.

Joyce, James, *Ulysses*, Paris 1922.

Joyce, James, *Letters* (edited by Stuart Gilbert and Richard Ellmann), London 1957 and 1966.

McCarthy, Michael J., *Priests and People in Ireland*, Dublin 1902.

Moore, George, *A Drama in Muslin*, London 1884.

Moore, George, *Parnell and His Island*, London 1887.

Moore, George, *An T-Ur Gort*, Dublin 1902.

Moore, George, *The Untilled Field*, London 1903.

Moore, George, *The Lake*, London 1905.

Moore, George, *Hail and Farewell*, London 1911, 1912, 1914.

Moore, Maurice, *An Irish Gentleman, George Henry Moore*, London n.d.

Noël, Jean C., *George Moore l'homme et l'oeuvre*, Paris 1966.

O'Conor, Norryes, *Changing Ireland, Literary Backgrounds to the Irish Free State*, Cambridge, Mass. 1924.

O'Donovan, Gerald, *Father Ralph*, London 1913.

O'Donovan, Gerald, *Waiting*, London 1914.

O'Donovan, Gerald, *Conquest*, London 1920.

O'Donovan, Gerald, *How They Did It*, London 1920.

O'Donovan, Gerald, *The Holy Tree*, London 1922.

Plunkett, Horace, *Ireland in the New Century*, London 1902.

Powell, Violet, *The Irish Cousins*, London 1970.

Ryan, W. P., *The Pope's Green Island*, London 1912.

Smith, Constance Babington, *Rose Macauley*, London 1973.

White, Terence de Vere, *The Anglo-Irish*, London 1972.

CHAPTER FOUR: THE THING THAT IS COMING

Boyle, J. W. (ed.), *Leaders and Workers*, Cork n.d.

Clarke, Austin, *A Penny in the Clouds*, London 1968.

Clarkson, J. Dinsmore, *Labour and Irish Nationalism*, New York 1925.

Colum, Padraic, *Arthur Griffith*, Dublin 1959.

Connolly, James, *Labour in Irish History*, Dublin 1910.
Connolly, James, *Selected Writings* (edited by Owen Dudley Edwards), London 1973.
Connolly, James, *Socialism and Nationalism* (edited by Desmond Ryan), Dublin 1948.
Connolly, James, *Labour and Easter Week, A Selection of the Writings of James Connolly* (edited by Desmond Ryan), Dublin 1949.
Davis, Richard, *Arthur Griffith and Non-Violent Sinn Fein*, Tralee 1974.
Dublin Housing Inquiry in Parliamentary Papers, Cd. 7273, vol XIX, 1914.
Dudley Edwards, Owen, *James Connolly, the Mind of an Activist*, Dublin 1971.
Dudley Edwards, Ruth, *Patrick Pearse, the Triumph of Failure*, London 1977.
Greaves, C. Desmond, *The Life and Times of James Connolly*, London and Berlin 1961.
Larkin, Emmet, *James Larkin*, London 1965.
Levenson, Samuel, *James Connolly*, London 1972.
Lyons, F. S. L., *The Irish Parliamentary Party 1890–1910*, London 1951.
McCay, Hedley, *Padraic Pearse*, Cork 1966.
MacDonagh, Thomas, *Lyrical Poems*, Dublin 1913.
MacDonagh, Thomas, *Literature in Ireland*, Dublin 1916.
Martin, F. X., *The Howth Gun-Running 1914*, Dublin 1964.
O'Brien, Conor Cruise (ed.), *The Shaping of Modern Ireland*, London 1959.
Pearse, Patrick, *Collected Works* (edited in three volumes), Dublin 1924.
Ryan, Desmond, *Remembering Sion*, London 1934.
Ryan, Desmond, *The Sword of Light*, London 1939.
Ryan, Desmond (ed.), *The 1916 Poets*, Dublin 1963.
Ryan, A. P., *Mutiny at the Curragh*, London 1956.
Wright, Arnold, *Disturbed Dublin*, London 1914.

The Easter Rising
Caulfield, Max, *The Easter Rebellion*, London 1964.
Coffey, Thomas M., *Agony at Easter*, London 1971.
Dudley Edwards, Owen, and Pyle, Fergus (eds.), *1916 The Easter Rising*, London 1968.
MacHugh, Roger (ed.), *Dublin 1916*, London 1966.
Nowlan, Kevin B. (ed.), *The Making of 1916*, Dublin 1969.

O'Dubhgaill, M. (ed.), *Insurrection Fires at Eastertide*, Cork 1966.
Ryan, Desmond, *The Rising*, Dublin 1949.
Stephens, James, *The Insurrection in Dublin*, Dublin and London 1916.

CHAPTER FIVE: THE SPRING OF 'SIXTEEN
Atkinson, Orianna, 'The Crock of Gold' in *The South and the West of It* (pp. 199–212), New York 1956.
Farrell, Michael, *Thy Tears Might Cease* (parts one, two and three), New York 1964.
Figgis, Darrell, *The Mount of Transfiguration*, Dublin 1915.
Figgis, Darrell, *Children of Earth*, Dublin 1918.
Figgis, Darrell, *Recollections of the Irish War*, London 1927.
Gibbon, Monk, 'Introduction' in *Thy Tears Might Cease*, New York 1964.
O'Faolain, Sean, *Vive Moi!* (pp. 373–4), Boston 1964.
Orpen, William, *Stories of Old Ireland and Myself*, London 1924.
Pyle, Hilary, *Modern Irish Art (Rosc Exhibition Catalogue)*, Cork 1975.
Yeats, Jack B., *Life in the West of Ireland*, Dublin 1912.
Yeats, Jack B., *Modern Aspects of Irish Art*, Dublin 1922.

CHAPTER SIX: A TERRIBLE BEAUTY
Murdoch, Iris, *The Red and the Green*, London 1965.
O'Casey, Sean, *Mirror in My House*, New York 1963.
O'Casey, Sean, *The Plough and the Stars*, London 1926.
O'Casey, Sean, *Inishfallen, Fare Thee Well*, London 1949.
O'Conaire, Padraic, *Seacht Buide an Eirigh Amact*, Dublin 1918.
O'Duffy, Eimar, *The Wasted Island*, Dublin 1920.
O'Flaherty, Liam, *Two Years*, London 1930.
O'Flaherty, Liam, *Shame the Devil*, London 1932.
O'Flaherty, Liam, *Insurrection*, London 1950.
Thompson, William Irwin, *The Imagination of an Insurrection, Dublin 1916*, New York 1967.
Townshend, Charles, *The British Campaign in Ireland, 1919–1921*, Oxford 1975.

CHAPTER SEVEN: THE SHAPE OF LIFE
Corkery, Daniel, *The Hounds of Banba*, Dublin 1920.
Farrell, Michael, *Thy Tears Might Cease* (part two), New York 1964.
O'Brien, Máire Cruise: 'The Two Languages' in *Conor Cruise O'Brien Introduces Ireland*, London 1969.
O'Connor, Frank, *An Only Child*, London 1961.

O'Connor, Frank, *The Big Fellow*, Dublin 1965.

O'Faolain, Sean, *Vive Moi!*, Boston 1964.

O'Malley, Ernest, *On Another Man's Wound*, Dublin and London, 1936. (In the U.S. : *Army Without Banners*, New York 1937.)

O'Sullivan, Tomas Ruadh, *Amhrain Thomas Ruaidh, The Songs of Tomas Ruadh O'Sullivan, the Iveragh Poet 1785–1848*, Dublin 1914.

CHAPTER EIGHT: ON A DARKLING PLAIN

Bowen, Elizabeth, *The Last September*, London 1929.

Bowen, Elizabeth, *Bowen's Court*, New York 1963.

Collis, Maurice, *Somerville and Ross*, London 1969.

Coxhead, Elizabeth, *Daughters of Erin*, London 1965.

Ellmann, Richard, *The Identity of Yeats*, London 1954.

Hone, Joseph, *W. B. Yeats*, London 1941.

MacManus, Francis (ed.), *The Yeats We Knew*, Cork 1965.

Powell, Violet, *The Irish Cousins*, London 1970.

Somerville, Edith, and Ross, Martin, *Mount Music*, London 1919.

Somerville, Edith, and Ross, Martin, *An Enthusiast*, London 1921.

Somerville, Edith, and Ross, Martin, *The Big House of Inver*, London 1925.

Robinson, Lennox (ed.), *Lady Gregory's Journals*, London 1946.

White, Terence de Vere, *The Anglo-Irish*, London 1972.

Yeats, W. B., *A Vision*, London 1925; new edition 1937.

CHAPTER NINE: A FELLAH IN A TRENCH COAT

Barry, Tom, *Guerilla Days in Ireland*, Cork 1949.

Breen, Dan, *My Fight for Irish Freedom*, Dublin 1924.

Butler, Ewen, *Barry's Flying Column*, London 1971.

Corkery, Daniel, *A Munster Twilight*, Dublin 1916.

Corkery, Daniel, *The Hounds of Banba*, Dublin 1920.

Deasy, Liam, *Towards Ireland Free*, Cork 1973.

Fallon, Gabriel, *The O'Casey I Knew*, London 1965.

Farrell, Michael, *Thy Tears Might Cease* (parts four and five), New York 1964.

Henn, T. R. : 'W. B. Yeats and the Poetry of War', in *Last Essays*, Gerards Cross 1976.

McInerney, Michael, *Peadar O'Donnell Irish Social Rebel*, Dublin 1974.

MacNamara, Brinsley, *The Valley of the Squinting Windows*, Dublin 1918.

MacNamara, Brinsley, *The Clanking of Chains*, Dublin 1920.

O'Casey, Sean, *Shadow of a Gunman*, London 1925.

O'Casey, Sean, *Inishfallen Fare Thee Well*, London 1949.

O'Casey, Sean, *The Letters of Sean O'Casey* (edited by David Krause), New York 1975.
O'Connor, Frank, *Guests of the Nation*, London 1931.
O'Connor, Frank, *The Lonely Voice*, London 1963.
O'Connor, Frank, *An Only Child*, London 1961.
O'Callaghan, Sean, *Execution*, London 1974.
O'Donnell, Peadar, *Storm*, Dublin 1922.
O'Donnell, Peadar, *Islanders*, London 1927.
O'Donnell, Peadar, *Adrigoole*, London 1928.
O'Donnell, Peadar, *The Knife*, London 1930.
O'Donnell, Peadar, *Wrack*, London 1931.
O'Donnell, Peadar, *Proud Island*, Dublin 1975.
O'Faolain, Sean, *Midsummer Night Madness*, London 1932.
O'Faolain, Sean, *Vive Moi!*, London 1963.
Rebel Cork's Fighting Story, Tralee 1949.
Ryan, Desmond : *Sean Treacy and the Third Tipperary Brigade IRA*, Tralee 1945.

CHAPTER TEN : THE SHAPE OF THE SWORD
Beaslai, Piaras, *Michael Collins and the Making of a New Ireland*, Dublin 1926.
Clarke, Austin, *A Penny in the Clouds*, London 1968.
Forester, Margery, *Michael Collins the Lost Leader*, London 1971.
Neeson, Eoin, *The Civil War in Ireland*, Cork 1966; 1969.
Neeson, Eoin, *The Life and Death of Michael Collins*, Cork 1968.
O'Connor, Frank, *The Big Fellow*, Dublin 1965. (In U.S., *Death in Dublin, Michael Collins and the Irish Revolution*, New York 1937.)
O'Faolain, Sean, *De Valera*, London 1936.
O'Hegarty, P. S., 'W. B. Yeats' in *The Dublin Magazine*, July–Sept., 1939, pp. 22–4.
O'Malley, Ernest, *On Another Man's Wound*, London 1936.
O'Neill, T. P. and Lord Longford, *De Valera, a Biography*, London 1971.
Taylor, Rex, *Michael Collins*, London 1958.
Younger, Calton, *Ireland's Civil War*, London 1968.
Younger, Calton, *A State of Disunion*, London 1972.

CHAPTER ELEVEN : THE HEART GROWN BRUTAL
Bowen, Elizabeth, *Bowen's Court*, New York 1963.
Gogarty, Oliver St John, *As I Was Going Down Sackville Street*, London 1937.
O'Connor, Ulick, *Oliver St John Gogarty*, London 1964.

O'Casey, Sean, *Juno and the Paycock*, London 1925.
O'Flaherty, Liam, *The Informer*, London 1926.
O'Flaherty, Liam, *The Martyr*, London 1927.
O'Flaherty, Liam, *Mr Gilhooly*, London 1928.
McInerney, Michael, *The Riddle of Erskine Childers*, Dublin 1971.
Ryan, A. P., 'The Life and Death of Erskine Childers', *The Listener* (London), 25 June 1970, pp. 853–5.
Yeats, W. B., *The Letters of W. B. Yeats* (edited by Alan Wade), London 1954.
Yeats, W. B., *Autobiographies*, London 1965
Yeats, W. B., *Memoirs*, London 1972.

CHAPTER TWELVE: THE WINTER OF 'TWENTY-THREE
Boyle, Andrew, *Erskine Childers*, London 1977.
O'Connor, Frank, *An Only Child*, London 1961.
O'Connor, Frank, *My Father's Son*, London 1968.
O'Donnell, Peadar, *The Gates Flew Open*, London 1936.
O'Faolain, Sean, *Vive Moi!*, London 1963.
O'Malley, Ernest, 'The Singing Flame', unpublished MS, Archives Department, University College, Dublin.
Stuart, Francis, *We Have Kept the Faith*, Dublin 1923 ('H. Stuart' on title page).
Stuart, Francis, *Things to Live For*, London 1936.
Stuart, Francis, *Black List, Section H*, London 1975.

CHAPTER THIRTEEN: AFTER AUGHRIM'S GREAT DISASTER
Bell, J. Bowyer, *The Secret Army*, London 1971.
Brody, Hugh, *Inishkillane, Change and Decline in the West of Ireland*, London 1973.
Coogan, Tim Pat, *Ireland Since the Rising*, London 1966.
Corkery, Daniel, *The Hidden Ireland*, Dublin 1925.
Corkery, Daniel, *Synge and Anglo-Irish Literature*, Cork 1931.
Cullen, L. M., 'The Hidden Ireland: a Reassessment of a Concept', *Studia Hibernica* (Dublin), vol. 9, 1969, pp. 7–47.
MacManus, Francis (ed.), *The Years of the Great Test 1926–1939*, Cork 1967.
Meenan, James, *The Irish Economy Since 1922*, Liverpool 1970.
Saul, George Brandon, *Daniel Corkery*, Lewisburg 1973.
White, Terence de Vere, *Kevin O'Higgins*, London 1948.
Whyte, J. M., *Church and State in Modern Ireland 1923–1970*, Dublin 1971.
Williams, T. D. (ed.), *The Irish Struggle 1916–1926*, London 1966.

CHAPTER FOURTEEN: GOING INTO EXILE (I)

Cosgrave, Patrick, 'Yeats, Fascism and Conor O'Brien', *London Magazine*, July 1967, pp. 22–41.

Krause, David, *Sean O'Casey, the Man and the Work*, London 1960.

Krause, David (ed.), *The Letters of Sean O'Casey*, New York 1975.

Manning, Maurice, *The Blueshirts*, Dublin 1971.

Marreco, Anne, *The Rebel Countess*, London 1968.

O'Brien, Conor Cruise, 'Passion and Cunning : the politics of W. B. Yeats' in *In Excited Reverie* (edited by A. Norman Jeffares), London 1965.

O'Faolain, Sean, *Constance Markievicz*, London 1936.

Tomorrow (Dublin), 1924, issues 1–4.

Ussher, Arland, *The Midnight Court and the Adventures of a Luckless Fellow* (with an introduction by W. B. Yeats), London 1926.

Ussher, Arland, *The Face and Mind of Ireland*, London 1949.

Ussher, Arland, *Three Great Irishmen*, London 1951.

White, Terence de Vere, *Kevin O'Higgins*, London 1948.

Yeats, W. B., *A Vision*, London 1937.

Yeats, W. B., *The Senate Speeches of W. B. Yeats* (edited by Donald Pearce), London 1961.

CHAPTER FIFTEEN: GOING INTO EXILE (II)

Figgis, Darrell, *A Chronicle of Jails*, Dublin 1917.

Figgis, Darrell, *A Second Chronicle of Jails*, Dublin 1919.

Figgis, Darrell, *The House of Success*, Dublin 1921.

Figgis, Darrell, *The Return of the Hero*, Dublin 1923.

Colum, Padraic, 'Darrell Figgis', *Dublin Magazine*.

Kiely, Benedict, *Modern Irish Fiction*, Dublin 1949.

O'Connor, Frank, *Guests of the Nation*, London 1931.

O'Connor, Frank, *The Saint and Mary Kate*, London 1932.

O'Faolain, Sean, *Midsummer Night Madness*, London 1932.

O'Flaherty, Liam, *The Puritan*, London 1932.

O'Flaherty, Liam, *Skerret*, London 1932.

O'Flaherty, Liam, *The Life of Tim Healy*, London 1927.

O'Flaherty, Liam, *A Tourist's Guide to Ireland*, London 1930.

Stuart, Francis, *Pigeon Irish*, London 1932.

Stuart, Francis, *Black List, Section H*, London 1975.

CHAPTER SIXTEEN: THE IMAGES OF THIRTY YEARS

Barrett, Cyril, 'Irish Nationalism and Art 1800–1921', *Studies* (Dublin), Winter 1975, pp. 393–409.

Berger, John, 'Jack Yeats' in *Permanent Red*, London 1960.

Gordon, D. J., *W. B. Yeats, Images of a Poet*, Manchester 1961.
Henry, Paul, *An Irish Portrait*, London 1951.
Henry, Paul, *Further Reminiscences*, Belfast 1973.
Lavery, John, *The Life of a Painter*, London 1941.
McGreevy, Thomas: *Poems*, London 1936.
McGreevy, Thomas, *Jack Yeats*, London 1948.
MacNeice, Louis, *The Strings Are False*, London 1965.
O'Malley, Ernest, 'Jack Yeats' in *Jack B. Yeats* (edited by Roger McHugh), Dublin 1971.
Orpen, William, *Stories of Old Ireland and Myself*, London 1925.
Pyle, Hilary, *Jack B. Yeats*, London 1970.
Ussher, Arland, *Yeats at the Municipal Gallery*, Dublin 1959.
White, James, *J. B. Yeats and the Irish Renaissance*, Dublin 1969.
White, James, *Jack B. Yeats, a Centenary Exhibition*, London 1971.
Yeats, Jack B., *Modern Aspects of Irish Art*, Dublin 1922.

EPILOGUE : LIVE AMMUNITION
Behan, Brendan, *Brendan Behan's Island*, London 1960.
Behan, Brendan, *Confessions of an Irish Rebel*, New York 1965.
Clarke, Austin, *Collected Poems*, Dublin 1974.
Devlin, Denis, *Selected Poems*, New York 1963.
Green, F. L., *Odd Man Out*, London 1945.
Kinsella, Thomas, *Downstream*, Dublin 1962.
McLaverty, Michael, *The Game Cock and Other Stories*, New York 1948.
O'Brien, Conor Cruise, 'The Parnellism of Sean O'Faolain' in *Maria Cross*, London 1953.
O'Donnell, Peadar, *There Will Be Another Day . . .* Dublin 1963.
O'Faolain, Sean, *Come Back To Erin*, London 1940.
Plunkett, James, 'Dublin' in *Conor Cruise O'Brien Introduces Ireland* (edited by Owen Dudley Edwards), London 1969.

Film list

The following is a short list of films related to the themes of this book. Some are well known, and can be seen in festivals and revivals frequently enough. Others are now almost forgotten. However no survey of this period would be complete without some reference to these achievements, which I hope to write about at a later date.

Irish Destiny (Dr Eppel, Ireland, 1925)
Ireland in Revolt (Edwin Weigle, U.S.A., 1925)
The Informer (Arthur Robison, British International Pictures, 1929)
Juno and the Paycock (Alfred Hitchcock, British International Pictures, 1930)
Man of Aran (Robert Flaherty, British-Gaumont, U.K., 1934)
Guests of the Nation (Denis Johnston, Ireland, 1934)
The Informer (John Ford, U.S.A., 1935)
Riders to the Sea (Brian Desmond Hurst, U.K., 1936)
Ourselves Alone (Brian Desmond Hurst, U.K., 1936)
The Plough and the Stars (John Ford, U.S.A., 1937)
The Dawn (Tom Cooper, Hibernia Productions, Ireland, 1937)
Odd Man Out (Carol Reed, U.K., 1949)
Mise Eire (George Morrison, Gael Linn, Ireland, 1959)
Saoirse? (George Morrison, Gael Linn, Ireland, 1961)
Ó Conluain, Proinsias : *Ár Scannán Féin*, Dublin, 1954.
O'Laoghaire, Liam : *Invitation to the Film*, Tralee, 1945.
O'Laoghaire, Liam : *Cinema Ireland 1895–1976* (Exhibition catalogue), Dublin, 1976.

Index

Dates are supplied for writers, artists and prominent political figures.